Praise for Nicholas Kristof and Sheryl WuDunn's

Tightrope

"Shocking . . . call to arms that warns that America is in deep trouble and needs to make big changes if it is to save itself. . . . *Tightrope* is a convincing argument that it's not too late to change the course of the nation. . . . It's also an agonizing account of how apathy and cruelty have turned America into a nightmare for many of its less fortunate citizens. . . . It was surely difficult to write, but it feels—now more than ever—deeply necessary."
　　　　　　　　　　　　　　　　　　　　　　—Michael Schaub, NPR

"*Tightrope* is a heroic, harrowing, and at times tender, look at the high-wire act that is survival for too many people today. Kristof and WuDunn know there are no easy solutions here, but that doesn't mean we can't take action, whether by pushing for better policies or changing our own attitudes."
　　　　　　　　　　　　　　　　　　　　　　　　　　　—Bono

"This is a must-read that will shake you to your core. It's a Dante-esque tour of a forgotten America, told partly through the kids who rode on Kristof's old school bus in rural Oregon. A quarter are now dead, and others are homeless, in prison, or struggling with drugs. They made bad choices, but so did America, in ways that hold back our entire country. *Tightrope* shows how we can and must do better."
　　　　　　　　　　　　　　　　　　　　　　　—Katie Couric

"While [Kristof and WuDunn] cover policy failures of the last half-century, they also affirm that we're no longer dealing in Republican or Democratic issues, but issues of Americans' very survival. Highlighting successful small-scale programs . . . they emphasize that there are potentially nationwide solutions. Both researched and personal, this will be hard for readers to stop thinking about."
　　　　　　　　　　　　　　　　　　—*Booklist* (starred review)

"With compassion and empathy, [the authors] pull readers into the lives of families who have been in a downward spiral for several generations. . . . They bring a human face to issues such as drug addiction, incarceration, family dysfunction, and declining prospects for employment. . . . Enlightening for all concerned Americans."

—*Library Journal* (starred review)

"While acknowledging the need for personal responsibility—and for aid from private charities—the authors make a forceful case that the penalties for missteps fall unequally on the rich and poor in spheres that include education, health care, employment, and the judicial system; to end the injustices, the government also must act. . . . An ardent and timely case for taking a multipronged approach to ending working-class America's long decline."
—*Kirkus Reviews*

"Kristof and WuDunn avoid pity while creating empathy for their subjects, and effectively advocate for a 'morality of grace' to which readers should hold policy makers accountable. This essential, clear-eyed account provides worthy solutions to some of America's most complex socioeconomic problems."
—*Publishers Weekly*

Nicholas D. Kristof and Sheryl WuDunn

Tightrope

Nicholas D. Kristof and Sheryl WuDunn are the first married couple to win a Pulitzer Prize in journalism; they won for their coverage of China's Tiananmen Square democracy movement as *New York Times* correspondents. Kristof, now an op-ed columnist for the *Times*, won a second Pulitzer for columns about the Darfur genocide. At the *Times*, WuDunn worked as a business editor and strategic planning executive. She now helps run FullSky Partners, which advises young companies, including those contributing social value.

Kristof grew up on a sheep and cherry farm near Yamhill, Oregon, graduated from Harvard College, and then studied law at Oxford University as a Rhodes Scholar. WuDunn grew up in New York City, graduated from Cornell University, and then studied public policy at Princeton and received an MBA from Harvard Business School. They have three children and live near New York City, while trying to manage timber and the production of cider apples and pinot grapes on the farm in Oregon.

Tightrope

Tightrope

Americans Reaching for Hope

NICHOLAS D. KRISTOF
and **SHERYL WUDUNN**

VINTAGE BOOKS

A DIVISION OF PENGUIN RANDOM HOUSE LLC

NEW YORK

For Ladis and Jane, David and Alice, who nurtured us.
For Darrell, Sirena and Sondra, who shaped us.
For Gregory, Geoffrey and Caroline, who exhausted us and enriched us.

And for all those passing through the inferno
who spoke to us honestly about their struggles so that the
public might understand and support wiser policies.

FIRST VINTAGE BOOKS EDITION, SEPTEMBER 2020

Copyright © 2020 by Nicholas D. Kristof and Sheryl WuDunn

All rights reserved. Published in the United States by Vintage Books,
a division of Penguin Random House LLC, New York, and distributed
in Canada by Penguin Random House Canada Limited, Toronto. Originally
published in hardcover in the United States by Alfred A. Knopf, a division
of Penguin Random House LLC, New York, in 2020.

Vintage and colophon are registered
trademarks of Penguin Random House LLC.

Photographs by Lynsey Addario copyright © 2020 by Lynsey Addario,
unless otherwise noted.

The Library of Congress has cataloged the Knopf edition as follows:
Names: Kristof, Nicholas D., author. | WuDunn, Sheryl, author.
Title: Tightrope : Americans reaching for hope / Nicholas D. Kristof and Sheryl
    WuDunn.
Description: First Edition. | New York : Alfred A. Knopf, 2020 | Includes
    bibliographical references and index.
Identifiers: LCCN 2019014592
Subjects: LCSH: United States—Social conditions—1980– | United States—
    Economic conditions—2009– | Poor—United States—Social conditions. |
    Working class—United States—Social conditions.
Classification: LCC HN59.2 K75 2020 | DDC 306.0973—dc23
LC record available at https://lccn.loc.gov/2019014592

Vintage Books Trade Paperback ISBN: 978-0-525-56417-1
eBook ISBN: 978-0-525-65509-1

Book design by Cassandra J. Pappas

www.vintagebooks.com

Printed in the United States of America
10 9 8 7 6 5 4 3 2 1

■

So be sure when you step.
Step with care and great tact
And remember that Life's
a Great Balancing Act.

—DR. SEUSS, *Oh, the Places You'll Go!*

Contents

Tightrope

The Kids on the Number 6 School Bus

Is this land made for you and me?
—WOODY GUTHRIE

Dee Knapp was asleep when her husband, Gary, stumbled drunkenly into their white frame house after a night out drinking. Bracing for trouble, Dee jumped up and ran to the kitchen. Gary, muscular and compact with short black hair above a long face, was a decent fellow when sober, a brute when drunk.

"Get me dinner!" he shouted as he wobbled toward the kitchen, and Dee scrambled to turn the electric stove on and throw leftovers into a pan. But she wasn't fast enough, and he hit her with his fist. A lithe brunette in her early thirties, with shoulder-length hair and calloused hands, Dee realized that this was one of those times she was destined to be a punching bag. Devoted to her five children, she especially hated to be beaten by Gary because of the loathing for their father this engendered in them.

"Dinner!" Gary roared again. "Get me dinner!" He grabbed his loaded .22 rifle and pointed it at her menacingly. She bolted past Gary and out the front door into the night.

Gary's shouting had awoken the children upstairs. "Mom," Farlan, her eldest son, hissed from the second-floor window as she ran around the side of the house. Dee looked up and he threw down a sleeping bag. She grabbed it in midair and ran into the protective darkness of their two-and-a-half-acre property, seeking a place to spend the night hiding in the tall grass, waiting for Gary to sleep off his rage.

"Damn that woman," Gary cursed from inside the house. Clutching his .22, he lunged out the front door, then looked wildly into the darkness. A white, wooden Pentecostal church was on one side, one of two churches serving the tiny hamlet of Cove Orchard, Oregon. Beyond the church was Highway 47, leading to the small town of Yamhill, three miles to the south. Dee was sheltering in the darkness somewhere between the church and the neighbor's fence line. Gary lifted the rifle to his shoulder and fired off a volley of shots into the field where his wife was cowering. Dee stiffened, hugging the ground.

The children listened, terrified. Helpless and furious, Farlan clenched his fists and vowed to himself that someday he would kill his dad. In the field, seventy feet away, with no trees to hide behind, Dee held her breath as bullets smacked into the ground nearby. This happened from time to time, and Dee knew that her husband would soon tire of shooting into the night.

Finally, Gary stumbled back into the house and ordered a sullen Farlan downstairs to cook dinner for him. Dee could hear all this from her hiding spot, for Gary didn't know how to speak softly. She gradually felt her heartbeat return to normal. She spread the sleeping bag and lay down inside it, listening to her husband's curses from the house, hoping that he wouldn't beat Farlan, praying that the other kids would stay quiet upstairs.

It was another violent, tumultuous evening, but strangely Dee says that she was still buoyed by hope that day in 1973, for despite the fear and violence, she believed that in some ways life truly was getting better—especially for her kids. Like her husband, Dee had been raised in a cramped household without electricity or plumbing. The youngest of ten children, she had grown up poor after her father, a construction worker, died when she was nine years old. Dee had dropped out of school in fifth grade, while Gary had had virtually no education and could barely write his name. She and Gary had started their married life as migrant farmworkers, or "fruit tramps," following the harvests around California and Oregon, paid according to how many strawberries or beans they picked, living in shacks without electric light or running water. As of 1960, only one migrant worker child in five hundred completed grade school. Dee wanted better for her children, and she announced that when their kids were old enough for school, the family was going to settle down.

That's how they ended up in Cove Orchard, population fifty, in northwestern Oregon, where the grasses of the Willamette Valley merge into the forests of the Coastal Range, where fields of grass seed, golden wheat and Christmas trees, and orchards abounding with apples, cherries and hazelnuts, blanket the earth to the horizon. Gary found regular work and at one point landed a good union job laying pipe, mostly for sewer lines, earning a solid income even if he spent much of it in the bars in Yamhill and nearby Gaston. Dee had a steady job driving

The Knapps around the Christmas tree in Cove Orchard, Oregon, circa 1968. Dee Knapp is in the back, and from left the kids are Nathan, Rogena, Farlan, Keylan and Zealan. At that time the family's prospects seemed to be soaring. *(Photo courtesy Dee Knapp)*

tractors on a hazelnut farm near Yamhill. She couldn't afford day care, so she brought along her youngest, Keylan, a toddler, and kept him on her lap as she worked.

The Knapps had been able to buy their property for $2,500 in 1963, and it had the first electricity they had ever enjoyed at home in their lives. Initially, there was no running water, but Dee was handy with tools, so she bought a pipe cutter and laid down pipes to bring water into the bathroom and the kitchen sink. They also earned extra money refurbishing cars together: Gary fixing the engine, and Dee upholstering the interior.

They were homeowners! They had risen from itinerant farmworkers, one of the lowest rungs on the American economic ladder, to the solid, union-fortified working class and were on a trajectory to claw their way into the middle class. Farlan in his early teens was already growing taller than his dad, perhaps a tribute to better nutrition; there was no shortage of food in the Knapp household. Dee canned beans, tomatoes, peaches, prunes and other kinds of fruit, she made her own fruit jellies, and the shelves were full. All the children—Farlan, Zealan, Nathan, Rogena and Keylan—were far outpacing their parents in education. It looked as if all five might graduate from high school, and maybe some would even attend college.

Farlan was adept with his hands and smart, a natural engineer. Maybe he would design pipelines, not lay them. Dee invested all her hopes in her kids. Yes, she inflicted punishment by hitting them with a stick on occasion, but they all knew how much she loved them. She made sure they got schooling, and she absorbed punches and black eyes to protect them from Gary's drunken furies. In the end, she was confident they would have opportunities that she and Gary had never enjoyed.

As she lay in the dark field, a bruise forming on her cheek where Gary had struck her, she was stubbornly consoled by faith in the future, by her belief that America was the land of opportunity, by the certainty that even Gary's drunkenness couldn't stop the Number 6 school bus from picking up her kids each morning and taking them to get an education at Yamhill Carlton High School, learning algebra, biology, the use of prepositions and other knowledge that no one else in her family had been exposed to. For ten generations, her forebears had struggled to scratch from the earth enough to eat, and now finally in her generation there was dizzying progress. Her kids were living their version of the American dream and inheriting a cornucopia. Electric lights. Tractors and cars. Education. Television. Medicare. Social Security. Tampons. John Denver and Johnny Carson. Vaccinations. Hot showers. Twinkies. Boom boxes. As Dee lay in her sleeping bag, this certainty sustained her: Life was getting better in spite of Gary, and her children would inherit the earth. Life in Yamhill back in the 1970s seemed to echo Curly's upbeat refrain from *Oklahoma!*, when he exulted, "Everything's goin' my way."

Tragically, it didn't work out as hoped. The Knapps, like so many other working-class families, tumbled into unimaginable calamity.

Farlan Knapp and Nicholas Kristof (below) next to each other as freshmen in the Yamhill Carlton High School yearbook. Farlan was the first in his family ever to reach high school.
(Photo courtesy Yamhill Carlton High School)

Gary and Dee were Nick's neighbors as he grew up outside Yamhill, and the five Knapp kids rode with him each day on the Number 6 bus to Yamhill Grade School and then Yamhill Carlton High School. When Gary fired his .22 rifle into the yard at his cowering wife, the gunshots echoed to Nick's farm half a mile away. Farlan was in Nick's class in school; his siblings were younger.

The Knapps' optimism at that time was shared by the entire community, and by millions of others throughout the country. We have no soggy sentimentality about those days: we recount Gary's violence precisely to cure anyone of false nostalgia. But life *had* improved dramatically, and most expected that rising education levels and improved social services would give the Knapp kids and almost everyone else a much better life. The kids on the bus as it careered toward Yamhill each morning were sure that their world would be better than their parents' had been.

Yet those kids ended up riding into a cataclysm, as working-class communities disintegrated across America, felled by lost jobs, broken families and despair. About one-fourth of the kids who rode with Nick on the bus are dead from drugs, suicide, alcohol, obesity, reckless accidents and other pathologies. A boy named Mike is dead from suicide, after struggles with drugs; Steve from the aftermath of a foolhardy motorcycle accident; Cindy from depression, obesity and then a heart attack; Jeff from a daredevil car crash; Tim from a construction accident; Billy from complications of diabetes while in prison; Kevin from consequences of obesity. There are different accounts of what Sue died of. Chris has gone missing after decades of alcoholism and homelessness. Others are alive but struggling with dead-end jobs or wrestling with drugs and alcohol. Of the two boys that Nick walked to the bus stop with each day, Mike is a homeless alcoholic living in a park, and Bobby is serving a life sentence in prison for offenses so harrowing that the family has cut him off.

THE AMERICAN ECONOMY HAS DAZZLED the world and its stock markets have created great riches, but the median American household is actually *poorer* in net worth today than it was in 2000. Median wages for the majority of the population that lacks a college degree are significantly lower today, according to the Bureau of Labor Statistics, than they were back in 1979. Gallup has been asking Americans once a month for decades if they are "satisfied" or "dissatisfied" with the way things are going in the United States, and for the last fifteen years a majority has steadily answered "dissatisfied." Gallup reported in 2019 that even as the economy grew steadily, "higher levels of stress, anger and worry nudged Americans' overall Negative Experience Index to 35—three points higher than any previous score." Gallup concluded, "In fact, the levels of negative emotions in the past several years are even higher than during the U.S. recession years." Gallup found that Americans were among the most stressed populations in the world, tied with Iranians and even more stressed than Venezuelans.

Life expectancy continues to rise in most of the rest of the industrial-ized world, but in the United States it has dropped for three years in a row—for the first time in a century. As we'll see, American kids today are 55 percent more likely to die by the age of nineteen than children in the other rich countries that are members of the OECD, the club of industrialized nations. America now lags behind its peer countries in health care and high-school graduation rates while suffering greater violence, poverty and addiction. This dysfunction damages all Ameri-cans: it undermines our nation's competitiveness, especially as growing economies like China's are fueled by much larger populations and by rising education levels, and may erode the well-being of our society for decades to come. The losers are not just those at the bottom of society, but all of us. For America to be strong, we must strengthen all Americans.

We set out in this book to explore that unraveling. We wanted to understand more deeply what had happened to Nick's friends on the school bus, how our country could have let tens of millions of people suffer an excruciating loss of jobs, dignity, lives, hopes and children, and how we can recover. The Knapps and many of the kids on the bus—and millions of Americans across the country—made terrible, self-destructive choices about using drugs or dropping out of school.

But we saw that these were compounded by terrible choices that the country made on multiple fronts. The kids on the bus who floundered weren't somehow worse than their parents or less prepared—indeed, they mostly had more education—and they didn't have weaker characters than their counterparts in other countries. American kids don't drop out of high school at higher rates than in other countries because they are less intelligent. So while we look unsparingly at failures of personal responsibility, let's also examine equally rigorously the failures of government, of institutions and of society. And let's seek solutions.

In doing our research and reporting for this book, we came to see that life's journey for affluent, well-educated American families is like a stroll along a wide, smooth path, forgiving of missteps. But increasingly, for those from lower on the socioeconomic spectrum, life resembles a tightrope walk. Some make it across, but for so many, one stumble and that's it. What's more, a tumble from the tightrope frequently destroys not only that individual but the entire family, including children and, through them, grandchildren. The casualties are everywhere in America, if we only care to notice.

Some 68,000 Americans now die annually from drug overdoses, another 88,000 from alcohol abuse and 47,000 from suicide. More Americans die from these causes every two weeks than died during eighteen years of war in Afghanistan and Iraq. Yet much of affluent America has shrugged, with elites paying little attention to the disintegration of communities across the country—or, worse, blaming the victims. In fact, plenty of blame could go elsewhere: Politicians, journalists, religious leaders and business executives were too often derelict as communities cratered and tens of millions of people endured the pain. The United States still doesn't have a coherent plan to address the challenges.

This journey of exploration has taken the two of us to all fifty states, and we tell stories here from Alabama, Arkansas, California, Florida, Maryland, New York, Oklahoma, Tennessee, Texas, Virginia, Washington, D.C., and elsewhere. But many of the tales are from Yamhill, because it is close to our hearts and because it reflects the challenges of working-class America. Another reason to write about the people of Yamhill is that they bared their souls to us. Nick has a lifetime of attachment to local friends, and Sheryl has been visiting Yamhill ever since our engagement, when she amused people by locking the car door. Our kids grew up partly on the Kristof family farm, and our ties to Yamhill give us a deep empathy for the community's struggles. The consequences of lost timber jobs in Oregon and disappearing coal jobs in Kentucky are not so different from the consequences of erased factory jobs in North Carolina, Maine or Michigan. In talking to our friend Wes Moore, an African American who grew up in poverty in Baltimore and New York, it struck us both how many commonalities there are between a white farm town in Oregon and a black neighborhood in Baltimore: what they share is deep pain.

This has been a wrenching book for us to write, because old friendships threatened to rob us of the protection of professional distance. In past books, we have tried to shine a light on urgent and neglected topics, such as the oppression of women around the world; now we are trying to illuminate similarly urgent and neglected crises in our own backyards. Some of these stories are of dear friends whom Nick had crushes on, passed notes to in class, danced with or competed against on the high-school track. Together we've covered massacres, genocide, sex trafficking and other tragedy and heartbreak around the globe, but these struggles hit so close to home because Yamhill and America *are* home.

THE KNAPP KIDS UNDERTOOK their own Dantesque journey through drugs, alcohol, crime and family dysfunction. Farlan, a talented woodcarver and furniture maker, died of liver failure from drink and drugs. Zealan burned to death in a house fire while passed out drunk. Rogena suffered from mental illness and died from hepatitis linked to her own drug use. Nathan burned to death when the meth he was making exploded. Four siblings, once happy kids bouncing on the seats of school bus Number 6, dead, dead, dead, dead.

Keylan, particularly smart and talented, whom Yamhill Grade School recognized as a math prodigy, is the lone survivor, partly because thirteen years in the state penitentiary protected him from drugs. He soldiers on with HIV, hepatitis and more broken bones than he can remember; he says he uses drugs much less now.

Today Keylan shares a home with Dee in Oklahoma. She survived Gary and, at seventy-nine, remains sound of mind and strong of body. She gets by on Social Security, doesn't touch alcohol or drugs, and makes daily visits to the grave site of her four dead children. Pulling out family photos, Dee pointed to her kids in happier times; over the doorway, the word FAMILY practically jumps off a wooden sign. "Our family is cursed," Keylan said. "Something went wrong with our generation, and so there was alcohol abuse. There was drug abuse. There was prison." He began weeping.

So many Americans have wandered off course "into a dark wood," as Dante described his journey in *Inferno*, exploring the corruption and hypocrisy of medieval Florence, then one of the world's great cities. Dee Knapp knows as well as anyone that the America of the old days was no simple *Leave It to Beaver* kaleidoscope of happy families passing the gravy around a dinner table. It was even more difficult for African Americans, Latinos, Native Americans and others who did not even have a seat at the table. Yet in those days the dream of advancement was real, and it sustained people like Dee through difficult times. For much of working-class America, of whatever complexion, the dream is now dead. It's dead along with all those children on the Number 6 school bus. It's dead along with Farlan, Zealan, Rogena and Nathan Knapp. Personal responsibility must be part of the turnaround, but so must collective responsibility, especially for children now struggling. We as citizens have failed in this, and so has our government, and that must change. The United States took a historic wrong turn over the last half century, and for the Knapps and so many others life has become an inferno. We will take you through that inferno, but also show how America can do better.

"We're Number 30!"

Civilizations die from suicide, not by murder.
—ARNOLD TOYNBEE, British historian

We Americans are a patriotic tribe, and we tend to wax lyrical about our land of plenty and opportunity. "We have never been a nation of haves and have-nots," Senator Marco Rubio once declared. "We are a nation of haves and soon-to-haves, of people who have made it and people who will make it." We proudly assert, "We're number 1!" and in terms of overall economic and military strength, we are. But in other respects our self-confidence is delusional.

Here's the blunt, harsh truth.

America ranks number 41 in child mortality, according to the Social Progress Index, which is based on research by three Nobel Prize–winning economists and covers 146 countries for which there is reliable data. We rank number 46 in internet access, number 44 in access to clean drinking water, number 57 in personal safety and number 30 in high-school enrollment. Somehow, "We're number 30!" doesn't seem so proud a boast. Overall, the Social Progress Index ranks the United States number 26 in well-being of citizens, behind all the other members of the G7 as well as significantly poorer countries like Portugal and Slovenia, and America is one of just a handful of countries that have fallen backward. "Despite spending more on healthcare than any other country in the world, the US has health outcomes comparable to Ecuador, while the US school system is producing results on par with Uzbekistan," the 2018 Social Progress Index concluded.

"Our country is failing on many of the things we hold most dear," noted Michael E. Porter, the Harvard Business School professor and expert on international competitiveness who designed the Social Progress Index. "And it's getting worse." Democrats blame President Trump, while Republicans blame President Obama, but the country has regressed under Democrats and Republicans alike. Professor Porter warns that "the fracturing of our society is grounded not in the weaknesses of a particular leader but in the inability of our institutions to deliver meaningful social progress for the average citizen."

What "the fracturing of our society" means in human terms is a dysfunction that statistics simply can't fully convey. It's a breakdown that rips apart families and tears the social fabric. Churches, social clubs and other civic organizations are not providing the social cohesion or assistance they once did. The government is unwilling to step in to fill the breach, so many children suffer needlessly and the dysfunction is transmitted to the next generation.

Molly is what we'll call a friend of ours who lives along the Number 6 bus route. She dropped out in the eighth grade and gave birth to a daughter when she was just fifteen. At the time, Molly didn't tell anyone who the father was, so she was assumed to be "loose" and "careless." Many years later, she acknowledged that her daughter, whom we'll call Laurie, was the result of a rape by her father. One of the first people she revealed her secret to was her mom.

"Your dad raped me, too, and that's how you got here," her mom replied. All this would be an enormous psychological burden for any family. Laurie, who grew up knowing that she was born of an incestuous rape, was homeschooled through grade school and then attended ninth grade for a few months before finding herself in over her head and dropping out. As an adult, Laurie is smart, plays the piano and is an excellent golfer, but she has five small children fathered by four dads.

Molly lives here with her son, along the Number 6 school bus route near Yamhill. *(Photo by Lynsey Addario)*

We were close friends with the paternal grandfather of two of the little girls, so we asked Molly about them.

"There are just too many kids for one person," Molly told us worriedly. Laurie's eldest boy was expelled twice from kindergarten, once for being disruptive and once for stealing the teacher's iPad. This upset Laurie, who now is homeschooling the five kids, even though she herself had only a few months of formal education. Laurie didn't want to talk to us about these issues, but Eric Pleger, a mutual friend of ours, sees the children periodically, so we asked him about the two toddler girls. He shook his head. "Sounds terrible to say this about two little girls," he said glumly, "but they're headed for the joint."

Some of the stories we tell here are unsettling. We share them because Americans must appreciate new realities, and the grimness may be mitigated by the suggestions we offer both for smarter policies and for individual philanthropy. It is heartbreaking to try to chronicle the suffering of a place you love, and we found it particularly painful to watch the dysfunction in old friends replicated in their children and their children's children. Yet that is the story of much of working-class

America. Yes, economic growth entails change, and "creative destruction" is as necessary as it is inevitable. But creative destruction need not mean the demolition of families for generations.

For starters, America doesn't adequately invest in children, whose potential so often goes unfulfilled. One reflection of the state of the American dream: 76 percent of adults expect their children's lives to be worse than their own. The World Bank Human Capital Project estimates that American children reach only 76 percent of their potential because of inequality and shortcomings in our health and education systems. That gives the United States a ranking of 24 out of 157 countries, in line with its score on the Social Progress Index. Many other countries, even much poorer ones, do better.

Math scores on standardized tests are a good predictor of future incomes, and one worrying omen is that the United States ranks below average in the industrialized world in math scores for fifteen-year-olds on the PISA test. Almost one-third of American fifteen-year-olds perform below the baseline that is believed necessary to thrive in the modern world. Indeed, the only area where the American students really excel is overconfidence, PISA found: they are more likely than pupils in other countries to believe that they have mastered topics, even as they do worse.

Undereducated children grow into troubled adults who die at higher rates partly because of despair and anxiety. Many fear the future, or doubt they will find meaning and purpose in today's society and economy. Suicide rates are at their highest level since World War II, and opioids and other drugs now kill more Americans each month than guns or car crashes. Every seven minutes, another American dies of a drug overdose, and one American child in eight is living with a parent with a substance use disorder. Dr. Daniel Ciccarone, professor of family and community medicine at the University of California, San Francisco, notes that drug abuse at the scale we see it is a symptom of a deeper malaise. "If we don't address the root suffering of Americans, even if you took every opioid pill away, that suffering will manifest into another social and public health problem," he told us. "If we want to end, truly end the opioid crisis, we need to understand the basic causes of suffering and pain in America."

These deaths from drugs, alcohol and suicide have been called "deaths of despair" by the Princeton University economists Anne Case and Angus Deaton, and that pretty much captures the mortality on the Number 6 bus. The despair arises in part from frustrations about loss of status, loss of good jobs, loss of hope for one's kids. Inequality is currently believed to be greater than it was in the Gilded Age of the nineteenth century, and just three Americans—Jeff Bezos, Bill Gates and Warren Buffett—now possess as much wealth as the entire bottom half of the population. Senator Mark Warner, a moderate Democrat from Virginia who before entering politics was a successful telecommunications investor and executive, put it to us bluntly: "I don't believe modern American capitalism is working." Ray Dalio, the billionaire founder of Bridgewater, the world's largest hedge fund, agrees, saying: "I'm a capitalist, and even I think capitalism is broken." Dalio added: "The problem is that capitalists typically don't know how to divide the pie well and socialists typically don't know how to grow it well."

That skeptical view of capitalism is shared by young Americans in particular. As recently as 2010, more than two-thirds of Americans aged eighteen to twenty-nine had positive views of capitalism; today, according to Gallup, Americans in that age group have more positive views of socialism (51 percent) than of capitalism (45 percent). The problems are most stark in America, but they are also evident in Britain and to a lesser extent in some other developed countries; Martin Wolf of the *Financial Times* argues that we are undergoing a "crisis of democratic capitalism."

The first lesson of our journey and theme of this book is that to a degree unnoticed in more privileged parts of America, working-class communities have collapsed into a miasma of unemployment, broken families, drugs, obesity and early death. America created the first truly middle-class society in the world, but now a large share of Americans feel themselves at risk of tumbling out of that security and comfort. There's a brittleness to life for about 150 million Americans, with a constant risk that sickness, layoffs or a car accident will cause everything to collapse. One in seven Americans lives below the poverty line, a substantially higher rate than in Canada or other OECD countries, and scholars estimate that half of all Americans will at some point slip below the line. A recent Federal Reserve survey found that almost 40 percent don't readily have the cash to cover a $400 emergency expense such as a broken car or a roof leak. They can't even think of retirement. When all else fails, they sell blood plasma, up to twice a week, for $30 or $40 each time.

The second theme of this book is that suffering in working-class America was not inevitable but rather reflects decades of social-policy mistakes and often gratuitous cruelty: the war on drugs that led to mass incarceration, indifference to the loss of blue-collar jobs, insufficient health-care coverage, embrace of a highly unequal education system, tax giveaways to tycoons, zillionaire-friendly court decisions, acceptance of growing inequality, and systematic underinvestment in children and community services such as drug treatment.

Government authorities too often sided with capital over labor, undermining unions and weakening wages for unskilled workers in particular. If the federal minimum wage of 1968 had kept up with inflation and productivity, it would now be $22 an hour instead of $7.25 (many states and localities have higher minimums). There have been intelligent debates about what the optimal minimum wage should be, how it should vary between cheaper and more expensive parts of the country and at what point it begins to undermine employment significantly, but almost every labor economist believes it should be substantially higher than it now is at the federal level. Many companies also subject hourly workers to unpredictable job schedules, sometimes working late one evening and then early the next morning, in ways that interrupt sleep and make it impossible to plan childcare, doctor appointments or parent-teacher visits. A 2019 study found that this kind of scheduling caused workers even more unhappiness and psychological distress than low wages, and it often seems unnecessary and callous.

A harshness and at times a nastiness have crept into American policy, rooted in the misconception that those who struggle with unemployment, finances, drugs and life's messiness are fundamentally weak, in danger of dependency, in need of hard lessons. During the Great Recession of 2008–09 and its aftermath, the government rescued Wall Street banks but approved an inadequate stimulus so that millions lost their jobs. The housing bubble reflected an orgy of white-collar greed and criminality, but the people who paid the price were the 10 million families who lost their homes.

The third theme we pursue is more hopeful: the challenges are not insurmountable, and we can adopt policies that are both compassionate and effective. While there are no magic wands, we will outline policies that can mitigate suffering and provide traction for struggling families. Early childhood programs for at-risk kids pay for themselves seven times over in reduced spending on juvenile detention, special education and policing, according to the Nobel Prize–winning economist James Heckman. Programs to help low-income teenage girls with family planning also save public money many times over, for an IUD is one-fifteenth the cost of a Medicaid birth. And initiatives like the Earned Income Tax Credit cover most of their own costs by nudging people into the labor force so that they become taxpayers.

We as citizens must also hold all politicians' feet to the fire. This is not a Democratic issue or a Republican issue; it is an American issue, and too many of our elected representatives have failed to grapple seriously with the humanitarian crisis unfolding in our own country. There has been a dereliction of duty by politicians of both parties. This is an appeal for a more responsible and compassionate, evidence-based and accountable approach to governance.

To achieve these smarter policies, we must transcend the customary narrative that focuses only on "personal responsibility" and on glib talk about lifting oneself up by the bootstraps. Wiser policy requires our country to possess a richer understanding of why people fall behind, a deeper comprehension of how many children grow up with the odds stacked against them. Yes, they make mistakes, but in some cases we fail them before they fail us. Self-destructive behaviors are as real as autoimmune disorders, but both can be treated. We aim to nurture understanding, empathy and a willingness to offer helping hands rather than pointed fingers.

The power of empathy can be formidable. Take a high-school drop-out named Mary Daly. She grew up in a small town near St. Louis and was mostly a good student. But then her dad lost his job as a postal worker, her parents fought and eventually divorced, and Mary found it impossible to concentrate on school. She dropped out at fifteen, moved in with friends and went to work at a doughnut shop operated by her grandparents; she aspired to be a bus driver. The high-school guidance counselor mentioned the case to a local college teacher, Betsy Bane, who spoke to Mary and urged her to get a GED. At seventeen, Mary passed the GED, earning a top score without much study, and Bane urged her to consider college. Daly had never thought of university and said she couldn't afford tuition, but Bane offered to pay for the first semester.

At the University of Missouri, Daly immediately excelled and earned a degree in economics in 1985, then a master's and a PhD. After post-doctoral work, she became a research economist in the Federal Reserve System in 1996, where she was mentored by another woman economist, Janet Yellen. Daly worked her way up, often focusing on inequality, and in 2018 was named president of the Federal Reserve Bank of San Francisco. In that role she is, as Heather Long of *The Washington Post* put it, "one of the most powerful shapers of economic policy in the United States." Daly set up a scholarship at the University of Missouri to honor Bane, who says that there are "a lot of little diamonds" who go unnoticed.

AS PAIN SEEPED ACROSS America, Yamhill became a microcosm of America's working-class dysfunction. The small high school in Yamhill endured two student suicides in a single year: a boy hanged himself at home, and a girl shot herself in her car in the school parking lot. Nick's successor as student-body president lost a son, greatly admired and much loved in the community, to a drug overdose.

One of Nick's schoolmates, Stacy Mitchell, a vivacious cheerleader and volleyball player while in high school, wrestled with alcoholism and ended up homeless, living in a tent. She froze to death on a cold winter night, at age forty-eight. The idea that a popular girl from a local family with deep roots in the community could freeze to death while homeless was shattering. It wasn't just Stacy who died that night; something in all of us perished as well.

Plenty of kids from Yamhill did just fine, and we'll later explore the lessons of some of these escape artists. But it isn't just the dropouts who struggled. In high school, Nick's rival to be valedictorian was Donna King, an exceptionally bright girl whose father was a truck driver for the county. Donna and Nick were neck and neck, and then she became pregnant. She explained to us that she knew about the county clinic that offered family planning but also knew that the clinic wasn't good at keeping secrets and that if she asked for contraception word might filter out to her dad and scandalize her family. The pregnancy caused a scandal anyway. Donna married her boyfriend, Marvin, and managed to finish school by force of discipline and intellect. Donna and Marvin didn't go to college, partly because of the baby and partly because of the cost, but they are smart, hardworking and law-abiding. They haven't abused drugs but have still struggled every step of the way. Marvin worked in a factory making trailers until it closed down. Then he worked as a logger until his back went out. Now he has reinvented himself as an information technology professional, working on computers on the Nike campus. Donna has likewise worked in a tax preparation office, in a hotel and for Amway. Mostly, she gets by cleaning people's houses.

In the end, Donna raised a wonderful, strong family that she is rightly proud of. But if she had grown up in an affluent home in New York, or if she had had some help with family planning when she was a teenager, she might have ended up a doctor. The problem wasn't Donna's ability, but limited opportunities for the working class.

There's sometimes an impulse to pit the suffering of the white working class against that of African Americans or members of other minority groups. That is a mistake. Government policies have poorly served the working class of every complexion, and we need solidarity rather than strife among those so overlooked. The challenges faced by Donna in a rural white community aren't always so different from those faced by brilliant working-class black kids in urban areas across the country. *The Boston Globe* tracked down ninety-three valedictorians who had appeared in its newspaper between 2005 and 2007 in a "Faces of Excellence" series. These were hardworking, smart, outperforming kids, mostly of color, and nearly one-quarter had aimed to be doctors. Yet not one has become a doctor, and one-quarter failed to earn a BA within six years. Four became homeless, one spent time in prison and one died. The *Globe* described "an epidemic of untapped potential," which seems about right whether one is talking about black neighborhoods in Boston or rural white communities in Oregon, not to mention Latino parts of Texas or Native American country across the West.

Some Americans assume that the grim difficulties affect only those on the bottom rung of the ladder, but that's incorrect. The economic and social fabric for much of America has been ripped apart, and this is expensive for everyone: the White House estimates that the opioid epidemic costs the United States half a trillion dollars a year—more than $4,000 per American household annually.

One mechanism by which pain on the bottom is transmitted throughout the nation is the political system. Some 60 million Americans live in a rural America that is suffering, and the U.S. political architecture gives the frustrations of these rural Americans disproportionate political influence. They have particular weight in the Senate, where each state has two senators, so a Wyoming voter has sixty-eight times as much clout in choosing a senator as a California voter. This baked-in bias in the Senate and Electoral College in favor of small, rural states will continue to give rural voters outsize influence for the foreseeable future, and rural America has for decades endured economic decline and social turmoil that have left voters angry and disillusioned. The political consequences are visible: Working-class Americans helped elect President Trump. The reasons they backed Trump were complicated and sometimes included nativism, racism and sexism, but about 8 million of these voters had supported Barack Obama in 2012. Many cast ballots for Trump as a primal scream of desperation because they felt forgotten, neglected and scorned by traditional politicians.

Yet once he was in office, Trump cold-shouldered the working-class voters who had supported him. He gave lip service to jobs in coal and manufacturing but took no significant step to assist workers, and he made things worse by chipping away at the Affordable Care Act. It was one more scene in a long drama of politicians' betrayal of America's working class.

A popular critique laments the indolence, irresponsibility and self-destructive behaviors of the working class. *National Review* in 2016 urged "an honest look at the welfare dependency, the drug and alcohol addiction, the family anarchy—which is to say, the whelping of human children with all the respect and wisdom of a stray dog" and concluded that "the white American underclass is in thrall to a vicious, selfish culture whose main products are misery and used heroin needles." It's true that too many working-class students drop out of high school and then have babies out of wedlock and that this is a prescription for poverty. Ron Haskins and Isabel Sawhill of the Brookings Institution have found that of people who follow three traditional rules—graduate from high school, get a full-time job and marry before having children—only 2 percent live in poverty. So play by these rules, called "the success sequence," and by and large one can avoid poverty. In contrast, of those who do none of those three things, 79 percent live in poverty. Overall, one-quarter of girls still become pregnant by the age of nineteen, so clearly there has been irresponsible behavior, by boys and girls alike.

Yet the irresponsibility is not entirely with adolescents. American kids have sex at the same rates as European kids, but European girls are one-third as likely to get pregnant—because European countries offer much better comprehensive sex education and easier access to reliable forms of contraception. So, yes, teen births reflect individual irresponsibility, but also collective irresponsibility on the part of society. If we're going to blame the kids, we should also acknowledge our collective failure to do a better job creating safety nets so that teenagers overcome by hormones don't damage their futures, not to mention their children's.

Something similar to today's malaise and falling life expectancy has happened before in the world, in the Soviet Union. In the 1980s, the USSR was still a superpower with a space program, magnificent orchestras and operas, impressive science and mathematics, an empire in Eastern Europe and the capacity to blow up the globe. It was easy for tourists visiting the Hermitage in Leningrad or Red Square in Moscow to be dazzled. Yet all of this rested on an economic and social foundation that was cracking because of the Soviet Union's disastrous policy choices.

Alcoholism and discontent were rife there, with men reaching for vodka by late morning and disappearing into a haze by afternoon. The old joke in the factories was, They pretend to pay us, and we pretend to work. Soviet officials knew of these deep and complicated social and economic problems but chose to ignore drunkenness, drugs and work-force absenteeism, which they believed wouldn't affect the Kremlin. Their solution was to stop publishing Soviet mortality data.

When substance abuse became inescapable, General Secretary Mikhail Gorbachev declared a war on drunkenness and closed liquor shops, viewing the problem as a moral one of personal weakness and irresponsibility. In fact, alcoholism and drugs were a symptom of far deeper structural problems, of policy mistakes such as agricultural collectivization, a dysfunctional command economy and the invasion of Afghanistan. These mistakes went back decades and finally became impossible to cover up. Hope had dissolved. When life expectancy declined in Russia, just as it has in America today, that was a sign of systemic troubles that patriotic rhetoric could no longer conceal. It should have been a wake-up call, just as America's declining life expectancy today should be our own alarm bell.

3

When Jobs Disappear

The test of our progress is not whether we add more to the abundance of those who have much; it is whether we provide enough for those who have too little.

—FRANKLIN D. ROOSEVELT, Second Inaugural Address,
   January 20, 1937

When Nick was growing up with the Knapps near Yamhill, one of their buddies on the Number 6 school bus was Kevin Green. Kevin and Nick both had brown eyes and brown hair, and both were distance runners in high school, so people would sometimes mix them up on the high-school track. "Go, Kevin, go!" people would shout during a race as Nick ran by. They both lived on farms north of Yamhill near Cove Orchard and picked strawberries as summer jobs, later graduating to better-paying jobs stacking hay bales. Along with Farlan and the other Knapps, Kevin and Nick took science classes in seventh and eighth grade from a teacher who taught that evolution was incorrect and showed religious films extolling creationism. In high school, Kevin and Nick both took welding and agriculture classes and joined FFA, the Future Farmers of America. After cross-country or track practice, Nick often drove Kevin home to his farm with its hogs, geese, chickens and two milk cows.

Granted, there were differences. Kevin's house had few books, while Nick's house was lined with shelves of them. Nick's parents, professors who believed passionately in education, read to him, took him to chess tournaments, discussed world affairs at the dinner table and infused in him a confidence that he would get A's and go to university. Nick's house wasn't dramatically nicer or more comfortable than Kevin's, but its ethos and expectations were a world apart. Kevin's dad, Tom, had only a fifth-grade education, mostly discussed car engines and was a disciplinarian with a temper.

"My dad cut his brother's finger off once with a hatchet," Kevin told us, with more awe than was appropriate. Kevin himself as a young child had a penchant for disastrous accidents with fire. "By second grade, Kevin had burned down parts of two houses," recalled his younger brother, Clayton, also an old friend of ours.

In high school, Kevin was a weak student but thrived in shop classes.

Kevin Green and Nick ran together on the Yamhill Carlton High School cross-country team. *(Photo courtesy Yamhill Carlton High School)*

Kevin Green in 1983 with a four-and-a-half-pound trout he had caught.
An enthusiastic fisherman, Kevin once dove into a river and caught a fish
with his hands. *(Photo courtesy Irene Green)*

He and Clayton could take any car apart and put it back together better
than ever. When Clayton was thirteen years old, he bought a beat-up
1955 Chevy for $20—the engine was dead—and spent several years
with Kevin painstakingly restoring it. When they finished, it gleamed
and ran beautifully. They sold it in 1985 for $1,500 to someone who
still drives it.

Friendly and relaxed, blessed with a sunny personality and a desire
to help others, Kevin got along with pretty much everyone. He was
famous for helping friends with chores and for his passion for fishing.
Once as he stood on a bridge, he saw a fish in the river below. He didn't
have a rod, so he jumped into the river to grab it—and cooked it that
evening. Kevin was less dedicated to his studies. He spoke of wanting to
become an architect but couldn't imagine how he could pay for college,
so he treated homework as optional, and at the beginning of his senior
year he was told he wouldn't have enough credits to graduate. He began

taking GED classes right away and earned his high-school equivalency papers before his classmates had even graduated. He became the first male in his family ever to have the equivalent of a high-school degree, and he had every expectation of going places. Kevin believed, as most people in Yamhill did then, in a piety that former House Speaker Paul Ryan liked to repeat: "In our country, the condition of your birth does not determine the outcome of your life."

The 1970s was an optimistic time in Yamhill, a town southwest of Portland with one flashing red light, four churches and, at that time, 517 people, almost all of them white. Built as an overnight stop for the stagecoach from Portland to the coast, it boasted about having been the first town in Oregon to get electric streetlights. One of Yamhill's early claims to fame was that Mary Pickford, the silent film star, lived there briefly in about 1900, above a hat shop on Main Street. At the time, she was eight years old, and her mom was teaching at Yamhill's elementary school; sadly, Pickford never seemed as proud of Yamhill as it was of her. A better claim is as the hometown of Beverly Cleary,

The center of Yamhill today with the general store still has charm, though that masks some of the struggles in the area. (*Photo by Lynsey Addario*)

the children's book author and creator of Henry Huggins and Ramona the Pest; Cleary told us that the town of Pitchfork, in *Emily's Runaway Imagination*, is based on Yamhill.

In the 1970s, it had a general store, a hardware shop, a farm supply store, a telephone booth, a barber and a bar. The economy was based on farming, logging and light manufacturing, and the biggest employer in the area was a glove factory in the nearby town of Carlton. The upbeat theme for Nick's high-school prom was "Stairway to Heaven," and that seemed about right. Many older people in Yamhill had grown up on farms without electricity, plumbing or telephones and then family fortunes had soared in the 1940s, '50s and '60s.

Kevin's dad, Tom, embodied that rise. He had grown up without electricity or running water in a shack by a river that regularly flooded. Tom was a proud Korean War veteran who became a good mason and cement finisher, and he married his sweetheart, Irene, who had grown up in poverty without toilets or running water. Tom was a hard worker, and by the 1970s he had a solid union job paying $43 an hour in today's money.

"His work meant a lot to him, and he was proud he had a good job," Irene recalled. Tom helped construct the Fremont Bridge soaring over the Willamette River in Portland, and he was able to access GI Bill benefits to buy his first home with just $99 down. The GI Bill was an enormous project to lift people toward the middle class, and it helped the Greens and millions of others. In 1972, Tom and Irene purchased a five-acre farm outside Yamhill for $51,000 in today's prices. Irene found full-time work at a cannery, paying about $12 an hour in today's money, and the family seemed on a solid upward trajectory.

"Tom ran a tight ship," recalled the Reverend Rhonda Kroeker, a family friend. "The place was clean. The boys had certain responsibilities. Everything was kept a certain way. You just knew. You respected Tom. He was a good man and you didn't throw down a cigarette butt in his driveway. You didn't do that."

Like their friends the Knapps, the Greens looked forward to continued improvements. They all had an impressive work ethic. Their first child, Thomas Jr., had died of meningitis at two months, but their next, Cindy, a sweet girl in Nick's class, worked full-time at a cannery during high school, surviving on a few hours of sleep each night. Kevin and Clayton worked on chicken farms two or three nights a week to make extra money, getting home in the wee hours to catch a bit of sleep before school. After Cindy graduated from high school, she took a correspondence class on managing a motel, a community college training program in nursing and vocational classes in fixing computers. She also took community college classes in health care and eventually became a hospital technician overseeing equipment in an intensive care unit. It was a responsible job in which she took pride.

The kids all looked up to Tom, who handled himself with dignity and self-confidence and was respected by neighbors and workmates. His kids weren't even aware that he was illiterate until they were on a road trip and he needed help deciphering the simplest highway signs.

"You can't read, Dad?" Clayton asked in astonishment.

"Never mind. What does the sign say?"

It was a reflection of the upward mobility of the time that an illiterate man born into poverty could learn a skill, buy a farm, earn a solid living and build a good life for his family. Yet in retrospect, that middle-class dream was becoming more elusive—in Yamhill and in the thousands of Yamhills across America. Soon after Cindy and Kevin left high school, lucrative union jobs like their dad's began disappearing, especially for young people without a high-school degree. The glove factory closed its doors. Sawmills closed down and farms consolidated and invested in technology, which resulted in fewer jobs. The Kristof farm was a part of that change: a cherry orchard that used to be picked laboriously by hand by dozens of workers is now serviced by machines. The machine picking is faster, cheaper and more efficient, and thus benefits farmers and consumers—but it spelled disaster for those who once made ends meet by picking fruit each summer.

Kevin at first found a good job at a company making storage racks, but it eventually went bust. Next he worked as a welder at a trailer factory, where the work was poorly paid and unsatisfying. Kevin had a girlfriend who had two daughters of her own, and they became a common-law

Kevin Green, his girlfriend, his twin boys, and her daughters by another dad in a family portrait in 1988, a happier time *(Photo courtesy Irene Green)*

couple after they were together for ten years. Kevin referred to her as "my wife," she sometimes used the last name Green and they had twin boys together, but he and the girlfriend never formally tied the knot. "I want to get married," he'd say, "but I just can't afford to now. I'll wait until my finances get better."

Then the trailer factory closed and Kevin lost his job. "It just kind of changed his whole world," his mother, Irene Green, recalled. "I don't think Kevin thought too well of himself. I think he thought he wasn't worth much." In contrast to his dad's steady rise, Kevin found himself scrambling but still falling behind. He began to make furniture and sell it, but that wasn't lucrative and didn't feel to him like the job a man should have to support his family. His girlfriend apparently felt the same way: after a decade together, she lost patience, moved out with the kids and found another boyfriend. "She dumped him because he wasn't able to make enough to get a place to live," Irene told us.

"It knocked him out, destroyed his self-esteem," Clayton remembered. (The girlfriend declined requests to be interviewed.) Kevin began drinking too much and putting on weight. He grew a long beard and increasingly looked like an overweight and out-of-shape lumberjack. He didn't shower enough, which turned people off. He developed diabetes and then injured his back as well. Social Security eventually paid him $520 a month in disability, a lifeline—but Clayton acknowledges that it also made him less inclined to search for another job. Kevin was assessed $350 a month in child support, which he often couldn't afford to pay.

Kevin's problem wasn't laziness. He would spend hours biking along Highway 47 north of Yamhill looking for bottles and cans to return for the deposits. He would walk for hours to get to a good fishing spot, and like us he enjoyed hiking on the Pacific Crest Trail to fish in mountain lakes. "Man, that guy was hard to keep up with," remembered Tony Kroeker, a hiking companion. "He was a workaholic. He was always wanting to do things. He'd come over to my place and help me work or put up a shed. But he didn't work enough for himself."

Getting behind on child support cost Kevin his driver's license, which made it more difficult to find a job. "If you can't drive, how can you work?" noted our mutual friend Rick "Ricochet" Goff. "So people drive without a license, and then they turn you into criminals." The policy of confiscating driver's licenses for nonpayment of child support or fines is shortsighted but widespread, affecting at least 7 million Americans. Hawaii, Kansas, Vermont and Virginia have all suspended the licenses of more than 9 percent of their adult populations.

Tom Green died in 1996 of heart troubles, at the age of sixty-three, and Kevin became the man of the house. But he wasn't the man he aspired to be. His debts soared to $35,000, making searching for a job less attractive, because his wages would be garnished. Without a decent job, he wasn't the role model for his twins that he aspired to be; he wasn't what his dad had been to him. His self-image suffered.

"My boys all tried to be like their dad," recalled Irene Green. "And they didn't feel like they were making the grade."

The problem is not the overall economy, which has been soaring. In

Kevin's lifetime, the U.S. economy quintupled in size, and American corporate profits rose tenfold. Just since 2000, private wealth in the United States has increased by $46 trillion, or an average of $365,000 per household. But that's like saying that when Jeff Bezos walks into a bar, the average net worth of tipplers there surges by a few billion dollars. True, but misleading. The gains in wealth and income have gone largely to a tiny share of the population, as is common knowledge by now. The people in the top 0.1 percent did fantastically well after 1980, those in the top 1 percent did very well, those below them in the top 10 percent enjoyed incomes growing at the same pace as the economy and those in the bottom 90 percent all lost ground—their incomes grew more slowly than the overall economy—during the last four decades. The Wall Street bonus pool at the end of each year exceeds the combined annual earnings of all Americans working full-time at the federal minimum wage. Average hourly wages were actually lower in 2018 ($22.65) than they had been forty-five years earlier in 1973 ($23.68 in today's prices), according to Bureau of Labor Statistics data. As for wealth, the median net worth adjusted for inflation of young and middle-aged Americans is lower than it was in 1989.

Raj Chetty, a Harvard economist, has found that for Americans born in 1940, roughly Kevin's dad's generation, 92 percent earned more at the age of thirty than their parents had at that age, after adjusting for inflation. That share declined steadily so that for those born in 1984, only half earned more than their parents had.

"Working-class America can't recover if we don't make work pay again," says Gordon Berlin, head of an economic research group called MDRC that studies ways to reduce poverty. Berlin says that if he could do just one thing to attack poverty, it would be to improve wages for people at the bottom. "I feel pretty strongly about this as the core underlying problem," Berlin told us. "If wages had continued to grow since the 1970s proportionately with the economy as they had in the post–World War II period, the average wage for a male full-time non-supervisory worker today wouldn't be $43,000 a year, but closer to $90,000. Think about that. It is likely that the poverty rate would be less than half of what we have today, it is unlikely that the nation's political fabric would be as riven by race and class, and the desperation that contributed to the opioid crisis would not be at its current crisis level."

Official unemployment rates today are impressively low, but they don't count people like Kevin who dropped out of the labor force: for every man aged twenty-five to fifty-four who counts as unemployed, three more don't have jobs but aren't looking for work. The percentage of these prime-age men who are out of the labor force has soared more than fivefold since the 1950s, although there has been significant improvement in recent years. When decent jobs disappear, the loss is not just economic but has consequences for self-esteem, family structure, substance abuse, hopelessness and even child abuse. One study found that for each percentage point increase in the unemployment rate in a county, the incidence of child neglect rose by 20 percent.

Disappearing jobs is a problem that varies greatly by region. Economists debate whether the American economy overall is at full employment, but it certainly isn't in Flint, Michigan, where 35 percent of men of prime working age were not employed in 2018. Hubs of the "knowledge economy," based on technology and education, have prospered, while rural areas and industrial regions continue to struggle. Half of all zip codes have less employment today than they did in 2007, while San Francisco, Seattle, Boston and New York are flourishing. Even more jobs may disappear in the coming years with the spread of artificial intelligence and machine learning. Truck drivers and cashiers, jobs that don't require much education, could largely be replaced by automation. The OECD estimates that 38 percent of jobs in rich countries are at risk, with 10 percent of jobs disappearing outright and another 28 percent requiring new skills and significant retraining. Experts have widely differing views about the severity of the challenge, but many agree that displaced workers will need substantial retraining to get jobs in the modernizing economy.

The late economist Alan Krueger found that almost half of prime-age men not in the workforce take pain pills every day, and the majority say that they are disabled or otherwise unable to hold a job. Many are like Kevin: poorly educated with criminal records, physically unhealthy, mentally unwell, and unhappy and lonely. Left and right may disagree about who is to blame, but fewer than one-third of Americans say in surveys that the country is headed "in the right direction," while large majorities say we're "on the wrong track." When pollsters asked Americans recently to offer a word to describe the times, among the top eight offerings were "worrisome," "chaotic," "exhausting," "hellish" and "hectic."

KEVIN'S SISTER, CINDY, also struggled. A wonderful homemaker who kept a vegetable garden and made delicious cookies and pies, she also became obese, had a son but never married and seemed lonely. She took medicine and eventually underwent surgery for her obesity, but the medication made her tired and she fell asleep on the job. The hospital warned her that it couldn't tolerate an employee in the ICU dozing when she was supposed to be monitoring equipment. The next time it happened, she was fired. Then, at age fifty-two, while walking from her car to the house, she dropped dead of a heart attack.

Ever since high school, Kevin had dabbled with marijuana, and increasingly he drank and took meth. With job troubles and other difficulties, Clayton said, "you start doing hard drugs or whatever, trying to make shit easier." Kevin also complicated his troubles with his temper. His ex-girlfriend periodically tried to drop the kids off with Kevin for a day or two, sometimes without letting him know ahead of time. Once she tried to drop them off for a weekend when he had to go to work.

"You can't," Kevin told her, as his mother remembers it. "You've got to take them back with you." When the ex-girlfriend refused and tried to leave, Kevin pulled a shotgun on her. "You guys get off this property," he ordered. She called the police, who arrested Kevin. He was convicted of drug-related felonies, making it even more difficult to find work, leaving him a poor role model for the boys and further eroding his self-esteem.

There were jobs around, but employers wanted people with a full high-school diploma and no criminal record. They certainly didn't want undereducated, overweight men with drug felony convictions, and when jobs turned up they were discouragingly poorly paid. Kevin couldn't even dream of getting the kind of well-paid blue-collar job that his dad had supported a family on.

Increasingly, we have come to believe that society needs to focus much more on jobs, for two reasons. First, it is more politically sustainable for the government to provide work for the needy than to mail benefit checks. Second, working-class jobs are often a source not just of income but of self-worth and identity. The sociologist Michèle Lamont wrote in her book *The Dignity of Working Men* that working-class white men often define their value in terms of their disciplined lives going to work to support their families, thus taking pride in themselves. This was true of Tom Green.

Because identity and self-esteem are closely tied to work, a poorly paying job may still be better for well-being than no job. In surveys, self-reported happiness drops ten times as much from a loss of a job as from a major loss of income. Long-term jobless men are three times as likely to be treated for depression as other men. Lack of employment is also associated with physical and mental-health problems, divorce, opioid use and suicide. The crucial gap on these metrics isn't between rich workers and poor workers, but between poor people who have a job and poor folks who don't.

Kevin may not seem like a sympathetic figure—an obese ex-felon deadbeat who pulled a gun on his ex-girlfriend. But, as Oscar Wilde wrote, "every saint has a past, and every sinner has a future." In many ways, Kevin encapsulates the crisis in the working class and the broken spirit among those who can't get work even after years of a roaring economy and end up beaten down by the marketplace. These are not Horatio Alger characters but complicated people who make serious mistakes and see their dignity, hopes and prospects deflated.

Kevin's self-destructiveness ironically was matched by his extraordinary generosity. When passing through the town of Sheridan once, he saw a homeless man without a shirt, badly sunburned on his shoulders.

"Why don't you put on a shirt so you ain't blistering?" Kevin suggested.

"I don't have a shirt," the man replied.

"Here," Kevin said, pulling off his own shirt. "Take this."

Had Kevin not had some bad breaks, this generosity might have been the dominant theme of his life, rather than joblessness, arrests and poverty.

Although he didn't talk about it much, Kevin was also frustrated by the path his kids were on. Beginning in fourth grade, the twins began getting into trouble, initially for petty offenses like stealing from the school, later for drug felonies, sexual abuse and probation violations. Neither boy finished high school. The Green family, so promising in the mid-1970s when we were in high school, now had gone backward. Friends tried to help with work or rides (Kevin sometimes cut firewood for Nick's mom on the Kristof family farm), but his health made it increasingly difficult to hold down a real job. Kevin's anguish has been repeated in millions of homes around America. As Langston Hughes put it, the "dream in the land" had "its back against the wall."

SOME OF THESE TALES are tragic, but this book is born of hope. Sheryl's grandparents were immigrants who fled Taishan in southern China and started over in America with a Chinese restaurant. Despite hostility and discrimination, including the Chinese Exclusion Act, the family invested in education and sent a granddaughter to three Ivy League institutions, which led to a job at *The Wall Street Journal*, where she met a young *New York Times* reporter who had grown up on a modest farm near Yamhill, Oregon.

We two are the fruits of America's progress, the beneficiaries of its opportunities. Because of our parents' passion for books and learning, we both were able to ride the education escalator upward, and we've witnessed breathtaking progress in our lifetimes. Today 80 percent of American households living in poverty have at least one air conditioner, while almost none did when we were children. Two-thirds of poor households today have cable or satellite television, and almost three-quarters have a car or truck. Health care is still profoundly unequal, but medical advances mean that even the indigent today get better care than, say, the family of a president a century ago; Calvin Coolidge's sixteen-year-old son developed a blister while playing tennis on the White House lawn in 1924, and the boy died of the resulting infection.

Consider also that when we were children, separate toilets and drinking fountains existed for blacks and whites in the South, same-sex relationships were felonious, contraception was still illegal in some states and the United States was so polluted that the oily Cuyahoga River in Cleveland caught fire in 1969.

The progress is undeniable and encourages us to ask: Why can't the gains be more broadly shared? Why do so many people end up left behind and dying young? Why are some statistics, like life expectancy, moving in the wrong direction? Why did the United Nations official in charge of extreme poverty visit not only Mozambique and Mauritania in Africa, but also Alabama? And why did he warn that the United States now has the lowest rate of social mobility in the rich world, and that "the American dream is rapidly becoming the American illusion"?

We are confident that the United States can do better partly because we have seen what is possible. Some organizations are already doing inspiring work addressing these challenges, providing models that government should adopt more broadly. And our peer countries have tested policies that work—however imperfectly—to empower individuals and, through them, entire communities.

In 1962, a young writer named Michael Harrington wrote an enormously influential book called *The Other America*, pulling back the curtain on poverty in the United States. Harrington laid bare misery, writing not as a scold but as someone who believed in the capacity for change. Though we disagree with some of Harrington's political views, his book opened eyes and galvanized a national debate about injustice and poverty; it helped midwife the War on Poverty a few years later. Likewise, we hope in this book to remind fellow citizens that there is another America where people are struggling and dying unnecessarily, often invisibly. "That the poor are invisible is one of the most important things about them," Harrington noted, and as long as that remains true their problems simply won't be addressed. Roman Catholic Cardinal Joseph Tobin put it to us this way: "We're developing a national cataract."

KEVIN HIMSELF NEVER WANTED to be remembered simply as a victim of large, impersonal forces, and he readily acknowledged that he had screwed up at times. He never liked to be pigeonholed as "poor," or "disadvantaged," and neither do most others in low-income communities. Kevin wouldn't seek your sympathy. He and others in similar predicaments are proud and complex, and they resist becoming caricatures to feel sorry for. What Kevin sought wasn't compassion or a handout but respect and a decent job.

He was lonely, embodying this social great depression. Naturally gregarious, he missed his kids; with his driver's license confiscated, he could no longer drop in easily on old friends. He was isolated on the farm, shorn of a support network, lacking the fulfillment that his dad had once found in his job. Indeed, across working-class America, we have an epidemic of loneliness. Older community institutions—churches, bowling leagues, poker evenings, clubs like the Elks, even dinner parties—have frayed, along with social ties. Instead of going out to a movie with friends, people sit on the couch to watch television.

"During my years caring for patients, the most common pathology I saw was not heart disease or diabetes," observed Vivek Murthy, the former surgeon general of the United States. "It was loneliness." He described it as "a growing health epidemic" that can lead to stress, inflammation, obesity, diabetes, heart disease and early death. It may be one reason suicide rates are at a modern high. Murthy calculates that loneliness and social isolation are even more associated with early death than obesity, and have approximately the same impact on lifespan as smoking fifteen cigarettes a day. That is why Great Britain in 2018 appointed a minister for loneliness.

Call this "social poverty." Americans think of poverty as lack of income, but educational failure, family breakdown and social dysfunction work together to destroy individual dignity and self-respect and to engender stress and cycles of self-destructive behaviors that cripple entire families. One consequence is an erosion of trust, accompanied by an increase in loneliness. Kevin struggled to find purpose and self-respect, especially after his girlfriend left him. For his dad, dignity had come from a job and a role as head of the household, but Kevin was able to derive satisfaction from neither. Unemployed men often just sit around and mope: one study found that they spend only an extra nine minutes a day caring for children or the elderly, but an average of five hours a day watching television. Not surprisingly, losing one's job is associated with divorce.

Kevin's problems were magnified because, without a wife and family, he was more inclined to treat doughnuts and soda as major food groups, and he ballooned to 350 pounds. In Canada or Europe, his diabetes and urinary issues might have been manageable, but Kevin regularly lacked health insurance. Emergency rooms cannot treat such chronic problems. His health steadily deteriorated, and he showed liver damage from drinking as well as heart problems.

Kevin eventually was able to get Oregon's version of Medicaid, which helped him get access to doctors, but it may have been too late. He was prescribed a multitude of medications but had difficulty following the doctors' instructions. He still found pleasure in fishing, at Hagg Lake and on the Yamhill River, but health problems made this less and less frequent.

"He was in school with you, Dad?" our daughter asked when she saw Kevin. "He looks so much older." His obesity made it hard for him to walk and hard to do even basic chores, let alone find a job. Then a flu shot led to health complications.

In the winter of 2014–15, Kevin's organs began to fail, and the hospital sent him home on Christmas Day 2014 with the message that his life was almost over.

"What are you crying about?" Clayton asked him.

"I have only two and a half weeks to live," Kevin replied through his tears. Clayton, who had had fistfights with his older brother, now cared for him lovingly. They watched movies together and talked about their lives and things they wished they had done. Kevin was back in the farmhouse in which he'd grown up, the farmhouse that at one time had embodied the Greens' hopes for a better future. In the will Kevin prepared, he left his tools to be divided among his sons, with the wish that they would get along, and allocated the tiny bit of money in his retirement account to pay for his cremation.

4

American Aristocracy

Every gun that is made, every warship launched, every rocket fired
signifies, in the final sense, a theft from those who hunger and are
not fed, those who are cold and are not clothed.
—PRESIDENT DWIGHT D. EISENHOWER

America's proudest boast throughout history has been that we
have no class system, and that opportunity is available to all.
Yet a starting point in an exploration of our nation must be to
acknowledge that today we do have a class hierarchy, and the Greens
and the Knapps are on the bottom tier. Billionaires like Jeff Bezos
are the new American aristocrats, while people like the Kristofs and
WuDunns, and probably you if you're reading this book, constitute
a new privileged class. This twenty-first-century version of feudalism
rests not only on money but also on access to education and the ability
to pass down inherited benefits and values to one's children. Children
from the richest 1 percent of households are seventy-seven times more
likely to attend an Ivy League college than children from the bottom
20 percent.

The writer Matthew Stewart noted that in the old aristocracies, the
rich were better nourished and thus were physically distinct from the

malnourished, stunted masses; in nineteenth-century England, upper-class sixteen-year-olds were eight inches taller than boys of the lower classes. These days, the physical difference isn't height but obesity, diabetes, heart disease, kidney disease, liver disease—all at least twice as common among low-income Americans as among wealthy ones.

In the feudal era, the lords lived in the manor house as the peasants worked the fields. There's an echo of that when the CEO of an agribusiness firm has a private jet at his disposal, while ordinary workers toiling on the assembly line wear adult diapers because they are not given adequate bathroom breaks, as was reportedly the case at poultry processing plants in the United States. In 2019, the hedge fund manager Ken Griffin purchased the most expensive home ever sold in the United States, a 24,000-square-foot penthouse on Central Park South in Manhattan, for $238 million—but because of a tax break for owners of condos in prime locations, he will pay property taxes as if it were worth only $9.4 million. In Florida, a developer is completing a home that is modeled on the palace of Versailles and has eleven kitchens, five swimming pools and a garage for thirty cars. These are monuments to today's inequality just as the original Versailles was such a symbol of the ancien régime. As in historic feudalism, the paramount need is not just for redistribution of income within an unfair system, but for a restructuring of the rules to create a more just society and greater opportunity for those below.

More than a century ago, Theodore Roosevelt described a similar crisis: "Exactly as the special interests of cotton and slavery threatened our political integrity before the Civil War, so now the great special business interests too often control and corrupt the men and methods of government for their own profit. . . . The absence of effective State, and, especially, national, restraint upon unfair money-getting has tended to create a small class of enormously wealthy and economically powerful men, whose chief object is to hold and increase their power. The prime need is to change the conditions which enable these men to accumulate power."

Education is supposed to be "the great equalizer of the conditions of men," as Horace Mann put it. The two of us were beneficiaries of an education system that became more meritocratic in the 1960s. But then our generation created a new elite caste preserved in part by large parental investments in kids. Today's youths get into Ivy colleges because of their perfect SAT scores, but they attain those scores because their parents have been reading to them since infancy, sending them to "enrichment" programs since they were toddlers and spending thousands of dollars on SAT preparation. Ivy Coach, a company based in New York City, charges $1.5 million for a five-year package: counseling to get a child into the right boarding school, then get top SATs, and finally acceptance into a top college—and it seems to work. There's not much room for scrappy, bright kids whose parents don't have a book in the house and are indifferent to schooling. College entrance may be based on metrics that seem meritocratic, like board scores and grades, but consider that 77 percent of kids in the top quartile of incomes graduate from college, compared to 9 percent of kids in the bottom quartile. This matters hugely for life outcomes and social mobility: a college degree on average is worth an additional $800,000 in lifetime earnings. Because Canada does not have such large educational disparities, low-income Canadian children are about twice as likely as their American counterparts to vault to higher incomes. As *The Chronicle of Higher Education* noted, America's education system is now "an inequality machine."

In most of the world, the public school system allocates more resources to disadvantaged kids than to rich ones. In the United States, we rely on local property taxes to fund public schools, so rich suburbs enjoy first-rate public schools that are a pipeline to the best universities, and underprivileged children suffer in third-rate schools with, often, the worst teachers. More than sixty-five years after *Brown v. Board of Education*, the disparities in public education between white kids and black and brown kids remain enormous, and this is a civil rights issue for this century. Since 1988, American schools have gone backward and become increasingly segregated by race. Today 15 percent of black students attend "apartheid schools," in which at most 1 percent of the student body is white, and they graduate at lower rates than in integrated schools. Black students are on average two grade levels behind white students, and kids in poor districts are four grade levels behind those in rich districts. "Quietly and subtly, the opponents of integration have won," writes Rucker C. Johnson in his book *Children of the Dream*, about school integration.

We came to a historic fork in the road in 1973, when this school funding system came within one vote of being overturned in a 1973 Supreme Court decision, *San Antonio Independent School District v. Rodriguez;* if it had been found unconstitutional, American education would look more like European and Canadian systems and we would be a more egalitarian country. The court based its decision in part on the idea that poor schools wouldn't necessarily have worse outcomes, but mounting evidence shows that that is as wrong as "separate but equal" was in 1896.

California's best public elementary schools are in Palo Alto, accessible to anyone who can buy a house in a district where the median home price exceeds $3 million. Next door in East Palo Alto, which is disproportionately poor and minority, children attend inferior schools that lead to an inferior future. In New York State, Governor Andrew Cuomo told us, per-pupil spending at public schools ranges from $11,000 to $33,000, with affluent suburban kids getting the higher sums. "We have to close that disparity," he told us, but he acknowledged that it's a third rail of politics to touch the issue. Liberal hypocrisy is at work here as well. Affluent liberals haven't agitated to address school funding inequity because their children benefit by attending elite, well-funded schools.

Some elements of America's modern feudalism are so embedded that we don't notice them. Dentists are paid substantially more in America than in Canada or Europe, and Americans often can't afford to care for their teeth, partly because the dental lobby has worked ferociously to block dental therapists (found in fifty other countries) from providing cheap and simple services, even in rural areas where there are few dentists.

Americans flying in coach class subsidize the tycoon flying in a private jet, because air traffic control is financed by commercial tickets. Tax depreciation rules subsidize the purchase of private planes. Everybody knows about the cost of food stamps for the poor, but few people are aware that the median taxpayer is also subsidizing the corporate executives whose elegant French dinner is tax deductible.

The public frets about cheating with food stamps (the fraud rate is about 1.5 percent) yet doesn't understand that zillionaires hide assets abroad and thereby deprive the Treasury of some $36 billion a year in taxes—enough to pay for high-quality pre-K and day care for all. Joseph Stiglitz, the Nobel Prize–winning economist, has said that "we confused the hard work of wealth creation with wealth-grabbing."

While the new aristocracy is opening up to women in some areas, in others, such as finance, it remains a white, male bastion. Only 2 percent of partners in venture capital firms are women, and—probably not a complete coincidence—about 2 percent of venture capital is directed to companies founded by women. Only one-fifth of 1 percent of American venture capital goes to companies founded by African-American women. Facebook, Google and Amazon soared partly because they were built by hard-driving, brilliant visionaries, and partly because those visionaries were white men who had access to capital.

The old feudal aristocracy kept its wealth through a combination of rules and norms, and so does today's new aristocracy. There are the subsidies to the wealthy, like the carried interest tax loophole or the mortgage subsidy for yachts. By some calculations, corporate subsidies, credits and loopholes are 50 percent higher than entitlements to the poor (not including Medicare and Medicaid). Some of the other subsidies are outlandish: put a few goats on your golf course and you can classify it as farmland, as President Trump did, and save large sums in taxes.

The tax code has come to serve the interests of the wealthy in myriad other ways. According to documents obtained by *The New York Times*, Jared Kushner appears to have paid zero federal income tax, year after year, even as his net worth quintupled to more than $300 million. In 2015, he had an income of $1.7 million. It's all quite legal, because lobbyists won loopholes for real estate tycoons. The custodians in the buildings don't have artful options like these to avoid paying taxes. Similarly, Amazon paid zero federal income tax in 2018 despite profits of $11.2 billion; indeed, it managed to get a $129 million "rebate" from taxes it didn't pay. That's an effective tax rate of negative 1 percent. Something is wrong with America's tax structure when the working poor pay taxes so the federal government can make a payment to an e-commerce giant owned by the world's richest man.

Then there are the incentives for economic development awarded by states and local areas, often never made public. Oregon awarded Nike $2 billion for five hundred jobs, or $4 million per job. Meanwhile, Louisiana paid $15 million for each of fifteen jobs with Valero Energy. In 2013, Washington State granted Boeing subsidies worth $8.7 billion over sixteen years, the largest subsidy in history for a company. By late April 2016, Boeing had laid off 5,600 workers.

Americans pay about $30 more per month for smartphone service than Europeans do, for the same-quality service. Researchers believe that's because European regulators pursue antitrust policy more aggressively, while for a generation, American antitrust regulators have been asleep at the wheel. "The United States invented antitrust and for decades has been the pioneer in its enforcement," Luigi Zingales, a finance professor at the University of Chicago, noted. "Not anymore."

The wealthy have also fought to underfund and defang the Internal Revenue Service, so it doesn't have the resources to audit or fight dubious deductions. Only about 6 percent of tax returns of those with income of more than $1 million are audited, along with 0.7 percent of business tax returns. Meanwhile, there is one group that the IRS scrutinizes rigorously: the working poor with incomes below $20,000 a year who receive the Earned Income Tax Credit. More than one-third of all tax audits are focused on that group struggling to make ends meet, even as the agency cuts back on audits of the wealthy—while the top 5 percent of taxpayers account for more than half of all underreported income. Overall, criminal prosecutions of tax cheats are now exceedingly rare, just one for every 385,000 households. Every dollar invested in the IRS for audits brings in $200 in new revenue—which is precisely why so many wealthy people want to starve it, while pretending that this is a populist move.

Criminal justice is a prime example of a two-tier system. Pass a bad check, and you may end up with a felony conviction, serve time in prison and lose your kids. But commit a white-collar crime like tax evasion or fraud, and in most cases crime will pay. Even if you are actually prosecuted and convicted, you're very unlikely to end up behind bars. For example, Joel Sanders, the former chief financial officer of the law firm Dewey & LeBoeuf, was convicted in 2017 of felonies for engaging in fraud while at the law firm, which collapsed. In a very unusual arrangement, Sanders was given no jail time, only a $1 million fine to pay over three years. Sanders found a new $375,000-a-year job as chief operating officer at a different firm and continued to hold on to a Long Island home, a top-floor oceanfront condominium in Miami and about $1 million in liquid assets, according to the Manhattan District Attorney's Office. He also leased two luxury vehicles, an Audi and a Mercedes-Benz, but in 2018 his attorney asked that the fine be canceled because paying it "would impose an undue hardship" on Sanders and his family.

As Heather Heyer, the young woman killed by a white supremacist in Charlottesville, Virginia, in 2017, observed in her last Facebook post: "If you're not outraged, you're not paying attention."

When we traveled to modern feudalist countries, like Pakistan, we were discomfited by the gaps between the high life inside the barbed-wire compounds and the struggle for survival in slums outside. It seemed ridiculous for tycoons to ride around in Mercedes-Benzes over deeply rutted roads. Yet that's the direction we're moving toward, with public goods like parks and libraries squeezed of resources. As a result, wealthy Americans have developed their own workarounds.

Public schools may deteriorate, but the aristocracy dispatches its children to private schools. If public security deteriorates, live in a guarded, gated compound or rely on a private bodyguard. If the public swimming pool becomes too crowded or limits its hours, build a pool in the backyard or get a weekend house. When airports become zoos, fly private. When the power grid becomes unreliable, buy a backup generator. When the subway is plagued by delays, rely on Uber.

Philip Alston, the United Nations special rapporteur on extreme poverty and human rights, has toured some of the world's poorest and most wretched countries to call attention to global poverty. But he also investigated the United States and wrote wonderingly and scathingly about American acceptance of poverty and inequality. "The United States already leads the developed world in income and wealth inequality, and it is now moving full steam ahead to make itself even more unequal," he declared. In particular, he called on the United States to, as he put it, "decriminalize being poor." It's worth quoting at length from his report:

> Punishing and imprisoning the poor is the distinctively American response to poverty in the twenty-first century. Workers who cannot pay their debts, those who cannot afford private probation services, minorities targeted for traffic infractions, the homeless, the mentally ill, fathers who cannot pay child support and many others are all locked up. Mass incarceration is used to make social problems temporarily invisible and to create the mirage of something having been done.
>
> It is difficult to imagine a more self-defeating strategy. Federal, state, county and city governments incur vast costs in running jails and prisons. Sometimes these costs are "recovered" from the prisoners, thus fuelling the latter's cycle of poverty and desperation. The criminal records attached to the poor through imprisonment make it even harder for them to find jobs, housing, stability and self-sufficiency. Families are destroyed, children are left parentless and the burden on governments mounts. . . . In the United States, it is poverty that needs to be arrested, not the poor simply for being poor.

The United States has been much more hostile to private labor unions than other countries have been, with fewer than 7 percent of private-sector workers now in a union—one reason almost half of American jobs pay less than $15 an hour. Consider this sentiment: "Labor is prior to and independent of capital. Capital is only the fruit of labor, and could never have existed if labor had not first existed. Labor is the superior of capital, and deserves much the higher consideration." Was that said by Karl Marx, Eugene Debs, Bernie Sanders or another socialist? Actually, it was said by Abraham Lincoln, in his first State of the Union address. Yet in recent decades, the political system has become more pro-business and suspicious of labor. "This country is the cesspool of labor relations," AFL-CIO president Richard Trumka told us. "It's much better in Europe." He argues that union membership brings a 30 percent wage premium for white men, and a somewhat greater gain for women and people of color.

Union featherbedding was real, but it has been replaced by corporate featherbedding with substantial interference in free markets. Noncompete agreements, which prevent an employee from getting a job at a competing company (even low-level jobs at fast-food outlets), constrain some 18 percent of American workers, or 30 million people, and have become a way for large corporations to intimidate employees, limit their mobility and keep labor costs down. Overall, economists have estimated that up to one-third of the increase in earnings inequality is a result of the weakening of unions.

In Denmark, partly because of strong unions, workers at McDonald's earn $20 an hour, have paid maternity and paternity leave, overtime, work schedules four weeks in advance, pension plans and five weeks of paid vacation each year. (Note also that while taxes are high, the average Dane works one-fifth fewer hours in a year than the average American.)

We once asked Alan Krueger, the late Princeton University economist who was previously chairman of the White House Council of Economic Advisers, about our perception that the American economy increasingly is structured unfairly to benefit corporations and hurt ordinary citizens. We thought he might push back, but he agreed completely. "The economy is rigged," he said.

That in turn reflects a political dimension that exacerbates the inequity: the *Citizens United* ruling by the Supreme Court and related cases in effect legalize graft by ruling that corporations and other players can spend "independent" money on campaigns without any limit. This legalized graft is accentuated by the revolving doors among industry, Congress and the federal bureaucracy. Of the senior congressional staff who worked on the 2010 Dodd-Frank law overseeing the financial industry, 40 percent have moved on to work on behalf of the finance companies that they purported to regulate. "The American people think this system is completely rigged," Fred Wertheimer, a longtime expert on government ethics, told us. "And they're correct."

One might think that economic inequality leads to self-correction in democracies, as the public becomes alarmed or outraged by income gaps and institutes taxes or other policies to take from the rich or give to the poor. But this doesn't happen often. Researchers have found that instead, in countries around the world, the accumulation of wealth also often leads to accumulation of political power that is then harnessed to multiply that wealth. Indeed, that's what we're seeing in America. Our political system responds to large donors, so politicians create benefits for the rich, who then reward the politicians who created them. How different is this from the symbiosis in the Middle Ages between a king and the nobility, elevating aristocrats who repressed the peasantry at the same time that they hailed their own magnanimity and rolled their eyes at the peasants' morals?

5

How America Went Astray

People who are hungry and out of a job are the stuff of which dictatorships are made.

—FRANKLIN D. ROOSEVELT, State of the Union Address, 1944

K evin Green died at home, age fifty-four, in January 2015, three weeks after leaving the hospital. So much had changed since the days when he was a sleek cross-country runner with a shining future.

Shortly after mourning Kevin, our mutual friend Rick "Ricochet" Goff himself was dying after a lifetime of drink, drugs and negligible health care. Ricochet was smart but had been expelled from school in eighth grade (as punishment for truancy!) and never recovered.

Then Mary Mayor, Nick's seventh-grade crush, a sweet, raven-haired girl who was the daughter of the county trapper, went off the rails. Mary was smart, hardworking and infinitely resourceful: when her parents moved away after her junior year of high school, she wanted to graduate with her friends, so she got a job at the Yamhill Café, rented a room and finished school on her own. But soon after graduation she was swamped by the wave of joblessness, despair, alcohol and drugs sweeping the area, and she didn't get the help that she needed. She spent seven years homeless, once putting a gun in her mouth to end it all. Her sister and three other relatives had already killed themselves. Just as she was about to squeeze the trigger, she thought of her daughter and paused; she decided to soldier on. Finally, with the help of a local church, Mary was able to start over. She is now sober and drug-free, making a living selling her own handcrafted birdhouses, though she still suffers pancreatitis from her drinking years. She was mortified to share details of her past but agreed to do so because she wants Americans to see those who struggle as real people. "I'd like to keep my personal life private," she acknowledged, "but then at the same time I want to let others know what it's like to be homeless and wonder where your next meal is going to be."

Kevin, Ricochet and Mary were good, capable, caring people who found themselves swamped by larger economic changes—and then that brokenness was passed to the next generation, with their children struggling with their own demons of addiction, unemployment or incarceration. Yes, people made bad choices, sometimes criminal ones.

Mary Mayor, after a great recovery from alcohol, drugs and homelessness, with one of the birdhouses she makes and sells for a living
(Photo by Nicholas Kristof)

But the essence of the problem is not individual behavior any more than the deaths of alcoholics were a problem of individual debauchery in the declining Soviet Union. In each case, the bad decisions were a symptom of larger economic malaise. In white America, the impact was focused on those who came of age in the late 1970s or afterward. Irene Green had lost Thomas Jr., Cindy and Kevin but was herself going strong physically and mentally at age eighty. Her own mother had died recently at ninety-seven. The younger generations of Greens were far more troubled, and you could see the declining well-being of working-class America—and a visualization of America's declining life expectancy—each time you looked around the Green dinner table. What we saw was a tragedy not just for one family, for the country cannot achieve its potential when so many citizens are not reaching theirs.

This is not an exclusively liberal or conservative issue. Conservative writers like Charles Murray and David Brooks have explored these chasms, with Brooks arguing that "the central problem of our time is the stagnation of middle-class wages, the disintegration of working-class communities and the ensuing fragmentation of American society." On the left, Senator Elizabeth Warren and many other Democrats have made similar arguments. Remarkably, this pain in white working-class America helped account for the rise of both Donald Trump on the right and Bernie Sanders on the left.

What went wrong?

For much of the nineteenth and twentieth centuries, the United States had pioneered efforts to create opportunity. The Homestead Acts, beginning in 1862, were a self-help program that gave American families 160 acres of land each if they farmed it productively or improved it over five years. Homesteads transformed the West and turned impoverished workers into landed farmers. One-quarter of Americans can trace some of their family wealth to that visionary initiative. Another historic program was rural electrification, which beginning in 1936 brought electricity (and later telephone service) to farmers across America, transforming rural life, improving productivity and multiplying opportunity.

The United States was one of the first regions of the world to offer near universal basic education, and then one of the first countries to introduce high schools for nearly all children. "By the early twentieth century America educated its youth to a far greater extent than did most, if not every, European country," Claudia Goldin and Lawrence F. Katz write in *The Race Between Education and Technology*, their exploration of how investments in human capital made America the world's leading country. "Secondary schools in America were free and generally accessible, whereas they were costly and often inaccessible in most of Europe. Even by the 1930s America was virtually alone in providing universally free and accessible secondary schools." A state university and community college system made tertiary education widespread, and the aforementioned GI Bill of Rights vastly expanded educational attainment and homeownership in America. Three-quarters of men who had served in the military took advantage of the educational opportunities in the GI Bill, and 5 million became homeowners as a result. The GI Bill was a major investment in ordinary Americans, and it paid huge returns by creating the modern middle class.

There were many other historic initiatives in the early twentieth century that put the United States on a progressive path. In the 1930s, America helped pioneer limits on guns with the National Firearms Act, in which members of Congress seriously considered banning handguns. In that same era, Congress approved social safety net programs like Social Security, unemployment insurance and jobs initiatives like the Civilian Conservation Corps. Other countries later adopted many elements of these programs.

Then in about 1970, for reasons we'll explore, America went off track, beginning a nearly half-century drift in the wrong direction. High-school graduation rates tumbled from the highest to among the lowest in the industrialized world. Incarceration rose sevenfold. Family structure collapsed. Single-parent households soared. Life expectancy peaked. Working-class incomes grew glacially, if at all. The top one-hundredth of 1 percent of Americans enjoyed a quadrupling of incomes since 1980, after adjusting for inflation, and the rest of the 1 percent saw a bit less than a doubling of real incomes. Those in the 90th through 99th percentiles simply stayed even, with incomes growing at the same rate as per capita GDP, or gross domestic product. And the bottom 90 percent lost relative ground, with their incomes since 1980 growing more slowly than per capita GDP. The result is that the top 1 percent now owns twice as great a share of national wealth as the entire bottom 90 percent. We went from being a world leader in opportunity to being a laggard.

The decline in education leadership is particularly significant, because good jobs increasingly require a solid educational foundation. Globalization, automation and a relentless focus on cost cutting led to a hollowing out of urban blue-collar and clerical jobs that in the past were often performed by people with limited education. David Autor, an economist at MIT, has found that as a result, urban workers with only a high-school education fill jobs that are actually lower skilled now than back in the 1970s.

One reason Kevin Green floundered was that he hadn't graduated from high school. That hadn't been an impediment for earlier generations of blue-collar workers, including his dad, for in the early 1970s some 72 percent of American jobs required only a high-school education or less. By 2020, that will have fallen to 36 percent. One consequence is a plunge in earnings for those with limited education. In the 1970s, a male high-school graduate earned on average almost four-fifths as much as a male college graduate, but that has fallen to just over 50 percent. And those like Kevin who didn't graduate from high school do even worse.

The last half century is also the period in which the American pathway began to diverge significantly from the paths of Canada and Europe. In the 1970s, the top 1 percent earned a similar share of income, 10 percent, whether in the United States or Europe. That rose modestly in Europe to 12 percent today; in the United States it doubled to 20 percent. That's the calculation of the economists Thomas Piketty, Emmanuel Saez and their colleagues; others offer different estimates that show a smaller increase in inequality.[*]

---

[*] We want to acknowledge the risk throughout of cherry-picking statistics. Reasonable people can examine data and reach varied conclusions. For example, here we cite the figures of Piketty and Saez on a soaring share of incomes among the top 1 percent. But

Former Treasury secretary Larry Summers offers another prism to look at inequality. He calculates that if we now had the same income distribution that we had in 1979, the bottom 80 percent of the distribution would have $1 trillion more, and the top 1 percent would have $1 trillion less. That means that the average family at the top would earn $700,000 less per year, and the average family in the bottom 80 percent would earn $11,000 more. For an average working family, that would amount to almost a 25 percent increase in income.

In 1970, tax revenue made up about the same share of gross national product in the United States as the average in the OECD, the club of industrialized nations. It then inched up in every other rich country, as one might expect when populations age and need more public services, while remaining unchanged in the United States. So people in other wealthy countries today pay about an extra ten cents on the dollar in taxes, but in exchange get health insurance, better infrastructure, less poverty, reduced homelessness and, we'd argue, a healthier society.

U.S. deregulation and pro-business policies do genuinely nurture economic growth and dynamism, but there are trade-offs. France's per capita GDP, for example, is well below that of the United States. Yet look at a typical citizen in each country, and the difference is not so clear-cut. One study finds that the average French citizen is 92 percent as well off as the average American, and that the average French per-

these are complex calculations subject to genuine disagreement. The economists Gerald Auten and David Splinter make various technical adjustments and conclude that the top 1 percent's share, particularly after taxes and transfers, has increased but by much less (partly because inequality in 1960 was worse than assumed). So please be aware that data sets and conclusions vary.

Likewise, there are disputes about median incomes. The Census Bureau calculates that median family income has grown only 7 percent in real terms since 1979. But the Congressional Budget Office shows a 51 percent gain in that period. The differences come from whether one looks at pretax income or after-tax income, how one adjusts for inflation and whether one adjusts for smaller family size. Similarly, poverty can be measured with official statistics (12.3 percent) or with a supplemental poverty measure (13.9 percent) that is generally regarded as superior, or with statistical analyses favored by some conservatives that look at spending by the poor and suggest that poverty is far lower (about 3 percent). We will try to avoid the temptation, as the saying goes, of using statistics as a drunk uses a lamppost, for support rather than illumination. We will focus on the weight of the evidence, which to us suggests that while any one statistic is open to interpretation, a large number of indicators converge to indicate a crisis for working-class Americans.

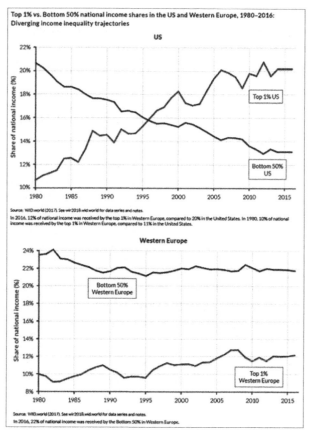

Top 1% vs. Bottom 50% national income shares in the US and Western Europe, 1980–2016: Diverging income inequality trajectories

This chart from the "World Inequality Report 2018" shows how the top 1 percent gained enormous ground in the United States since 1980, but only modestly in Western Europe.

son also lives longer than the average American, is less likely to have a child die, is less likely to die in childbirth, works 310 fewer hours in a year (more than an hour less per workday), is less likely to be murdered and is less likely to die of a drug overdose. The two of us prefer the American life, but not everyone, particularly those left behind, would make the same choice.

"American exceptionalism" these days often runs in the wrong direction: we're frequently exceptional because of economic and social pathologies that we suffer to a much greater degree than other advanced countries. A woman in America is now roughly twice as likely to die in childbirth as a woman in Britain. Shouldn't this be an embarrassment to every American? We forged a different path over the last half century from the rest of the advanced world, and it has turned out to be a dead end for millions of Americans.

ONE SIGN THAT the United States was moving rightward and following a different trajectory than the rest of the West was the election of Ronald Reagan in 1980. Reagan both reflected and shaped the country's mood in the 1970s when in his speeches he regularly denounced a Chicago welfare recipient: "She has eighty names, thirty addresses, twelve Social Security cards and is collecting veteran's benefits on four nonexistent deceased husbands."* After his election to the presidency, he famously declared in his inaugural address in 1981, "Government is not the solution to our problem; government is the problem." He broke the air traffic controllers' union, worker protections declined and the business world became much more powerful.

As hostility toward government spread in America, there have been determined efforts to cut taxes, particularly for the wealthy, and then "starve the beast"—using reduced revenue to justify cuts in services for the disadvantaged. This is both disingenuous and cruel, as well as out of step with the advanced world. Other countries over the decades expanded health-care coverage, adopted family-leave policies, extended mass transit and implemented child allowances to reduce poverty, while the United States bucked the trend by slashing taxes, cutting back hours at public libraries, raising tuition at state universities and allowing infrastructure to decay. Grover Norquist, an influential Republican advocate

---

* Reagan's denunciation was exaggerated but based on a real Chicago woman, Linda Taylor, who used at least thirty-three aliases and bilked government programs as well as private individuals; she was also suspected of homicide and baby trafficking, so welfare fraud may have been the least of her offenses. She did drive a Cadillac and wore furs, and the *Chicago Tribune* dubbed her a "welfare queen." But most studies have found that cheating of public assistance programs is quite modest, perhaps 2 percent—less than tax evasion by the wealthy.

for lower tax rates, captured the small government ideology: "My goal is to cut government in half in twenty-five years, to get it down to the size where we can drown it in the bathtub."

Why did the United States drift so far rightward in a way other countries mostly did not? We wonder if one reason wasn't national anxiety about race, violence and unrest beginning in the mid-1960s. This was the time of assassinations of John F. Kennedy, Robert Kennedy and Martin Luther King Jr., of political riots in Chicago, of race riots in Los Angeles, Newark, Detroit and other cities, of domestic terrorists like the Weathermen, of talk of revolution, of hippies and yuppies, of furious debates in households across America. Repeated psychology experiments have shown that fear makes us more conservative in our political beliefs, and Richard Nixon seized upon the fears in 1968 when he ran for president with coded dog whistles playing on white apprehensions of black unrest.

This "southern strategy" turned the South into a GOP bastion, and the fearmongering has often extended into social policies as well. Welfare was portrayed as handouts to lazy blacks, and immigration as a threat to American culture and jobs. The lack of social-support policies then led to a certain despair and disintegration of traditional communities, amplifying fears that traditional values were being lost and pushing states that once had progressive streaks, like Iowa and Oklahoma, firmly into the Republican camp. Kent Hance, a Texas politician who defeated George W. Bush in a 1978 congressional race, told us that the lesson his victory taught Bush was, "He wasn't going to be out-Christianed or out-good-old-boyed again." That was broadly true in much of the South and middle of the country, as "God, guns and gays" became dominant issues that helped conservatives.

Another factor was the inflation of the 1970s and the recognition that American business had grown too complacent, too blasé about efficiency and shareholder return, so that the economy really did need a kick in the pants. European and Japanese corporations were gaining ground, and some union rules did suppress innovation and labor-saving efficiencies. There were legitimate grounds for deregulation and also a genuine need for new industries like venture capital and private equity that forced efficiencies in the bloated private sector. But we then went too far in unleashing unfettered capitalism. In the 1970s, we undermined our international competitiveness because our companies looked after all stakeholders, employees included; today we've gone to the other extreme, as ruthless corporations scurry to the beck and call of shareholder capitalism. Our international competitiveness is damaged because the American economy has created a Hobbesian world in which life is "solitary, poor, nasty, brutish and short." As the business writer Steven Pearlstein put it: "What began as a useful corrective has, 25 years later, become a morally corrupting and self-defeating economic dogma that threatens the future of American capitalism. . . . Our current prosperity is not sustainable because it is not producing the kind of society that most of us desire."

In the mid-twentieth century, Big Business was kept in check by Big Government and Big Labor, but that balance faded and business now faces fewer constraints. As society fractured, the sense of everyone being in the same boat faded, so that it became more acceptable to flaunt wealth. Indeed, riches became something to be celebrated; in 1984, the television series *Lifestyles of the Rich and Famous* made its debut. The writer Michael Tomasky puts it this way: "Americans became a more acquisitive—bluntly, a more selfish—people."

In 1965, the average chief executive earned about twenty times as much as the average worker; now the average CEO earns more than three hundred times as much. A Walmart employee earning the median salary at the company, $19,177, would have to work for 1,188 years to earn as much as the chief executive did in 2018 alone. Companies also changed the ways they operated, outsourcing custodial jobs and eliminating pensions in ways that raised share prices but left many families more vulnerable. Historically, corporations that prospered returned significant sums to workers, but increasingly investors protested solicitude to employees. When American Airlines announced in 2017 that it would reinvest a share of its hefty first-quarter earnings in pay raises for staff, Wall Street erupted in jeers. "Labor is being paid first again," protested an analyst for Citigroup. "Shareholders get leftovers." Morgan Stanley downgraded American Airlines shares, citing the "worrying precedent," and the airline's share price tumbled 8 percent over two days.

Oren Cass, a former management consultant at Bain & Company who was domestic policy director for Mitt Romney's presidential campaign, understands the arguments for business efficiencies. He notes that the erosion of the old labor market resulted in strong overall economic growth and cheap products. But the trade-off was not worth it, he adds. In his book *The Once and Future Worker,* he cautions, "What we have been left with is a society teetering atop eroded foundations, lacking structural integrity, and heading toward collapse."

Whereas government historically had helped struggling Americans with measures like the GI Bill of Rights, it retreated just as disappearing jobs, proliferating drug use and disintegrating families increased the need for social services. The churches, schools and community organizations could not respond adequately when faced with these dark new forces, so government officials instinctively lashed back with mass incarceration that only compounded the problems. In medieval Europe, villages responded to inexplicable crop failures from the "Little Ice Age" by burning witches; in the twenty-first century, we built prisons instead. Neither was a successful strategy.

Increasingly, government not only refused to help but also seemed to adopt petty cruelty as a principle of governance. More states and localities, for example, imposed an array of fines on even minor offenders as a way to fund agencies—and then locked people up when they couldn't pay. The civilized world had begun to close debtors' prisons in the 1830s, seeing them as barbaric. Yet when we dropped in on the Tulsa jail one day, we found twenty-three people inside simply for failing to pay government fines and fees. One gray-haired woman, Rosalind Hill, fifty-three years old with a long history of mental illness and drug addiction, had spent eighteen months incarcerated for failure to pay a blizzard of fees and fines. With penalties and interest, her total owed had soared to $11,258, but her depression and bipolar disorder made it impossible for her to hold a job. So she was periodically imprisoned

The Tulsa jail, where one day we found twenty-three people locked up simply for failure to pay government fines *(Photo by Lynsey Addario)*

for failure to pay, and then new fines would be tacked on top of the old ones.

In Oklahoma, criminal defendants can be assessed sixty-six different kinds of fees, ranging from a "courthouse security fee" to a "sheriff's fee for pursuing fugitive from justice." There's even a fee for an indigent person applying for a public defender, even though the indigent by definition can't pay; once they confirm their indigence by failing to pay, they are arrested. The sums accumulate to staggering levels. Cynthia Odom, an office worker in Tulsa, told us that she owes $170,000 and is constantly at risk of being carted off to jail, away from her two children. Even the Tulsa district attorney, Stephen Kunzweiler, told us, "It's a dysfunctional system."

That's not simply Oklahoma. In New York City, detainees were regularly held for failure to pay a one-dollar bail. Typically, this happened when someone was arrested on multiple charges, with $500 bail on the primary charge and one-dollar bail on the secondary charge. But then the main charge was dropped, and the person remained stuck in jail because the computer showed a remaining one-dollar debt. Even if the inmates had healthy bank accounts, they couldn't access them to pay any sum, and sometimes they had no one to ask for help; the obstacle wasn't the money but finding a friend or relative with the time and English-language ability to confront the system and pay the bail. One mother missed her child's funeral because she was jailed on one-dollar bail. Some inmates were held for days, weeks or occasionally months for failure to pay the same amount. Finally, a group of New York University students came up with a solution: they formed the Dollar Bail Brigade, a collection of volunteers who would periodically go to jail and bail out inmates for one dollar. Even for elite university students, the bureaucratic challenges can be staggering: it took one volunteer twenty-four hours and three jail visits to pay an inmate's single dollar of bail.

It's puzzling that many politicians fear that poor people are trying to milk the system, while they don't seem to fear rich people doing the same with far more dollars at stake. The latest fashion for smacking the downtrodden among some lawmakers: work requirements to receive benefits such as Medicaid. In theory, requiring certain people to work in return for benefits could be a useful way to nudge the long-term unemployed back into the labor force. But in practice these requirements are often just an excuse to cut off benefits. Arkansas in 2018 became the first state to impose work requirements for Medicaid. It also required participants to log their work hours online with an email address and a code sent by mail, and proceed through several successive web pages. Unfortunately, Arkansas ranks forty-eighth among states in internet access, and many Medicaid recipients have no email or internet. Even months later, in early 2019, Arkansas's Medicaid website had no clear explanation of the new work requirements or how to reapply or input work hours. Of the first group subjected to the requirement, 72 percent could not comply. So families lost health insurance, and then some people were unable to get medication and, their sicknesses flaring, lost *jobs*. This is a reminder that work requirements are often a camouflaged and mean-spirited move to kick people out of the safety net. Meanwhile, from 2007 to 2016, the state granted subsidies of $156 million to corporations, including HP and Caterpillar, under an "economic development" program that researchers found had almost no correlation to increased employment.

Some local leaders are refusing to expand social programs even when voters demand it. After residents in Utah and Idaho voted to expand Medicaid in November 2018, the Republican legislatures tried to roll back those votes. The ethos of the country changed in this half century. Many Americans came to celebrate wealth as a prime metric of success and became more judgmental of those who lost jobs, went bankrupt, used drugs or otherwise stumbled; the acme of this changing ethos was the election in 2016 of a billionaire president who was best known for ostentatious living and for his reality TV refrain: "You're fired!"

THE CAUSES OF ECONOMIC DISTRESS included automation and globalization, which affected workers in many countries, and real wages for low-skilled workers fell not only in the United States but also in Britain and Germany. So as part of our journey to understand what went so badly wrong, we wanted to see if workers battered by these global forces had suffered as severely across the border in Canada. As it happened, a sociologist named Victor Tan Chen had explored precisely that question after the Great Recession of 2008–09. Chen, a professor at Virginia Commonwealth University, spent weeks talking to autoworkers laid off by General Motors and Ford in Detroit and also in Windsor, Ontario, its sister city just across the border. Global economic forces had disrupted auto plants in both countries, but Chen found that laid-off autoworkers fared worse in Detroit. That's partly because of a better Canadian safety net, including a national health-care system, and partly because of a vigorous Canadian effort to cushion the blow. Within twenty-four hours of a big layoff on the Canadian side, the government set up an "action center" to help with job searches, government benefits and access to focused retraining programs. Peer aides would help with preparing résumés and finding solutions. When Ford laid off workers in Windsor, some of them hoped to study nursing, but the local college program was oversubscribed. So the action center convinced the college to start a new nursing program immediately.

Canada did relatively better because it didn't as firmly buy into the narrative that outcomes are simply about personal responsibility, a doctrine that left workers in the United States often feeling like failures and, in Chen's words, "sinking into apathy, despair, and self-blame." Chen argues that the psychological blow of losing a job (and, we would argue, a home) was particularly demoralizing, and he argues for more supportive government policies, like the Canadian action centers or retraining programs and education benefits. He calls for a return to social balance through a "morality of grace," an ethic that relies more on compassion and egalitarianism, less on scolding about personal irresponsibility. The morality of grace arises from the theological concept that everyone can be saved by God's grace, even the undeserving, the uneducated, the jobless, the addicted and the homeless.

Canada is not unusual in its jobs efforts; the United States is. As a fraction of GDP, the United States spends on job-training and assistance programs barely one-fifth as much as the average among industrialized countries. Moreover, the United States has significantly cut spending on these programs in recent decades, while significantly increasing spending on prisons instead.

The lesson is that the tragedies that befell so many working-class Americans were not inevitable. "A lot of people put this on globalization, but the thing about globalization is that it's global," Princeton professor Angus Deaton, the Nobel Prize–winning economist, told us. "And none of this stuff is happening in Germany or France or Spain. The deaths of despair are just not happening in Europe. So something is happening here, and I think it's that over the last forty years a lot of policy has been directed against the working class." Canada and Europe were also roiled by trade disruptions and global recession, but they preserved some space for labor unions and used higher taxes to protect citizens with more comprehensive social safety nets, job retraining, universal health care and strict regulations limiting the marketing of prescription painkillers. So unemployed workers in Canada and Europe were less likely to lose their homes, to see their families break up, to die of overdoses—and they were in a better position to find new jobs and restart their lives when the economy revived. Where was the American government?

America took a half-century detour that has failed particularly in creating inclusive growth. Poor parts of the country had been catching up with the rich parts for much of the twentieth century. Mississippi went from 30 percent of the per capita income in Massachusetts in the 1930s to almost 70 percent by 1975, and similar trends were apparent in other southern states. But that trend slowed and then reversed, so that Mississippi is now down to 55 percent of the Massachusetts per capita income. The reasons seem to be in part self-inflicted. There has been a growing premium in the labor market for educated workers, but Mississippi and other southern states have underinvested in education and other forms of human capital, particularly for blacks but also for whites. The South's strategy was to cut taxes, on the theory that low taxes would attract businesses and boost the economic growth rate, but this was not terribly effective in the age of the knowledge economy. High-paying, high-technology employers want low tax rates, of course, but above all they require a pool of educated workers, so they often end up investing in high-tax, high-education states like California, Massachusetts and New York. This is amplified when right-wing politicians in the South defend Confederate statues or demonize gays or transgender people, and the result is further economic backwardness and frustration. And the cycle repeats.

Not since the Great Depression has America experienced the kind of working-class stagnation that we've seen in recent decades, and it has fed polarization, racism and bigotry, gnawing away at our social fabric. Resentment has grown toward Latinos, Muslims and African Americans, and sometimes toward upwardly mobile women as well. White supremacists gained ground, and on websites and social media Americans glibly trumpet their bigotry. Hate crimes have increased in the United States for three years in a row, the FBI reported. On one ultra-right website we visited, people posted venomous statements about Muslims and called for mass deportation. One woman proposed, "Any Muslim man wanting to come into our country must be castrated first."

Is this America?

The white working class has genuine grievances. It has greatly suffered from rising inequality, from a minimum wage falling in real terms and from inattention by Washington politicians. Perhaps as a result, this demographic is also extremely distrustful of politicians and political solutions—93 percent say they have an unfavorable view of politicians.

"This creates a dilemma for Democrats," the economist Isabel Sawhill notes in her book *The Forgotten Americans.* "Any activist agenda risks driving even more of the working class into the Republican camp, especially if that agenda relies on Washington-led policy making and new taxes." So far, these voters have doubled down on politicians who want to move the United States farther away from the trend in the Western world.

President Donald Trump's election in 2016 was a manifestation of that trend. Trump did extremely well in areas with high death rates for whites aged forty to sixty-four. Many of these working-class white voters had previously supported President Obama and President Clinton, but now they switched sides and backed Trump. "People felt ignored," the pollster Frank Luntz told us. "And Donald Trump spoke to them." Once in office, of course, Trump chipped away at the Affordable Care Act, so that fewer Americans were insured than would otherwise have been the case. Less insurance in turn means that more die from heart disease, cervical cancer and liver ailments, and fewer have access to addiction treatment, a tragic wrong for his working-class supporters.

In Oklahoma, we met a kindergarten teacher named Rhonda McCracken who fervently supports the local domestic violence intervention center, which she said had helped her escape a brutal ex-husband who beat and choked her. "I remember thinking, *He's going to kill me,*" she recalled. "There was hitting and kicking, but choking was most common." Staff at the domestic violence center helped McCracken escape that relationship and start over.

"They saved my life, and my son's," she told us, her eyes liquid.

So how does McCracken vote? "I voted for President Trump," she told us, noting that she is a Republican, and it seemed natural to support him. "I'm conservative, and he was the conservative choice," she explained. Soon after taking office, Trump attempted to cut funds that finance the domestic violence center, and McCracken was aghast. "My prayer is that Congress will step in" to protect domestic violence programs, she told us. Yet she did not regret her vote for Trump, and she was generally sympathetic with his desire to cut spending. She said she might support his reelection.

Because many readers are likely to find the support for the GOP unfathomable in places that are hurting so badly, we asked our Yamhill friend and neighbor Dave Peper to explain his politics. As we'll see later, Dave has endured tough times—including seven episodes of homelessness—but he is a firm supporter of Trump. One reason is that he's a firm believer in gun rights and carries a loaded handgun on his hip at all times. But Dave says that he's also fed up with paying taxes to support social programs that, as he sees it, go to support deadbeats who don't want to work.

"I think we need welfare reform like you can't believe," he said. "I believe there's a ton of people out there milking this system to death. I'm sick and tired of paying for it. I really am. My taxes tend to go up, but my road never gets fixed." As examples of people milking the system, he cites people in the area who don't seem much interested in working hard but get food stamps or disability. Dave and April once tried to help a local meth addict, a construction worker who was homeless, by letting the man stay on their property in his truck. Then the man refused to move out, continued to use drugs and became confrontational. After five months, Dave ordered the man away at gunpoint.

"I really liked the guy and I felt for him, because I had been there," Dave recalled. "He reminds me so much of myself." He shook his head. "We wanted to try and help him, but it seemed that his addiction was more important than trying to find himself a place to live."

Our understanding of politics and the world often differed from Dave's, partly because his version of reality relies heavily on Fox News. "Yes, I watch Fox News," he told us, "but I also watch CNN because

I do like to kind of get a point of view from the other side. I'll be honest, it's kind of hard for me to watch it very long because it feels like lies to me." People like Dave living in a conservative news orbit become inflamed by issues that liberals never even hear about. Dave was incensed that Google Home speakers, when asked questions like "Who is Allah?" or "Who is Buddha?" gave immediate answers but could not readily answer questions like "Who is Jesus?" This was a tempest in the right-wing media world in 2018, prompting accusations that Google was anti-Christian or trying to promote Islam. Google responded by tweaking the algorithm so that it answered all such questions the same way: "Religion can be complicated and I'm still learning."

For all his strong support for Trump, Dave acknowledged being troubled by the polarization and nastiness of politics today. "I don't know what the solution is," he added, "but I just pray every night for my country and my home." Dave reflected local sentiments. In Yamhill in 2016, Trump captured 57 percent of the vote, and Hillary Clinton 32 percent (most of the rest went to Gary Johnson, the libertarian candidate). The Green family also supported Trump, as did so many others who were struggling and whose lives were on the line. As went Yamhill, so went much of white, working-class America. One of the strongest predictors of support for Trump in any county was the share of whites with just a high-school diploma or less. Friends in Yamhill often saw Trump as the outsider who would drain the swamp, bring back jobs in manufacturing and primary industries and restore a period when working-class lives were steadily getting better.

Working-class voters are not uniformly conservative in their views. Polls show that they favor higher taxes on the rich, paid family leave and a higher minimum wage. But the working poor are disdainful of government benefits, even though they sometimes rely on them, partly because they often see firsthand how neighbors abuse those benefits; there's far more anger at perceived welfare abuses than at larger subsidies for private jets. The resentment is more visceral when it is people around them who are bending rules and benefiting unfairly.

Rev. Rhonda Kroeker in Yamhill shares some of that concern, and she, too, is sympathetic to Trump. "People just want a more simple life," she told us. "They want America to be great again. The way it was when we were kids. Maybe they just trusted that this man could actually help make that happen." Pressed on what that simple life would look like, she thought for a moment and answered, "Just the America we grew up in. I was proud to be an American girl. Families were important. It was important to go to school. It was important to have a job. Try and do the right thing for your family. I don't know. Maybe they see that in Trump."

WE BELIEVE THAT NOSTALGIA is widespread, and we wholeheartedly agree that schools, jobs and family are all extremely important. We also argue that this supposed golden era had a dark side: in the early 1960s, before the wave of changes in America, women had few opportunities, African Americans lived under Jim Crow laws and family planning was banned in a majority of states for unmarried women. As recently as 1987, only half of Americans said that it was always wrong for a man to beat his wife with a belt or stick. A 1963 poll found that 59 percent of Americans believed that black-white marriages should be illegal, and interracial marriage was still banned in sixteen states as recently as 1967, when the Supreme Court overturned such laws in the case of *Loving v. Virginia*. Some of those laws banned only black-white marriages, but as of 1950 fifteen states specifically banned all interracial marriages, including those like ours between an Asian American and a white person.

Anyone prone to nostalgia for a "golden era" should remember Gary Knapp firing his gun at the field where Dee lay cowering. Yet it's true that there were indeed elements of that era that were important and that have been lost. Inequality was lower, and working-class families enjoyed huge gains in education, in incomes, in standard of living. Families had their problems, but children were far more likely to be raised in intact, robust two-parent households, and there was very little homelessness. One simple gauge of well-being: suicide rates were much lower than today. Few of our friends understood the plight of those struggling more viscerally than Mary Mayor, Nick's old friend who had spent years homeless and once put a gun in her mouth. So we asked Mary if she supported politicians who would take a different course to fix America. Yes, she said, although she acknowledged that she wasn't terribly interested in politics and had never actually voted until recently. "It was just too complex," she told us. "And I got confused with this or that." But finally, she said, she voted for change in the 2016 general election because the stakes were so high. Casting a ballot for the first time in her life, she voted for Donald Trump.

"Trump is our only hope," Mary told us. "The man's dirty, you know? But he's still plugging forward." She said she wished that Trump would get off Twitter, but added that the economy was doing better, with more jobs available. The media are unfair to Trump, she said, while giving Democrats a pass.

In the fall of 2018, when Taylor Swift endorsed two Democratic candidates, Mary wrote on Facebook, "Taylor Swift, all your music I've collected over the years just became fire starter."

In the middle of a series of Trump scandals, we asked Mary how she thought Trump was doing so far. She paused thoughtfully and said firmly, "He's done a good job."

"He believes in the American people," she added. "I feel great to call myself an American once again."

6

Drug Dealers in Lab Coats

OxyContin is our ticket to the moon.
—DR. RAYMOND SACKLER, Purdue Pharma

D aniel McDowell is a solidly built thirty-two-year-old of Gua-
temalan origin, an olive-skinned refrigerator of a man with
forearms that look like Popeye the Sailor's. He is also addicted
to heroin, and because he lives in Baltimore, which for decades has
been notorious for its narcotics trade, you might think that he became
addicted because of some street-corner dealer. In fact, the people
responsible wore three-piece suits and lab coats, and they never saw
the inside of a jail cell—although Daniel did. We went to Baltimore
because as a city with a large black population it offered a counterpoint
to Yamhill, but we found many parallels in the suffering as well as a
uniquely American story about betrayal.

Daniel joined the army in 2004 after graduating from high school
and was an immediate star. He was in the top 10 percent of his class
at noncommissioned officers school and was promoted on a fast track,
soon commanding soldiers who had been in basic training with him.
Military life appealed to Daniel and for a time brought out the best in
him: he was courageous and liked the camaraderie and sense of mission,

while senior officers found him dependable and purposeful. He served in Afghanistan and Iraq and then signed up for another tour while still in Baghdad. He decided that he was a military lifer, and his wife supported him even as she worried about him.

One day, in southern Afghanistan in the summer of 2006, Daniel's Humvee hit an antitank mine set by the Taliban. A dozen years later, telling us the story in his cramped windowless room in a low-rent district in Baltimore, Daniel was shaky as he remembered the scene. He recalled a sudden concussing boom and then smoke filling the Humvee as pain shot through his body. "My legs hurt so bad that I remember I didn't know if I still had my legs. So I reached down because I couldn't see anything and I felt my legs and in my head I was like, *Thank God.*"

Daniel's knees had been permanently damaged, earning him a Purple Heart and leaving him smoldering with anger at Afghans. Less than a month later, he was caught in a brutal nine-day firefight in which his friend Staff Sergeant Robert J. Chiomento, age thirty-four, took a rocket-propelled grenade in the chest. Daniel's rage at Afghans grew. His job was to operate a .50 caliber machine gun, a monster weapon that can fire ten rounds a second and has a range of four miles. In the firefight, Daniel was frantically firing at everything that moved, every mud-brick compound, anything that looked as if humans might be nearby.

In that moment, Daniel wanted an outlet for his fury at the enemy and at the Afghan people. "We were some bad dudes, we fuck shit up," he told us. "I shot at compounds, I shot at anything that moved, you know what I mean? I was an angry guy. They killed my friends and they hurt me, so at the time I killed anything that walked."

After the battle, rage ebbed and shame grew. It wasn't that Daniel had deliberately massacred women and children in his rifle sights, but he had fired on homes, and his mind conjured terrified kids huddled inside as his fire cut them in half. Long after the firefight was over, the people he had killed inhabited his nightmares. "That's the shit I think about, and the shit that bothers me," he said softly. "I come off as a hard person, but I still have feelings."

Back in the United States in 2009 as a drill sergeant, Daniel found that both his knees and his conscience troubled him. In addition, post-

Daniel McDowell, a war veteran now in a different kind of fight for his life, to overcome drug use, in Baltimore *(Photo by Lynsey Addario)*

traumatic stress disorder left him with nightmares that frightened his wife. "I'd be having the worst dreams, dreams of being over there, getting shot, and I'd be crying in my sleep or sometimes screaming in my sleep," he told us. "She'd be trying to wake me up, whacking me."

Daniel received treatment for his knees, including meniscus surgery, and was prescribed a potent synthetic opioid called Tramadol. He welcomed medication to numb his physical and emotional pain. Military doctors soon referred him to an outside pain clinic that prescribed him large quantities of oxycodone and other opioid painkillers. When Daniel switched doctors, the new physician looked at his medical record in horror.

"You're on more medication than someone with terminal cancer would be on," he told Daniel, and he cut back on the dosing. Now desperate for pain pills and running out, Daniel scrambled for alternatives and raged at the new doctor. *Fuck that guy*, he said to himself. *He cut me off my pills. He doesn't know what I'm going through.*

Daniel knew he needed help, but it would be humiliating to turn to army doctors and explain that he was dependent on pills, plus it might hurt his military career. So instead he took private advice from an army buddy with a neck injury who was a bit ahead of him in the addiction cycle: crush pills into powder, mix with water, and inject the mix into a vein. That helped for a while, but soon Daniel was again running out. For a time he purchased prescription pain pills on the black market, but that was ruinously expensive. So the same army pal introduced Daniel to heroin, a cheaper way to get opioids.

"That started the monster I'm struggling with," Daniel told us. He didn't know it, but this was the most common American route to heroin addiction in modern times: use prescription painkillers, become addicted, scramble to buy them illegally, and when the habit becomes unaffordable, switch to street heroin.

Daniel's descent into addiction has been repeated all across the country on a vast scale, creating individual tragedies and bringing down national life expectancy. In Daniel's case, his work ethic collapsed, he became disheveled, his performance reviews suffered and he faced a violation for being disrespectful.

"You've got an issue with drugs," his wife told him. "You've got to stop."

"Look, I've been through all this shit and I just had this surgery and my back hurts," he retorted angrily. "I work all day long."

So his wife, whom he describes as "the best wife ever," left him.

"I basically ruined our marriage," he explained. "Pills were more important to me than she was."

Stuck with a $150-a-day heroin habit, Daniel soon found himself in debt, and then the army pushed him into early retirement. To pay for his habit, he began dealing heroin. Soon he was arrested and spent eight months in jail on drug charges. On his first night out, he got high again.

Finally, Daniel found a rehab program that would take him. It lasted only twenty-eight days—far too short—but he still managed to stay off drugs for six months. Things looked up: he and his new girlfriend, Megan, had a son, Braydon, whom Daniel doted on. He cared about Braydon more than anything in the world, except one thing—his craving.

"I loved to get high," he told us. "Honestly, that was the main thing. I just loved how it felt. There's no other feeling like that. I would pick being high over sex, over eating, over spending time with my family." The other reason to keep taking heroin, despite the peril, was more banal: avoiding becoming "dope sick" from withdrawal. For anyone dependent on opioids, the physical pain of going without is terrifying. "It's the flu times ten, plus having a baby," one heroin user, Shawn Price, told us. "You can't control your bowels; you're going to throw up everything you eat. I've been shot, and I'd rather be shot again than be ill from heroin withdrawal."

Although Daniel is devoted to Megan and Braydon, heroin upends his priorities. "When I'm using," he told us, "I'm going to do what I have to do to get it. Lie. Cheat. Steal." Sure enough, Daniel soon relapsed and was back to heroin. He stole from Megan and lied to her, so she kicked him out, and Daniel wound up homeless in Baltimore. He had plenty of company, for the U.S. government estimates that there are about forty thousand homeless veterans across America.

Daniel, the once meticulous drill sergeant, now found himself sleeping on the streets, smoking crack and injecting heroin. "I was stinking and hungry," he recalled. He tried twice to kill himself by overdosing but wasn't competent even at that. "You hit the point in your life where you're just like, I don't want to live," Daniel said heavily. "I'm like, I'm tired of hurting. I'm tired of being in pain. I'm tired of doing all the shit that I've been doing to get by. It just gets old."

His efforts to mislead Braydon failed. "He found out I was in jail," Daniel told us, looking down at his shoes. "I was a shitty father." Daniel tried to buy his son birthday and Christmas presents, but heroin was the priority and somehow the money disappeared before he managed to buy the gifts for the person he cared most about. "I hated myself," he said. "I hated what I had become."

Daniel's father is a policeman who broke off ties with him, and they haven't spoken since 2013. The only person to stand with Daniel is his mother, who has repeatedly driven long distances to rescue her son and try to admit him into rehab programs. He acknowledges manipulating her and lying to her to get money for drugs.

"My mom loves me; she's my angel," he explained. "There's no point in time where I couldn't rely on my mom to help me out. And I know I abused that." When desperate for a fix, Daniel would beg her for cash and make up excuses. "I've got a ticket, and if I don't pay it I'll go to jail," he told her once. Another time, it was, "Somebody stole my money."

"I can give it to you on a gift card," she would say, trying to keep him from drugs.

"No, I need it in cash."

They would argue a bit, and finally his mom would relent because she didn't want to see him suffer. Still, it was his mom who saved Daniel with her unconditional love, repeatedly rescuing him and finding new rehab programs for him. Eventually, she helped him get a referral to the Baltimore Station, a two-year residential program for veterans struggling with addiction, supported by the Department of Veterans Affairs—part of a campaign to end veteran homelessness.

The Baltimore Station (an old firehouse, hence the name) has an excellent record helping people overcome addictions and recover their lives. It's a model of the kind of programs we need around the country,

Daniel McDowell in a group discussion about managing addiction at the Baltimore Station, a program for veterans *(Photo by Lynsey Addario)*

and not just for veterans. At the Baltimore Station, Daniel received counseling and was put on Suboxone, an opioid medication that stabilizes people with addictions, and he began to put his life back together. We visited him in his dorm room at the Baltimore Station, and he hadn't used street drugs for three months but was still fragile and mortified. For a proud army man to talk about how far he had fallen was humiliating, but he did it because he wanted people to understand the plight of the addicted.

"Honestly, it just sucks, man," Daniel told us. "The potential I had when I was younger, I could have been a sergeant first class. Now, I'm a felon. No house. I ain't got shit but a bag of clothes upstairs, so it's a fight. Every day is a fight, man. You want to use every day, but you know you ain't going nowhere if you do."

What motivates Daniel is his determination to rebuild his relationship with Megan and be a dad to Braydon. "She loves me to death," he said of Megan, "but she can't trust me. It's my fault." He paused and added wistfully, "I want to get back to being a family again. I want to take Braydon to football practice." He hopes eventually to return to college and emerge as a drug counselor to help other struggling veterans.

We asked Daniel whom he blames for his addiction. The Taliban, for laying the antitank mine that caused his knee injuries? The army, for negligently prescribing him Tramadol and referring him to the outside clinic? The pharmaceutical executives who marketed the opioid painkillers and claimed they weren't so addictive? The doctors who gave him the medications that got him hooked? Daniel wasn't buying any of that.

"I blame myself," he said. "At any point, I could have said, I don't want to do this," he explained. "I chose to do what I did."

At one level, it may be useful for Daniel to blame himself. Grassroots addiction programs emphasize that participants must take responsibility for their own actions, never making excuses, because patients have better outcomes when they accept this mantra of personal responsibility. As Plutarch said, "What we achieve inwardly will change outer reality."

Yet in a larger sense, Daniel was unfair to himself. He was betrayed by the government he risked his life to serve. By official estimates,

2.1 million Americans suffer opioid addiction, and some scholarly estimates run many times higher. When so many Americans simultaneously make the same bad choice, that should be a clue that the problem is not simply individual moral failure. It is a systemic failure.

Here's one way of looking at what happened: Daniel was injured on the job, and then doctors in and out of the military prescribed highly addictive opioids that got him hooked. That was because the government, through lax oversight, empowered pharmaceutical companies to profit from reckless marketing. Once Daniel was addicted, the army didn't try adequately to help him, but rather spit him out, and then he became a target not of public health efforts but of the criminal justice system. The government failed him, blamed him and jailed him. A couple of generations ago, the United States rewarded veterans by affording them education and housing benefits. More recently, the United States helped get veterans hooked on drugs and then incarcerated them.

THE STORY OF AMERICA'S current addiction nightmare begins in the 1990s, when the pharmaceutical industry was looking for a new blockbuster drug to market. Opioids were then seen as addictive and useful only for extreme pain or for those with terminal cancer, but business executives believed that opioids could be hugely expanded into a lucrative market. So the pharmaceutical industry, led by Purdue Pharma and the Sackler family who owned it, marshaled a sophisticated campaign to treat pain more aggressively—with their opioid prescription painkillers. Those OxyContin pills that got Daniel addicted were manufactured by Purdue.

Pharmaceutical companies commissioned reports arguing that doctors were allowing patients to suffer unnecessarily. There was an element of truth to this critique, and that recognition helped the pharmaceutical marketing campaign gain traction.

There had always been four "vital signs"—temperature, pulse, respiration, blood pressure—but in 1995 the American Pain Society (financed partly by Purdue) urged adoption of pain as a fifth vital sign. This became standard, adopted by veterans hospitals and by the American Medical Association. Consumers were asked in hospital assessments, "How often was your pain well controlled?" and "How often did the hospital staff do everything they could to help you with your pain?" Reimbursement levels later depended in part on patient satisfaction, and not surprisingly, painkiller prescriptions surged in the United States, though much less abroad. The American Pain Society acknowledges that in practice what happened at many institutions was: "Ask people if they have pain. If they do, give them opioids."

It wasn't just Purdue that was reckless. McKinsey & Company, the global consulting firm, advised Purdue on how to "turbocharge" sales of opioids, how to resist drug enforcement agents and how "to counter the emotional messages from mothers with teenagers that overdosed." Insys Therapeutics, a pharmaceutical company, allegedly paid $175,000 to an Ohio doctor, Gregory Gerber, in kickbacks to promote a prescription version of the powerful synthetic opioid fentanyl. Insys achieved 1,000 percent growth in earnings from fentanyl from 2012 to 2013 by paying doctors to join a speakers program and promote the drug, and by paying sales representatives bonuses for aggressive marketing of it. Insys was effectively manipulating doctors to get patients addicted.

"Every time a doc tells you they prescribed, the very next question should be, 'How many units? And what dose?'" Frank Serra, a regional sales manager, instructed his sales representatives in 2012. Congressional investigators obtained internal Insys documents that emphasized the importance of "owning" a physician or nurse.

Medical staff not only sold their souls but did so remarkably cheaply. One study found that the pharmaceutical industry spent an average of $588 per doctor from 2013 through 2015 marketing opioids to 68,000 of them, including paying for meals and trips. That's a modest sum over three years, but it was effective in increasing both prescriptions and deaths. The study found that the number of payments to doctors in a particular county correlated to overdose deaths from prescription medications in that county a year later.

Heather Alfonso, a nurse practitioner, admitted in a plea agreement that she received kickbacks on the way to becoming the largest prescriber of Insys fentanyl in Connecticut. As part of the Insys speakers program, she had received $1,000 per session for about seventy speeches—except that they weren't actually speeches. Instead, they amounted to dinners at nice restaurants where she gave no presentation and often there was no one present who was able to prescribe the drug anyway, according to a Senate report. In 2015 alone, Alfonso wrote 1,162 fentanyl prescriptions, the Senate report said. One can only guess at the misery that caused. She completed paperwork for fentanyl prescriptions for people with neck pain, back pain, leg pain, and shoulder pain. There are reasonable uses for fentanyl—such as patients with terminal cancer—but prescribing it for chronic back pain is a recipe for addiction.

McKesson Corporation, another giant pharmaceutical company, in just two years shipped nearly 9 million prescription painkillers to a single pharmacy in Kermit, West Virginia, population 400. Predictably, the result was addiction, overdoses and funerals—while McKesson profited from its recklessness. The government eventually fined McKesson $163 million, but the company board specifically excluded the fine in calculating profits to determine the bonus for the chief executive, who over a decade earned more than $600 million.

We reached out to Daniel's doctor at the outside clinic who had prescribed large quantities of opioids to tell him that Daniel had become addicted to heroin and ask if he regretted his prescription practices. He declined to comment.

Purdue was later convicted of a felony for fraudulently marketing its opioids by downplaying the risk of addiction. The company was vigorously defended by Rudy Giuliani, and its $600 million fine was negligible compared to the $35 billion that it is estimated to have earned from OxyContin. Individual executives from Purdue were also convicted and made to pay substantial fines, but they never served a day of jail time. Purdue was allowed to continue selling opioids, and the Sackler family is now worth $13 billion.

Some 80 percent of Americans addicted to opioids began with prescription painkillers, not with illegal street drugs. Essentially, pharmaceutical executives acted like Colombian drug lords, with legal approval. Many cities and states, including Baltimore, are now suing Purdue and other pharmaceutical companies to recover some of the costs of treating the opioid epidemic, but no one can ever give Daniel back what he lost.

"The biggest drug dealers wear white lab coats or pinstripe suits, not hoodies or the gang garb of street-level dealers," Jonathan Caulkins of Carnegie Mellon University and Keith Humphreys of Stanford University have noted.

The failure to imprison any of the Purdue executives shouldn't surprise us. America rarely prosecutes white-collar criminals. Even after the 2008 financial crisis, despite widespread illegal conduct that destroyed lives around the country, just one banker went to jail; in contrast, back in the 1980s, almost nine hundred bankers were jailed in the aftermath of the savings and loan scandal. Without much discussion, we have created a two-tier justice system. If you shoplift at the grocery store, you can be carted off to jail. But if you steal tens of millions of dollars from the tax authorities or fraudulently peddle dangerous drugs from a corporate suite, you'll be hailed for your business savvy.

THE AUTHORITIES SHOWED none of this leniency to ordinary drug users and distributors, and we wanted to see firsthand what has happened to small-bit drug peddlers like Geneva Cooley, so we went to Alabama to find out. A seventy-one-year-old black woman, mild-mannered, graying and husky, Geneva grew up in Harlem and was orphaned as a teenager. Living in a neighborhood where drugs were easily bought and sold, she began taking heroin half a century ago after surviving brutal sexual and domestic violence. Soon she had a daily habit and began selling heroin as well. She was twice convicted in New York of felony forgery, writing bad checks to pay for her habit.

In 2002, while working as a secretary for an accounting firm on Long Island, Geneva visited a friend in Birmingham, Alabama. She says he met her at the train station, handed her a green sock that she realized must contain drugs and asked her to take it to his mother's house. In retrospect, she thinks the friend set her up, because a plainclothes police officer immediately confronted her:

"Are you Geneva Cooley?"

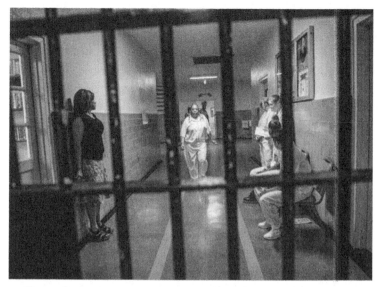

Geneva Cooley in a women's prison in Alabama, where she was sentenced
to life without the possibility of parole for drug trafficking
(Photo by Lynsey Addario)

"Yes."

"May we search your bag?"

"Sure." One woman began searching her bag.

"May we search your clothes?"

"No," Geneva said, and then she rushed to the bathroom, where she
threw the bulging sock into the garbage. But it was too late.

"Police! You're under arrest."

That sock contained 5,600 opioid pills and 90 grams of heroin. The
prosecution said Geneva was a drug mule, carrying narcotics from New
York City with a street value of a quarter-million dollars. In 2006, after
a trial that lasted only about an hour, Geneva was convicted of trafficking narcotics and, because of her previous felony convictions, was
given a mandatory sentence of life without the possibility of parole.
The Alabama prison computer system logs that sentence as 999 years,
99 months and 99 days.

"I felt like that was the end of my life," Geneva told us. "I felt like committing suicide."

We visited Geneva in the Julia Tutwiler Prison for Women in Alabama, where she has a bottom bunk in a bare, open room full of bunk beds for fifty women. This is the "honor dorm" for those with good behavior records, and Geneva keeps her bed area tidy. A row of exercise equipment is available for inmates, though Geneva doesn't use it much.

One of the more elderly inmates, Geneva is a calming influence and often intervenes when tempers get hot and arguments get out of hand. She uses the prison library to read novels, especially David Baldacci mysteries, and at times she has taken classes on anger management, drug rehabilitation and history. She also loves to visit the prison flower garden, but otherwise the prison is drab, dull and forever.[*]

Neither her son nor anyone else in her family uses drugs, Geneva says, and she tries to be upbeat with her grandson and granddaughter. "I write them positive things to do in life," she said. While she talks on the phone regularly with family members, she has never let any of them visit her in prison—because she couldn't bear them leaving.

Geneva certainly committed a crime, but the contrast is brutal: a marginalized black woman sentenced for the rest of her life to a prison in Alabama, her world revolving around her neatly made bunk bed, while members of the rich white family that helped create America's opioid epidemic became billionaires. We asked the Sacklers at Purdue what they thought of the comparison; they declined to comment.

---

[*] Because of heroic legal work by Courtney Cross, an assistant professor at the University of Alabama law school, Geneva was resentenced in March 2019 to life *with* the possibility of parole. Professor Cross is now trying to get her paroled. Geneva's case was championed by Susan Burton, who runs A New Way of Life in Los Angeles and alerted both us and Cross to the sentence.

7

Losing the War on Drugs

The Nixon campaign in 1968, and the Nixon White House after that, had two enemies: the antiwar left and black people. You understand what I'm saying? We knew we couldn't make it illegal to be either against the war or black, but by getting the public to associate the hippies with marijuana and blacks with heroin, and then criminalizing both heavily, we could disrupt those communities. We could arrest their leaders, raid their homes, break up their meetings, and vilify them night after night on the evening news. Did we know we were lying about the drugs? Of course we did.

—JOHN EHRLICHMAN, President Richard Nixon's
   domestic policy adviser

America's drug policy over the last five decades has been a tragedy that grew out of tragedies. It emerged from frustration at cases like that of Len Bias, arguably the greatest basketball player who never made it to the NBA. A black kid who grew up in the Maryland suburbs of Washington, D.C., Bias was an All-American forward two years running at the University of Maryland, sometimes compared to Michael Jordan. He could leap like an acrobat, scoring thirty-five points in his final college game—after which, fans in the gymnasium wept at the ending of his college career.

Bias was the local boy made good, a hometown hero in the Washington area. He was a clean-cut kid who did well in school, went to church every Sunday and never smoked, drank or used drugs. "He loved his body," his mother, Lonise Bias, told us, so he never wanted to taint it. He was also proud of his musculature, including a six-pack of abdominal muscles that he would show off to his mom.

"Ma, take your fist and hit me in the stomach," he would dare her.

"I would take my fist and hit him in his stomach," Lonise recalled. "And it was like hitting a brick wall. He would laugh."

In 1986, Bias was drafted by the Boston Celtics as the second overall draft pick, and Reebok began pursuing him for a huge endorsement deal. Two days after he was drafted, Lonise Bias received the call that would shatter her life.

"I was in bed, six thirty in the morning on one of the most beautiful days I had ever seen," she remembered. "I received the call and someone said, 'Len is sick.'"

Lonise and her husband rushed to the hospital. "Is he alive?" she asked a nurse, who told her that he was on life support. Soon after, a doctor came out and told them that their son was dead. An investigation found that he had partied with friends in his dorm room, ingesting cocaine perhaps for the first time and suffering a fatal overdose.

Len Bias's death rocked the nation, including his fans in Congress. One result was the Anti-Drug Abuse Act of 1986, sometimes called the Len Bias Law, followed by a further tightening with the Anti-Drug Abuse Act of 1988. We traveled around Maryland to learn about the origins of these flawed laws; they had created mandatory minimum sentences of five years for drug crimes, even involving marijuana, but it turns out they reflected more of a cry from the heart than a thoughtful examination of policy proposals.

"There was no evaluation of what this law might do," said Eric E. Sterling, who as a young lawyer working for Congress helped draft both drug laws. "It was emotional. It was visceral. It was not tied to the understanding of whom it might affect." Sterling recalls that the talk was simply about the importance of passing harsh drug laws to "send a message."

IN THE 1980S AND 1990S, Portugal also had a terrible drug problem, one of the worst in Europe, and lawmakers there, too, debated
how to respond. In the end, the two countries took precisely opposite paths. The United States doubled down on the war on drugs and
"zero tolerance" criminal justice approaches. In contrast, Portugal
convened a commission and ended up adopting—under then prime
minister António Guterres, now the secretary general of the United
Nations—a public health approach instead. Portugal treated drug
addiction like a disease, rather than a crime. It decriminalized possession of all drugs, even heroin and cocaine, and focused on prevention
through public education, as well as treatment of those with addictions
to try to wean them of substance abuse.

Many people around the world were horrified that a major nation
like Portugal was abandoning the war on drugs and decriminalizing
drug use. There was legitimate concern that this would lead to soaring use of hard drugs. We now have almost two decades of experience
with these two diametrically opposite approaches, and it's clear which
worked better.

In the United States, drug use and fatalities have soared, thanks
partly to street fentanyl. There were 6,100 deaths from illegal drugs in
1980, compared to 68,000 in 2018. Every fifteen minutes in America,
another child is born with an opioid dependency. In contrast, Portugal's
experiment proved a huge success. The number of people with addictions has fallen by about two-thirds, and its rate of drug-related deaths
is now the lowest in Western Europe. In Portugal, 6 persons die of
drug-related causes per million people between the ages of fifteen and
sixty-four. In the United States, the figure is 348.

Crackdowns on small-time drug offenders in the United States devastated many low-income families, especially in African-American communities, and the resulting felony records left black men in particular
less employable and less marriageable. The United States has spent
more than $1 trillion on the war on drugs, money spent locking up

two-bit users rather than educating children. The war on drugs has been perhaps the worst single policy mistake of the last half century.

One legacy of this policy blunder is that 70 million Americans now have a criminal record, according to the Brennan Center for Justice. That's slightly more than the number of Americans with a college degree, and we have more jails and prisons than four-year colleges. The war on drugs even reached into schools. In Ohio, a fourteen-year-old girl named Kimberly Smartt was suspended from a public junior high school for four months in 1996 after she gave a thirteen-year-old girlfriend a Midol tablet for menstrual cramps (Midol is a mild over-the-counter pain reliever).

Portugal's experience helped convince us that the United States and other countries should try the public health approach, too, and it's encouraging that more localities are moving in that direction. One reason is simply that the opioid crisis, while still disproportionately affecting low-income families, increasingly is striking middle-class communities as well. In Ohio, the lieutenant governor discovered that both her sons were wrestling with addictions. The public is showing far more sympathy to middle-class white kids struggling than it ever showed to blacks like Geneva Cooley. The mantra moved from "lock 'em up" to "treat addiction like a disease." The recent emphasis on treatment rather than punishment, now that white kids are overdosing in large numbers, is welcome and long overdue, but those in the black community have reason to see it also as hypocritical.

AS ERIC STERLING DRAFTED tough drug laws, and Daniel McDowell broke them, it was up to officers like Baltimore Police lieutenant Steve Olson to enforce them. In the 1990s and early 2000s, Baltimore and many other cities had a zero-tolerance approach to narcotics, and Olson participated in waves of drug arrests.

"We made a boatload of arrests, we took a lot of people to jail and the end result is it's not any better," he told us as we drove in a police cruiser through tough neighborhoods. "The vast majority of arrests didn't make a difference."

Steve, an athletic jokester with a fondness for bicycle policing and marathons, comes from a military family with a precise sense of order and propriety. He despised the chaos and violence of the drug world, and he still carries scars from an incident in 2013 when a criminal ran him down with a motorcycle. But Steve eventually came to view the crackdown as more harmful than helpful. He loved traveling overseas, and he would notice that other countries frequently handled drugs with a lighter touch and seemed to have fewer problems.

As Steve was having these doubts, something happened in his personal life that also changed how he saw the problem. In 2016, Steve was raising money for Habitat for Humanity, his favorite charity, by offering to do chores for people. His sister volunteered to donate if Steve would clean their dad's truck, so he did so with his usual meticulousness—and was rocked when he found drug paraphernalia. The issue wasn't his

Baltimore Police lieutenant Steve Olson writes down information for a woman he meets on the streets. Steve used to arrest people with drug problems but now realizes that isn't much of a solution.
(Photo by Lynsey Addario)

dad, he realized, but Steve's brother Mark, age thirty-four, who often used the truck.

To Steve, all the things he hadn't understood about Mark suddenly made sense: "Why he couldn't pay his rent, why he couldn't hold a job, why he had a dirty appearance, why some of his actions were just completely out of character, why he would explode in rage." It was also clear why Mark hadn't applied for jobs that his brother had recommended: he knew he would fail the drug test. Steve had once found Mark's vehicle in a notorious drug zone, but Mark—who worked on cell phone towers—explained that he was checking on the local tower. "Addicts are great liars," Steve noted resignedly.

So he phoned his brother. "Mark," he told him. "I'm cleaning Dad's truck." Mark immediately understood and overdosed in an effort to kill himself. He failed, and then he and Steve had a heartfelt conversation. Mark confessed that he had a $300-a-day habit. The family tried to get him into a long-term rehab program and initially couldn't find one that would accept Mark's health insurance. That's all too common. Finally, the family found one, and Mark stayed off drugs for three and a half months. He struggled with his cravings, calling his brother several times a day. Once he explained that the downside of sobriety was the need to face up to a wrenching world. "Sober," he added, was actually an acronym for "son of a bitch, everything's real."

Then, a few months after Mark went into rehab, Steve was in Malawi volunteering with Habitat for Humanity when he received an urgent text message to call his wife.

"I knew what that text message meant," he said. "It meant my brother was dead."

Craving a fix, Mark had been driving ninety miles an hour on the highway to buy a $20 bag of heroin when he lost control of his vehicle. He was killed in the crash. The tragedy made Steve more sensitive to what families were going through. When fellow police officers referred contemptuously to "junkies," Steve would respond, "Oh, you mean like my brother?"

The tragedy also made him more aware of the barriers to treatment. He saw how difficult it was for people to get help, and he became more understanding of the need for public health approaches to addiction in addition to criminal justice approaches.

"When my brother first started down this road, he did something wrong," Steve told us somberly. "He broke the law. He made a decision, and that was a moral decision. And somewhere down the line during his course of addiction, during the way he lived his life, it stopped being a moral issue, it started being a health issue.

"When you feel as though you're lost, as my brother felt, you're not going to seek the resources. And it's not made easy. There are so many different loopholes and hurdles and doors to go through."

The year after Mark's death, Baltimore began a pilot program called LEAD—Law Enforcement Assisted Diversion—that attempts to address these barriers. LEAD responds to drug users not with arrest and imprisonment but with social services, working with users rather than handcuffing them. LEAD started in Seattle, where it led to a 60 percent drop in recidivism, and it has now been copied in many cities around the country. It marks a step away from the traditional American approach toward a Portugal-style decriminalization of narcotics, and it is long overdue. We followed Steve as he made the rounds, looking for people on the streets with addictions, not to arrest them but to guide them toward LEAD counselors.

"Joe!" he shouted jubilantly to one scruffy, bearded man carrying pipes over his shoulder. Joe greeted Steve warmly, although perhaps a little guiltily: he said he had found the pipes in a dumpster, but that didn't seem terribly credible. In the old days, Steve later explained, the police might have arrested Joe for one thing or another, but now officers were focused on getting Joe into treatment.

After a bit of chitchat, Steve made his pitch: "Joe, what if I told you that the people I want you to talk to will help you get back to your family?"

"Give me the name and number and I'll call."

"I'll take you there."

"I know you got my back all the time," Joe replied, but then he wavered and said he was too busy.

"My guys might come to you. Can you stay here for a few minutes?"

Joe shuffled his feet and looked uneasy, then tried to put Steve off.

"I'll come down," he said, referring to some vague point in the future. "You know how difficult it is to make that first step. You know that, Mr. Olson."

"Here's my big thing. Can you give me fifteen minutes right now? Just fifteen minutes? I'm not going to take you anywhere. I'm not going to ask you to go anywhere. I'm going to bring people to you. Just fifteen minutes. I know you've got to go. I know how much fifteen minutes means to you. But at the same time, fifteen minutes can be the difference. You know that discomfort you're feeling right now? How would you like it to go away?"

"I want everything to go away."

While Steve got on his cell phone to track down a social worker who could come over, we asked Joe why he was wary of visiting the LEAD office. "That step is the hardest," Joe said nervously. "You walk into a place where you don't know anybody. You wonder, are they going to welcome you, or treat you like a piece of shit?"

Soon Steve came back, dejected. The social workers were busy, he explained, taking another young man to get a haircut so he could go to a job interview. But he pleaded with Joe to go to the LEAD office.

"I'll go," Joe promised. "I really will." He seemed heartened when Steve told him that some of the social workers themselves had previously been addicted and know that world well. Joe added that he would prefer to have Steve escort him, because he feels overwhelmed in strange settings.

"Joe, you call, I'll come running," Steve promised.

Joe was sweating, probably a little dope sick and in need of a fix. That may have been why he was impatient to go, and Steve watched him walk away with his pipes over his shoulder.

"The hardest thing about watching them walk away is this is how it happens all the time," Steve told us when we were back in the cruiser. "I've been talking to Joe quite a bit for a number of weeks. And it's always closer and closer and closer to it being a success. Today was the closest it's ever come."

We asked Steve if this kind of policing is enormously rewarding, and

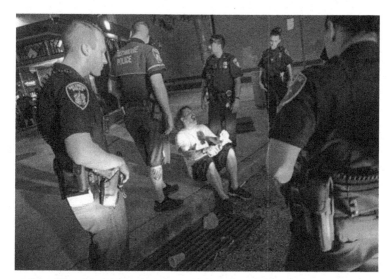

Steve Olson, with his back to the camera, tending to a man who police believed was suffering a drug overdose. Under the LEAD program (the letters stand for Law Enforcement Assisted Diversion), Steve doesn't arrest people with addictions but tries to steer them into treatment. *(Photo by Lynsey Addario)*

he nodded and said he was sure that he was saving lives. Then he sighed. "It's also exhausting," he said. "It's mentally and physically draining to scream without raising your voice eight hours a day. And to know that when I go home at night, the people that were resistant or I couldn't get through the door or don't want to talk to me are still out there." He paused, shook his head and added, "It's not something that I can do for the rest of my career, I can't do this. Physically, mentally, I can't do this."

Baltimore is pioneering a public health approach to drug addiction in part because of its former health commissioner, Dr. Leana Wen. Like many other experts in the field, Wen argues that we need to treat addiction as a chronic health problem like diabetes or heart disease. Not everyone agrees, and it's true, of course, that addiction depends partly on circumstance and behavior, and that users should be encouraged to say no to drugs—just as diabetics should reject cinnamon buns. Many people do manage to overcome substance abuse without medication, by sheer force of will. But addiction, like diabetes, is about the body's physical wiring, as well as about behaviors. As Wen noted, "We'd never tell someone with diabetes, 'Why can't you get off insulin?' We'd never ask someone with high blood pressure, 'Why do you need medicine, why aren't exercise and diet enough?'"

There are signs of a bipartisan shift from an approach based solely on criminal justice to a more effective one that also relies on treatment. Portugal's sensible and effective public-health-focused drug policy has been the trend in Canada and Europe. In the United States, such an approach would include three crucial elements.

First, treatment must be available to all 21 million Americans who need it, and this should include both psychosocial counseling and medication-assisted treatment. An astonishing one in seven young adults, ages eighteen to twenty-five, need treatment, the government estimates. Back in 1971, President Nixon ordered that treatment be made available for all people with drug addictions, without fear of criminal sanction, and obtained substantial funding from Congress to provide that treatment. For a time there was real progress against heroin, but, sadly, in the decades afterward, treatment actually became less available. Barely one in ten Americans with substance abuse disorders now receive any treatment. That is an astonishing failure of our government and health-care system, and the Trump administration arguably made it worse by chipping away at the Affordable Care Act and Medicaid. "I cannot imagine if we said only one in ten people with cancer can get chemotherapy, or one in ten patients who need dialysis is able to receive it," Wen told us. "But that's what happens for addiction."

The Affordable Care Act included mental-health care and treatment of drug-use disorders as essential health benefits, but reimbursements for addiction treatment and mental health are very low and many users have no health insurance at all. A much more comprehensive and better-funded national program is needed. We've spoken to people who tried to get into rehab but were told that their addictions weren't yet serious enough to qualify; in effect, they were told to wait, deteriorate and try again. That's obviously shortsighted, particularly because researchers find that increasing access to drug treatment pays for itself by reducing crime. Outpatient substance abuse assistance costs about $4,700 a year; incarceration costs five times as much, according to the National Institute on Drug Abuse. It says that a dollar invested in addiction treatment programs saves $12 in reduced crime and court costs, plus health-care savings. The Baltimore Station's program that helped Daniel is an example of an effective program that could be replicated.

A second step is to make drug use less lethal for those who resist treatment. The United States has succeeded in making naloxone, an antidote for opioid overdoses, far more available, so that police officers like Steve Olson now carry it with them to administer in an instant. Naloxone truly is a miracle drug: jab someone comatose from an overdose and, astonishingly, he or she will typically revive and, just minutes later, seem almost as good as new. Wen issued a citywide prescription to all 620,000 Baltimore residents for naloxone, and she worked to distribute naloxone to high-risk communities, such as the red-light district.

Promoting needle exchanges to reduce transmission of HIV and hepatitis also helps, and this is now widely accepted in the United States. More controversial are safe injection sites, where users can go to use their own heroin or other illicit narcotics, while monitored by a nurse or health aide. The injection site will supply needles, but not the drugs themselves. When users overdose, they can receive immediate treatment, rather than dying on a park bench. There are some ninety safe injection sites in other countries, including Canada, and not a single fatal overdose has been reported despite millions of injections. Dozens of studies have found that they not only save lives from overdoses but also allow health authorities to connect with drug users and gradually reel them in for treatment. At the first safe injection site in North America, in Vancouver, British Columbia, the result was a 35 percent reduction in fatal overdoses in the area. One study estimated that a safe injection site in a U.S. city would not only save lives but also some $3.5 million. Unfortunately, the Trump administration has threatened to prosecute local officials who try to operate safe injection sites.

The third step is the most complicated—to focus on prevention, education and reducing the stigma that hampers users from getting help. "Society needs to change its attitude to drug users," Wen said, reiterating her point. "They are patients with a disease that needs treatment." One element of prevention is to reduce opioid prescribing by doctors and dentists, and that is belatedly taking place, but the numbers are still far higher than in our peer countries; in 2016, doctors wrote more opioid prescriptions in the state of Michigan than the number of people living in the state.

When Wen had a baby in 2017, she was prescribed a thirty-day supply of oxycodone.

"Why do I get this?" she asked.

"Just in case you need it," the doctor explained. "We don't want you to be in pain."

Prevention also means criminal prosecutions of major drug smugglers and in particular targeting Chinese businesses that operate fentanyl supply houses. But the broadest challenge in prevention is to recognize that addiction is a symptom of a deeper malaise and that a strategy also has to offer jobs, education and hope. Whether in Baltimore or in Yamhill, drug use is often not just a trip but also an escape from a place that has become unendurable.

The 2018 First Step Act was an example of bipartisan criminal justice reform and may benefit thousands of federal prisoners by lightening sentences, but it should be just the beginning of greater change in incarceration policies. Eric Sterling, who helped write the harsh drug laws of 1986 and 1988, has completely reversed his perspective and is now working to undo those laws. "That Congress has been unable so many times to change these laws is a real indictment of its unwillingness to fix injustice."

"It was tragically misguided," he said of the war on drugs. "Everything needs to change."

8

Up by the Bootstraps

It is a cruel jest to say to a bootless man that he ought to lift himself up by his bootstraps.

—DR. MARTIN LUTHER KING JR.

At Kevin Green's funeral in Yamhill, the church was packed. Rev. Rhonda Kroeker, who had known Kevin since she was thirteen years old, noted that the crowd reflected his extraordinary loyalty as a friend. Yet she was also blunt about the toll of drugs: "Using these drugs unfortunately becomes a way of life. They take the pain, emotional and physical, and put it on hold. For a while."

Rev. Kroeker says that officiating at Kevin's funeral was difficult partly because she was emotional. "I was mad," she told us. "Mad that the drugs he chose to use for years had caused his body to fail him. I was mad that he had made these bad choices that had placed him into the small box in front of this weeping crowd. I was mad at the people in the crowd who I knew he hung out with, who did the dope with him and supplied it freely."

Rhonda knew this world well. She had dropped out of Yamhill Grade School at age thirteen, in the eighth grade, when she became pregnant with her first child. She then abused alcohol and drugs herself. She was

Clayton Green in his shop in 2018. He was a master mechanic and could fix anything. *(Photo by Lynsey Addario)*

close to the Knapps and to the Greens. When she married, Clayton Green was the best man. She and her husband eventually gave up partying and became born-again Christians. They remained friendly with the Knapps and the Greens but broke away from drugs.

Although she never reached high school, let alone attended divinity school, Rhonda became a nondenominational minister with a predilection for faith healing (she says she can lay hands on people and cure them of cancer). She came to lead My Father's House Church, which moved from one borrowed location to the next, and the Blessing Room Free Store, which gathered donations from the public and offered them to the needy. Some one thousand people each month came to get food, clothing, toys and other items, a huge number in a rural area like Yamhill. By day, Rhonda works as a car saleswoman in the nearby town of Newberg, but her passion is finding ways to help people struggling in the Yamhill area.

At the funeral service, Irene Green was now mourning her third child, after Cindy and Baby Thomas. Rhonda, her voice breaking, told those assembled that she did not want anyone else to be the next one in a box. She did not want to perform another premature funeral. "The crowd was so full of broken people," Rhonda recalled. "When I was finished, they just sat there and looked at me. No one moved. I realized they needed more. I began to sing over them and pray for them. I spent the next twenty minutes ministering to the crowd."

WHEN NICK POSTED on social media to tell Kevin Green's story and mourn him, the reaction was sometimes scornful. "Kevin made choices," Libby scoffed on Twitter. "He had free will. Obesity kills, not inequality."

On Facebook, José said, "Blaming the system is just an excuse for your mistakes." Ayden was similarly unsympathetic: "This man CHOSE to live that way and made decisions that ultimately were detrimental not only to him, but also to his offspring."

"He was a food and drug addict," offered Nancy. "He was a dead-beat dad. He made bad decisions." When another person on Facebook remonstrated that this was harsh, Nancy followed up: "Did I miss the part where this deadbeat dad got up off his fat ass to support his children?" Nancy said that she worked hard, never got a handout, earned an MBA at night, invested in her children's college funds and would never be like Kevin. "No sympathy whatsoever," she said. "None."

Nancy, we wish there were more people with your drive and diligence. You're also in prominent company. Dr. Ben Carson, who oversees housing for the poor as secretary of housing and urban development, describes poverty as "really more of a choice than anything else." It's true that some extraordinary individuals like Dr. Carson manage to clamber to the top despite very difficult childhoods, but these are exceptions. The economist Alan Krueger noted that income in America is approximately as heritable as height. "The chance of a person who was born to a family in the bottom ten percent of the income distribution rising to the top ten percent as an adult is about the same as the chance that a dad who is five feet six inches tall has of having a son who grows up to be over six feet one inch tall," Krueger observed. "It happens, but not often."

The harsh assessments of people like Kevin miss the mark. They reflect an increasingly cruel narrative that the working-class struggle is all about bad choices, laziness and vices. Over the last fifty years, poverty has come to be seen not just as an economic failing but also as a moral one, prompting a pervasive suspicion that the poor are secretly living cushy lives on government benefits. A Pew poll found that wealthy Americans mostly agreed that "poor people today have it easy because they can get government benefits without doing anything in return." Ted Nugent, the musician, suggested that those who receive benefits are "takers," "entitlement chumps" and "gluttonous, soulless pigs." The conservative author Neal Boortz compared the poor to toenail fungus. This "bootstraps narrative," that all people need to do to get ahead is lift themselves up, is at the root of our failures to adopt policies that would have helped the country and given opportunity to children. If you believe poverty is a choice, then you try to stigmatize and punish it, rather than focusing on interventions to ease it. Looking back, it seems to us that the bootstraps narrative began to gain traction in the 1970s, at about the same time the United States started pursuing misguided policies at odds with those in Europe and Canada. That's when the discourse about the poor became nastier, and when the aggressive push began to send drug offenders to prison for life.

Years later, former House Speaker Paul Ryan was among those arguing that the best solution to disadvantage was for the poor to "pull themselves up by the bootstraps." In fact, that expression originally signified the opposite of what it does today: in the early 1800s, it meant to do something impossible, for it is of course physically impossible to pull oneself up by one's own boots. Not until the twentieth century did Americans begin to assign the phrase its current meaning.

As the bootstraps narrative of personal responsibility gained ground, it was easier to avoid investing in early childhood programs, or in drug treatment. The narrative became an excuse for passivity and harsh social policies. It became an ideology. That's why Professor David Ellwood of Harvard says that the first step in tackling poverty must be to challenge the idea that the major problem is personal failure. "It all starts with changing the narrative," Ellwood says.

At one level, the narrative is factually flawed. Sure, some are lazy. Others are not. Kevin Green toiled all day with his bicycle and a little trailer to collect cans by the roadside, earning about $20. He also built furniture, worked odd jobs as a logger and supplemented this income with a huge vegetable garden that constantly required weeding and watering. Yes, Kevin received food stamps and disability benefits, but his early death meant that while he had contributed to Medicare and Social Security, he never received a retirement pension or Medicare health coverage.

"We are the richest country on the planet with the worst poverty," Professor Matthew Desmond, a Princeton University sociologist, told us. "There's no advanced industrial society with the kind of poverty that we have and the level of poverty that we have. So if we are going to accept this kind of individualistic theory of poverty—the reason so many people are poor in America is because of something they did— then we have to accept this idea that there's something disproportionately wrong with the stock of Americans. I do not believe that's the case. I believe that there have been decisions that have led to poverty, but those decisions have not solely been made by those who are suffering from it."

Yet the cruelty to those left behind isn't just factually problematic. It also speaks to a skewed moral compass, not to mention a dollop of hypocrisy, since the wealthy also receive substantial financial subsidies. Americans used to extol good-hearted Robin Hood, taking from the rich to give to the poor, and now we've stepped into the shoes of the Sheriff of Nottingham. When as a society we shrug at 30 million children living in low-income families in America, slashing their benefits while urging them to pull themselves up by their bootstraps, we need to look in the mirror and have a good talk with ourselves.

"It's not like I woke up one day and decided I wanted to be a drug addict," said Michelle Vavrick, a young woman now thriving in a new job in Tulsa after getting help overcoming her struggles with drugs, alcohol and crime. "I was seriously sexually abused, and the only coping mechanism I had was doing drugs."

The bootstraps narrative emerges from a growing empathy gap in America, one consequence of which is a scorn for those left behind. Stuart Varney, the Fox News host, has absorbed the personal responsibility narrative and propagates it. He has a penchant for attacking those left behind in America, those he refers to as the "so-called poor." Noting that many have cars and televisions, he declared, "The image we have of poor people as starving and living in squalor really is not accurate. Many of them have things; what they lack is the richness of spirit." On another occasion, he acknowledged that "I am being mean to poor people."

Although Varney is British, he is a great believer in the American dream, in the idea that success rewards those who work hard and play by the rules. In 2011, he invited the Cornell University economist Robert Frank on his show, and he was outraged when Frank said that luck was an important factor in success. That didn't fit with Varney's view of his own trajectory. Here's a bit of the conversation:

VARNEY: Am I lucky or not, being who I am and where I am?

FRANK: Yes.

VARNEY: I'm lucky? I'm lucky?

FRANK: Yes, you are. And so am I.

VARNEY: That's outrageous. That is outrageous. What about the risk I took? Do you know what risk is involved in coming to America with absolutely nothing? Do you know what risk is involved in trying to work for a major American network with a British accent, a total foreigner? Do you know what risk is implied for this level of success?

FRANK: I do.

VARNEY: Is it luck that you hold a tenured position?

FRANK: Yes.

VARNEY: That's nonsense. I'm insulted by what you say. You're going against the American dream. Look, if you come to America with nothing, and you play by the rules, you work hard, you get discipline inside yourself, you marry and have children, in that order, okay, you do all of those things, you play by the rules, you will make it in America and luck has nothing to do with it.

FRANK: That's not true, sir.

Varney is right that he worked hard, took risks and played by the rules (not counting spending hundreds of thousands of dollars on a mistress, according to the divorce complaint filed by his wife), and we don't begrudge him his success. But he doesn't seem to appreciate that his luck began when he was born to a loving, married, middle-class family in England, his mother a teacher. Later he graduated from the London School of Economics, one of the world's great universities, and spent time in Kenya and Hong Kong. He didn't arrive in America with "nothing," but with a tremendous amount of human capital—which, to his credit, he amplified with intelligence and hard work. Varney's successful trajectory began with the nurturing womb in which he happened to be conceived.

That doesn't mean that personal responsibility is immaterial. There's some risk that when affluent liberals talk about these issues, they adopt a counter-narrative in which every poor person or criminal is a noble victim of circumstances, denied all opportunity and sucked into an irresistible whirlpool. That's condescending and robs people of agency, for poor people can be every bit as mean and dumb and narcissistic as rich people.

Liberals often explain bad behavior in part by looking at difficult circumstances and shortcomings of society, while conservatives often emphasize bad choices by individuals. So liberals perceive exploited victims, and conservatives scorn lazy parasites. In truth, people are invariably complicated, and both difficult circumstances and bad choices are real; each compounds the other. Kevin acknowledged his own poor choices, and the rest of us should as well. Anybody who has worked at the grassroots level has seen plenty of irresponsibility, but also seen that it's far more complicated than the narrative of personal irresponsibility conveys.

One hazard of our social Darwinism is that it is absorbed even by those who are themselves on the bottom, leading them to stigmatize themselves. On a street in Baltimore, we chatted with a man named Jackson Phillips Jr., a twenty-eight-year-old who was standing beside the tent in which he was living alongside a highway. Jackson, a lean man with a scraggly beard, said he had been homeless for the last eight years and thought this was in part his own fault. "I had multiple chances," he told us. "I made some bad choices."

By blaming himself, he seemed to us to be assuming *too much* personal responsibility. When we asked about his background, Jackson's "choices" seemed awfully limited. His mom had been a drug addict, and he may have been exposed to narcotics in the womb. His siblings had acute lead poisoning, so he may well have cognitive and behavioral problems from lead exposure as well. When he was three years old, Jackson saw his brother shot dead. Two years later, when he was five, he himself was shot in the head by a drug dealer. "Here's my scar," he said, pointing it out. He never got much of an education and formally dropped out of school in the eighth grade.

Sure, we advised Jackson, he had made some bad choices, but so would most people who went through those ordeals. Professor Esther Duflo of MIT, a prominent economist, told us that she wonders if America's ideology of mobility, the idea that anyone can achieve anything, empowers some poor people but leaves others feeling like failures and more prone to making bad choices.

AFTER KEVIN DIED, Clayton Green tried to take over and run the farm, but he had many of the same problems as his brother. Clayton struggled with his weight, couldn't find good jobs and occasionally ended up in jail for drug offenses—all of which made him less employable. Clayton also had a speech impediment that sometimes made him difficult to understand; he had never received speech therapy in school. The impediment sometimes left people thinking that Clayton was dim, but he was very bright, and particularly talented as a mechanic.

Clayton sometimes worked on the Kristof farm, regularly repairing tractors and the Caterpillar bulldozer. When Nick drove the tractor through the sheep shed wall (the second time), it was Clayton who

Clayton Green, right, with our mutual friend Ricochet Goff, in 2015,
as troubles began to take over *(Photo by Nicholas Kristof)*

helped fix the shed. Or there was the time Clayton managed to kill
hundreds of yellow jackets and destroy their nest after Nick had fled
in defeat.

One of the problems was Clayton's temper and propensity to solve
problems with fists rather than words. That reflects a self-destructive
element in some working-class cultures—a prickliness about matters
of honor, a dependence on fists and a sense that only sissies resort to
teachers, police or courts. When kids grow up with violence and are
beaten when they misbehave, they absorb it as a norm. This perceived
nobility in fisticuffs perhaps is a modern echo of nineteenth-century
dueling, and you see it in the way men boast of their battle scars and
the way they raise their sons.

"My dad told me, 'Don't walk away from nothing; don't lose a fight,'"
Clayton remembered. He followed that advice. On the Number 6
school bus, most kids sat wherever they chose (typically high schoolers in the back, grade schoolers in front), but Clayton was enough of a

troublemaker that he had an assigned seat near the front. In ninth grade alone, Clayton participated in five fistfights—at which point the school expelled him and his education ended.

Clayton found a girlfriend with whom he had a son, Eathan, and they soon married—with Eathan, still a small child, serving as best man. Within a couple of years, the marriage soured and Clayton's wife took off for Idaho with Eathan. Solving problems in customary fashion, Clayton drove to Idaho, took Eathan and started driving home. A posse of his wife's friends chased after Clayton, caught him, beat him and recovered Eathan. After further negotiations, Clayton was able to get custody of Eathan and raise him in Yamhill on the family farm, although the father-son relationship was often strained.

A devil-may-care recklessness frequently shadows single men, and that was true of Clayton. Riding too fast on a motorcycle, he lost control and went careering off the road. Another time, Clayton disagreed with a man about who owned a trailer, and the other man solved the problem by hooking it to his truck and driving it away.

"It's not your trailer," Clayton yelled at him, trying to block the truck. In the commotion, the truck and trailer rolled over Clayton and disappeared down the road. Badly injured, Clayton staggered to a neighbor's house to call 911. At the hospital, it turned out that he had injured his liver and burst a lung, in addition to breaking twenty-eight bones. "I got beat up pretty good," Clayton recalled with a touch of pride.

Always entrepreneurial, Clayton found ways to make money when decent jobs proved elusive. After leaving high school, he grew marijuana for a time, sometimes on distant corners of other people's property so that if found it couldn't easily be traced back to him. Once he was caught only because a farmer fell asleep on a tractor and inadvertently drove into Clayton's marijuana patch. Later, although he had never taken high-school chemistry, he began to make and sell meth; he and Nick's classmate Farlan Knapp, whose father had shot at his mother cowering in the field, became the local pioneers in cooking meth. Over three years in the early 2000s, Clayton told us, he earned a profit of $125,000 from his meth business (other estimates of his earnings were much higher). His nickname in the drug community was "Candy Man," and he had a reputation as a talented chemist who could turn out both simple crank meth powder and also crystal meth. In those flush years, he bought the custom license plate NAST-1, a play on nasty. He also put up an array of signs to keep intruders out: as you enter the Green driveway even today, there are five No Trespassing signs and two Beware of Dog signs. In any case, after a couple of felony convictions, the drug business model didn't seem so appealing, and Clayton gave up his lab equipment and moved on, the felonies impeding his efforts to find other jobs.

Previous generations in Yamhill and elsewhere in working-class America found sustenance and support in churches or social organizations, even in the bowling clubs that have been fading away, as Harvard professor Robert Putnam noted in his book *Bowling Alone*. Yamhill used to have a Masonic Lodge, an Odd Fellows secret society, a women's association, a Veterans of Foreign Wars post and a good-size band, as well as the weekly *Carlton-Yamhill Review* reporting on social interactions such as, say, Mrs. Withycombe calling on Mrs. Laughlin. There's quite good evidence that this kind of social cohesion is good for us. One famous study of Roseto, Pennsylvania, a tight-knit Italian-American community, found that close social bonds resulted in a lack of stress and enormous reduction in heart disease. The people in Roseto smoked, drank and ate fatty sausages, but they didn't have heart attacks, and this protective influence of a close-knit community on mortality is called the Roseto Effect.

It's also notable that Latinos have significantly lower suicide rates than other Americans, and often lower death rates generally, especially once lower average incomes are factored in. In other words, the Latino working class—especially people born abroad—has been somewhat protected from the factors that have caused such devastation among the white working class. This is sometimes called the Hispanic paradox, and there are many theories about why this is and how real it is. One explanation is that the strength of Hispanic families and community, especially among new immigrants, creates cohesion and a protective social fabric that shields workers from the loneliness, frustration and stress that are so debilitating in working-class white communities.

Clayton Green and Nicholas Kristof on the Kristof farm in Yamhill in 2015. Clayton fixed the sheep shed in the background when Nick drove through it with the tractor. *(Photo courtesy Kristof family)*

While once a model of a close-knit farm town, Yamhill now finds its social fabric frayed. Today the town still has four churches and a volunteer fire department, but the other institutions are gone, and the old social glue has dried up remarkably quickly. Clayton was typical of his generation: he wasn't active in a church or another community organization. Those social networks and local institutions had frayed, so while Clayton had friends, he didn't really belong anywhere, and he didn't have a social role that gave him fulfillment and meaning.

Increasingly, Clayton seemed to be following in Kevin's footsteps. He, too, grew a big beard and became so overweight that it was difficult for him to work. He crossed four hundred pounds, and doctors told him he was diabetic and had congestive heart failure with fluid rising in his lungs. He tried to get gastric bypass surgery but was told that he needed to improve his health first. We gave him a diet book, but he never managed to lose much weight.

Paul Ryan probably would have seen in Clayton a man who refused to lift himself up by his bootstraps. We saw a deeply loyal friend who had never managed to get an education and struggled ever after, often working long hours at difficult physical labor despite many ailments. Once Clayton emerged from the hospital after nearly dying from heart problems and staggered over to the Kristof farm a few days later because he had promised to fix a tractor. We had complete confidence in him, for Clayton had proven ferociously loyal to Nick's mom and to his old friends like Ricochet Goff. In a tribute to his loyalty, he once fired Goff's son from a work crew on our farm for showing up high on meth, an ironic move given Clayton's own towering status in the meth world. Clayton reassured us periodically that he had warned people in the drug community that he would personally kill anybody who messed with Mrs. Kristof. We mumbled thanks but added we hoped it wouldn't come to that. Yes, there were times when he took gasoline from our farm tank without asking, but he would also hand out cash to friends who needed money and show up whenever we needed help. In retrospect, the school had shown irresponsibility in expelling Clayton and in failing to provide speech therapy, and he then responded with his own irresponsibility in cooking meth, but to think that an obese ninth-grade dropout with an outdated blue-collar skill set could lift himself up by his bootstraps is magical thinking.

Like Kevin, Clayton had lost his driver's license for failing to pay child support. But while Kevin was cautious about driving without a license, Clayton was less inhibited. He drove around openly in his black pickup truck. Once he was summoned to the district attorney's office in the county seat, McMinnville, for driving without a license. "You didn't drive down here by yourself, did you?" the prosecutor asked.

"No, I wouldn't do that," Clayton replied. "I took my dog with me."

9

Deaths of Despair

Poverty entails fear, and stress, and sometimes depression; it means a thousand petty humiliations and hardships. Climbing out of poverty by your own efforts—that is something on which to pride yourself, but poverty itself is romanticized only by fools.

—J. K. ROWLING, *Very Good Lives*

In the early 1800s, by far the richest man in the world was Nathan Mayer Rothschild, a founder of the Rothschild banking dynasty, the man who bailed out the Bank of England in 1826. Adjusted for inflation, he was wealthier than John D. Rockefeller or Bill Gates or Jeff Bezos. Yet in 1836 he suffered a boil on his buttocks, surgeons lanced it and it became infected. Doctors performed more painful surgeries, but nothing helped, and the wealthiest man in modern times died for want of what would now be a dollar's worth of antibiotics.

For the last 150 years, life expectancy has soared around the world because of antibiotics, blood transfusions, vaccinations, sterilization, sanitation and other innovations that have had a stunning effect on health care. Even the poorest American would not normally die today of an infected abscess of the kind that killed Rothschild. Life expectancy rose in the United States from less than 35 in 1860 to almost 77 in 2000, and continued to creep up before peaking at 78.9 in 2014.

Then, beginning in 2015, something disquieting happened: life expectancy began to tumble again in America, falling for three consecutive years, the first three-year decline since 1918, when people were dying from the worst flu pandemic in modern history. The fall in life expectancy underscores that something is profoundly wrong even at a time when the overall economy has been booming.

"We should take it very seriously," said Bob Anderson of the Centers for Disease Control. "If you look at the other developed countries in the world, they're not seeing this kind of thing." Indeed, once impoverished South Koreans already live to eighty-two on average, substantially longer than Americans, and demographers predict that by 2030 Mexicans will enjoy a longer lifespan as well.

Everything depends on your social stratum. Low-income American men have a life expectancy comparable to men in Sudan or Pakistan, while rich American men live longer than the average in any country in the world. The average American lifespan is falling because of people like the Greens and the Knapps—whites with a high-school education or less. Meanwhile, black life expectancy is still rising, although it remains lower than for whites as a whole. Anne Case and Angus Deaton, the Princeton University economists who first highlighted the trend, attributed the falling life expectancy to "deaths of despair" from three main factors: drugs, alcohol and suicide.

"They're a symptom of this deeper thing: the meaningfulness of the working-class life seems to have evaporated," Professor Deaton told us. "The economy just seems to have stopped delivering for those people." Thinking of the trajectory of the Knapp kids on the Number 6 school bus, that seems about right.

WHENEVER GARY KNAPP BEAT UP Dee and reached for his rifle, she would run outside and cower in the darkness. Then he would begin shooting.

"I just stayed low and stayed hid and stayed still and hoped to God he didn't hit me," she said.

It was more unnerving when Gary picked up the shotgun and pointed it at her. A .22 bullet, a woman could survive; a 12-gauge shotgun blast in the chest, not so much. What Dee feared wasn't just death, but also the trauma to her children if they witnessed her murder. The kids were already scarred by seeing Gary beat her, and Farlan was talking darkly about killing his father.

To try to rescue the kids from this trauma, Dee visited the sheriff's office to complain and seek help. The deputies in the 1970s, though, weren't interested in domestic violence. "No, it's a family problem," one explained. So Gary became increasingly violent toward Dee and the children, although she did her best to distract him when he lined the kids up to whip them with his belt. She usually succeeded, but only at the price of being beaten herself. Three times she had to replace the door because Gary pushed her through it.

One evening, Dee was cooking dinner for the kids when Gary demanded that she drive him to the bar in Gaston. "I'm not going to go off and leave the kids hungry because you want to go to the bar," she replied. "The kids are going to eat before I leave." She had already started dinner, with hot grease in the skillet ready for cooking. Furious, Gary threw the skillet at her, burning her with sizzling grease. Then he grabbed a knife, saying, "You stand still or I'm going to kill you." And then he started cutting her clothes off.

"Kids, you go upstairs," Dee shouted at them, helpless, not wanting them to see her humiliation. They went, and Gary systematically used his knife to cut off every stitch of clothing she wore; he then punched her and shoved her through the wall.

One Easter Sunday morning, after an all-night fight, Dee and Gary drove the kids to an Easter egg hunt. Gary had been drinking whiskey all night and soon started taking pills as well, and the combination overwhelmed his body. He turned gray, lost his sight and began walking into walls. Dee and Farlan wrestled Gary into the car and drove him to the hospital. He died two hours later, age thirty-nine.

For Dee, the main reaction was relief. "I knew he couldn't come back and hurt me anymore," she said. At the funeral service, she sat impassively, with a black eye and split lip to commemorate the relationship. Surprisingly, the one true mourner was Farlan, who was wracked by guilt for having worked out schemes to kill his dad. Superstitious, he wondered if he was responsible in some way.

"I think Farlan would have figured out some way to kill his dad, he hated him that bad," said Dee.

With Gary gone, the Knapp home was more tranquil, and prospects seemed better. Poverty shouldn't be romanticized, but neither is it unremitting bleakness. Other kids noticed the Knapps at times having plenty of fun. The difficulties were real, but so were the practical jokes, the joys of fishing, the warmth of a large family gathered around the table. The kids did everything together, from canning tomatoes to tinkering with carburetors. For all the quarrels and fistfights within the family, there was also a profound bond. The Knapps exasperated one another, sometimes bloodied one another, but also protected one another and depended on one another. The kids were one another's best friends, and they all knew their mom's unconditional devotion to them. From her meager income, Dee scraped together the cash to buy sixteen-year-old Farlan his first car, a Mustang, and the entire family marveled at the love and sacrifice the gift reflected.

The Knapp household was newly upbeat, but getting ahead proved complicated. Schooling was the escalator to a better life, but because Dee herself was a fifth-grade dropout, she wasn't in a position to coach her kids or provide much oversight. She was an exhausted single mom driving a tractor all day and then struggling to raise five children. So the escalator broke, and the kids dropped out of school one after the other. Farlan quit after the ninth grade to help the family with money. Zealan was essentially illiterate and had paid no attention to school for years before he formally dropped out. Nathan skipped school constantly, bored and resentful of discipline, and dropped out in tenth grade. Rogena was sixteen when she dropped out.

Keylan got into trouble regularly. When he was in the third grade, he brought the hallucinogenic drug PCP to Yamhill Grade School and tripped with Zealan and a friend, requiring a visit to the hospital. Yet Keylan was exceptionally good at math and science. In fifth grade, the teachers sent him up to join the eighth-grade math class, his feet dangling from the big chairs; he outperformed most of the eighth graders. Maybe at that moment the right teacher could have nurtured in him a passion for math and put him on a path toward college. Instead, he ran out of challenges and grew bored.

Dee complains, probably rightly, that the schools weren't much interested in her kids, seeing them as disruptive white trash, and were happy to push them out the door. From a principal's point of view, a school ran more smoothly without the Knapps and without the Greens, but the policy of pushing out troublesome kids simply turned them into society's problems.

The Knapp home had guns but not books; the children were taught how to tinker with cars but not to read. Dee had never acquired the middle-class skill set to negotiate with a bureaucracy like a school. "They said they didn't have the manpower to help the kids that were slow learners," Dee recalled, and she didn't know how to push back.

When her family did protest, it was in the wrong way. The cultural honor code stipulated that indignities merited a violent response. After Keylan, in a bad mood, flipped over his teacher's desk and was suspended for three days, his uncle sought vengeance by going to the school and wrestling the teacher against the wall. This made the school even more eager to see the Knapps drop out.

Other problems may have been the lack of role models and the absence of self-confidence. The Knapps lived in Cove Orchard, a hamlet built around a tiny store with a gas pump, north of Yamhill. Cove Orchard groundwater was salty, so wells weren't much good, and there was no sewage system other than outhouses and septic tanks. Human waste flowed in the ditches, black and stinky. "Many of the ditches were an extreme health hazard from raw, untreated sewage," recalled Joe Petrovich, a county sanitation official at the time. All this made property prices cheap, attracting people at the bottom of the social pecking order. The Knapps' neighbors included several families with alcoholic fathers, an old drunk whom people called "the wino," a couple of widows living in shacks without electricity or plumbing, and a young single mom who, when boys came to court her pretty daughter, propositioned them. Nick still blushes at the memory.

"If you lived in Cove Orchard, that shithole of Yamhill, you were trash," Keylan recalled.

That sense of degradation, of being labeled inferior, is a central feature of the whirlpool of the working poor. The Nobel Prize–winning economist Amartya Sen has said that shame is the "irreducible absolutist core" of the experience of poverty. Poverty is about not just income but also humiliation, social exclusion, the stress of being forever lower on the social ladder.

Some will say—or at least think, for this is politically incorrect to express publicly—that the poor are poor because they received a third-rate intellectual inheritance. There's reason for strong skepticism (and not only because arguments about inherited deficiency have historically been used without basis to justify racism and bigotry).

Researchers have looked closely at genetic factors relating to how long people stay in school, partly because education data are widely collected and fairly objective. They do find that genetic factors play a small role, although they probably have to do not just with cognitive skills but also with persistence, ability to concentrate and neuron-to-neuron communications. An enormous study of 1.1 million people published in *Nature Genetics* in 2018 found 1,271 genetic variations that correlated to differences in how long people stayed in school. Among the one-fifth with the genetic variations most highly correlated with education, 57 percent graduated from college; among the bottom one-fifth, 12 percent did. The study found that these genetic factors played a role only for whites of European background and were not predictive of how long blacks remained in school. More significantly, even for whites, these genetic elements were less important in determining time in school than environmental factors such as parental wealth or parental educational level. Research, therefore, suggests that while genetic factors may play a role, they are much less significant than geography, parental circumstances, access to good schools and other criteria.

Hope matters, too. There has been important scholarship in recent years showing that when people despair of their situations and see no way out, they are more likely to surrender and engage in self-destructive behaviors that make the despair self-fulfilling. If they don't feel they can escape from poverty, they don't. Conversely, as Esther Duflo of MIT has shown, if they're given hope that there is a way out, then they are more industrious and the hope becomes self-fulfilling, allowing them to escape.

The wisdom that people tend to live up to expectations, or down to them, helps explain success and failure, particularly for men (for reasons we don't understand, this effect is greater on boys than on girls). There is evidence that this is one of the most insidious consequences of racism, nurturing insecurities and hopelessness, but, as in Cove Orchard, it can also be true of struggling whites. At some level, the Knapps and the Greens absorbed the idea that they were screw-ups, that they wouldn't get ahead, and then it became easier to console themselves with alcohol and drugs. It also became easier to violate norms and laws, both because the "system" appeared less legitimate and because jail is less humiliating if you're already an outcast.

So Farlan, like Clayton Green, became a self-taught chemist and manufactured some of the first methamphetamine in the Yamhill area. He rented a building in Gaston and became a successful entrepreneur noted for his high-quality meth. "This is what I was made for," he once told Clayton. Unfortunately, Farlan also sampled the merchandise and became addicted, while replicating his father's penchant for alcoholism.

An excellent woodworker and furniture maker, Farlan dreamed of opening his own furniture store, which he would call "Farlan's Far Out Fantastic Freaky Furniture." But it didn't come to pass, for alcohol and drugs were taking a steady toll on his liver. By his late forties, he was dying from cirrhosis and liver failure. He was hollow-cheeked, gaunt and frail.

"Mom, how old are you?" he asked Dee one day.

"Seventy," she replied.

"Why can't I live that long?" he asked wistfully. He was forty-nine then. He died in 2009, just after his fifty-first birthday.

Zealan, who had spent years shooting heroin in Oregon, moved to

Dee Knapp visiting the grave site of four of her five children, above her house (Photo by Lynsey Addario)

Luther, Oklahoma, along with his mom and much of the family. It was there that his mobile home mysteriously caught fire. Others in the mobile home escaped, but Zealan, passed out drunk, died, even though his body was found near the back door. Dee told us she thinks the home caught fire from chemicals that Zealan was using to make meth. She had taken photos of the home and the drug apparatus but had recently thrown the photos away.

"Why would you do that?" protested Keylan. "I would have liked to see them."

"It was bad memories, son."

The tragedies continued with Nathan, who was also in Luther, living next to Dee in a trailer home and making meth with his son using the dangerous "shake and bake" method. The concoction blew up, and Nathan came staggering out toward Dee. "He melted away," she recalled. Rushed to the hospital by helicopter, he died later that day.

Rogena had the same affinity for alcohol and drugs as her siblings, complicated by mental illness that in turn was aggravated by the drug and alcohol abuse. She worried that airplanes were following her around, and once when driving from Oregon to Oklahoma she was so oblivious that she continued hundreds of miles past her destination and stopped in Missouri only because her engine blew out. One July 4, she stopped at a party but was offended that she was told to have only one hot dog because there were few left. She started a fight, and when the police came, she retreated. The police angled their car sideways across the driveway so that she couldn't drive past and escape. An angry Rogena crashed her car into the side of the police vehicle. Then she backed up and did it again. The police officers dragged her out of her car and took her to jail. After years of suffering from hepatitis C and liver cancer related to longtime abuse of drugs and alcohol, Rogena passed away in 2016. She was the fourth child that Dee had buried in five years. Behind her house was her children's grave site, which she visited every day.

Rogena was part of a wave of increasing deaths related to alcohol—an important component of the "deaths of despair," according to the Centers for Disease Control and Prevention. A study in the *British Medical Journal* found that between 1999 and 2016, cirrhosis-related deaths in the United States rose 65 percent and those from liver cancer doubled. The increases were driven primarily by alcohol abuse, the study found. While drugs get more attention, the CDC calculates that excessive alcohol kills more Americans each year (88,000) than drug overdoses do (68,000).

Why did deaths of despair claim Farlan, Zealan, Nathan, Rogena and so many others? We see four important factors.

First, good union jobs disappeared, because of technology, automation, trade, political pressure on unions and a general redistribution of power toward the wealthy. As well-paying jobs for the less educated disappeared, the self-esteem of workers who couldn't find new jobs plummeted and some obtained prescription painkillers for health conditions and soon abused the medication.

Second, there was an explosion of drugs—oxycodone, meth, heroin, crack cocaine and now fentanyl. The proliferation of drugs was partly driven by the professionalization of drug cartels and by the reckless marketing of prescription painkillers by pharmaceutical companies.

Third, the war on drugs meant that addiction became far more difficult to reconcile with daily life than in the old days when substance abuse involved alcohol. In the past, alcoholics like Gary Knapp remained somewhat functional and could hold on to jobs, avoid felony convictions and afford their habits. In contrast, people in Farlan's generation used illicit drugs and so were much more likely to get criminal records, which made them less employable and marriageable. There was also the temptation to make money by manufacturing or peddling illegal drugs, even at the risk of a meth lab explosion of the kind that killed Nathan Knapp. In any case, one can feed an alcohol habit for $20 a day, while a drug habit may cost ten times as much and is far more likely to lead to robbery or prostitution.

Finally, mass incarceration for drug-related offenses broke up families and meant that millions of boys were raised without the presence

Keylan Knapp, the sole survivor among the Knapp children, comforting his mother in the house they share *(Photo by Lynsey Addario)*

of a dad or any other positive male role model, helping transmit the problems to the next generation.

The government intervened with the Knapp kids not to keep them in school, but only to arrest them. The kids were bright, and with outreach from social workers or economic support they might have been able to finish high school, even attend college or join the military. Keylan survived in part because he and Nathan were convicted of armed robbery, of a gas station, and spent nine years in the Oregon State Penitentiary. They shared a cell there, a symbol of the strong family bonds among the Knapps but also of a family gone astray. Keylan worked in the penitentiary metal shop and invested in stocks: he says he made about $25,000 with his stock market trades while incarcerated.

Once freed from prison, Keylan ran amok again. He bought a monster pickup truck with huge wheels. "I could set all the car alarms off going down the road," he says, and he did so—usually at three a.m. After police found meth in his vehicle, he served another forty-seven months in prison. He says that he found God while inside and, after his release, traveled to Oklahoma to be with his mom. He arrived with just $35 and two pairs of jeans but found work doing construction.

In 2018, Keylan had another mishap reflective of a penchant for risk-taking: while working on a roof, he fell forty-five feet and broke his pelvis, his hip, both legs and his right arm. He accumulated $700,000 in medical bills and was supposed to spend three months in the hospital and rehab but managed to get out after a month. When we caught up with him a few months later, he walked stiffly but was ready to go back to work.

For an armed robber and lifelong drug abuser, Keylan brims with charm, intelligence and insouciance. With a different beginning, one can easily imagine him having ended up as a successful engineer or sales executive. He exudes an easy humor that belies his life, as well as a surprising optimism. "I've been fortunate," he told us—not the term we would have picked to describe his trajectory. "I don't know why God loves me."

It was getting late and we had just a few final questions.

"Are you clean now?"

"Yes, except for the weed. I mean, I still like my weed."

"But other than that?"

"Every once in a while I might bust out and do a little bit of meth."

"I see. And do you abuse alcohol?"

"I don't abuse it," he said impishly. "I drink it, daily."

10

Interventions That Work

What's the use you learning to do right when it's troublesome to do right and ain't no trouble to do wrong, and the wages is just the same?

—HUCKLEBERRY FINN

ollectively, the seventeen women had 260 years of drug addiction, an average of 15 years each, plus long experience in crime, poverty and homelessness. All were on probation. They had lied to, stolen from and cheated just about everyone around them for years. But the jubilant crowd of three hundred was giving them a standing ovation. On this night in 2018 in Tulsa, Oklahoma, the seventeen women stood proudly before the crowd in beautiful dresses, their hair and nails elegant, to raucous cheers from family members and even police officers who previously had arrested and scorned them. This was a graduation ceremony from Women in Recovery, a diversion program from prison for nonviolent drug offenders, and these women were now emerging to reenter society as productive workers, taxpayers, voting citizens and moms. We had come to Tulsa not for a grim tour of human devastation but to celebrate a triumph and explore a program that has been astonishingly successful in helping shattered people rebuild their lives and families.

Several judges who had frequently encountered these women in their courtrooms were in the front row, applauding wildly. The sheriff was beaming. The district attorney told us how these women inspired him. Oklahoma's state attorney general was a graduation speaker and called the women "heroes." That drew smiles through tears from a group of women more used to being reviled as "junkies" or "whores."

"I thought we'd be planning a funeral instead," said one audience member whose younger sister had started using meth at age twelve and was now graduating at thirty-five.

Ken Levit, who runs the George Kaiser Family Foundation and helped launch Women in Recovery, told the audience that the program had saved Oklahoma more than $70 million in prison spending. "You and your stories have singlehandedly transformed the trajectory of criminal justice policy in this state," he told the women.

Toward the end of the ceremony, the audience gave the women graduates another standing ovation. Then the graduates shouted, "Thank you, judges," and gave a return standing ovation to the judges. The giddy scene offered a crucial lesson that the rest of the country hasn't appreciated: there is hope even for people with addictions whom society has given up on—if they get the right help.

"It'd be a horrible injustice for them to be in prison," Judge William J. Musseman Jr. told us. "It'd be an injustice because the system didn't recognize that treatment could provide a sufficient wedge in conduct, that treatment could in fact change the trajectory of their lives."

Women in Recovery is just one modest-sized program in a single city, but it can be replicated. It also underscores the point that with encouragement and the right resources for many Americans left behind, there is hope. While we worked on this book, colleagues so often made comments like, "That must be terribly depressing." Yes, of course there have been grim moments, but we have also seen uplift and inspiration. We fear that too many Americans believe that addiction, homelessness and criminality are intractable, that nothing can be done. Anybody attending the Women in Recovery graduation saw immense joy and exhilaration, as well as a path to a better future. Those of us who care

Tanitoluwa Adewumi,
a homeless refugee from
Nigeria who studied chess
while lying on the floor
of his shelter, beaming
beside the trophy he won
as the 2019 New York
State chess champion
for his age bracket
(Photo by Russell Makofsky)

about improving outcomes can't just wag our fingers and scold; we also must point out successes that are possible if we pursue different policies that consistently deliver opportunity.

Flashes of hope burst out in unexpected places, and they give us optimism about what can be achieved. One of our most thrilling moments in recent years was watching a homeless eight-year-old boy named Tanitoluwa Adewumi—he goes by Tani—lug a trophy almost as big as he was through his homeless shelter in Manhattan. Tani had arrived in New York City only a bit more than a year earlier, after his family fled Nigeria because of Boko Haram terror attacks on Christians like themselves. A pastor helped them get settled in a homeless shelter, and Tani attended the neighborhood elementary school, PS 116, where 10 percent of the pupils are homeless. The school had a part-time chess teacher, Shawn Martinez, who was passionate about the game and came every Thursday to teach Tani's second-grade class how to play. Tani had never encountered chess before and joined the school halfway through the year, but he quickly caught up with his classmates. Impressed by Tani's start, Coach Martinez encouraged the boy to sign up for the school's chess club. The club required fees to cover the cost of attending tournaments, but Tani's mom, Oluwatoyin Adewumi, emailed the head of the chess program and explained that the family was living in a homeless shelter and couldn't pay anything. The fees were waived, Tani showed up at chess club meetings, and everybody could see that he had promise. Nobody had any idea yet just how much promise.

CHANGING THE TRAJECTORY of lives is the ambitious goal of Women in Recovery, and its alumnae show it can be done. One of those alumnae is Rebecca Hale, who spoke at the Women in Recovery graduation. With fine brown hair framing sparkling green-brown eyes, Rebecca grew up in Tulsa and told us that she drifted to prison the usual way, through an obstacle course of neglect, trauma and physical and sexual abuse. For as long as Rebecca could remember, her mother, Joyce King, had sold meth from their home, and people would traipse in and out constantly. Joyce was also a user and often high. When Rebecca was about six, Joyce was imprisoned on drug charges, so her father took care of her. But her dad was drinking heavily and also using drugs at the time, Rebecca said, so she and her father ended up homeless over the summer after she completed first grade.

When Joyce left prison, Rebecca went to live with her, but her mom returned to selling drugs and was sent to prison again. At the age of thirteen, Rebecca found herself effectively an orphan, her father already in prison for burglary. Rebecca was placed in a children's home but wasn't happy there, running away to stay with friends. But she wanted to continue school, so when ninth grade began she went to her local school to register on her own. She picked up enrollment papers, took them to prison to get her mom's signature and finally went to school to sign up for classes.

"Where's your mom?" a woman in the school office asked.

"She's at work and can't come in today."

The woman asked her more probing questions. Finally, Rebecca owned up.

"Look, I'm homeless," she admitted. "My parents are in prison. Please just let me enroll in school."

"Oh, honey, we can't do that," the woman replied. "There are laws and rules. We can call somebody who can help you."

The woman telephoned the police, and as she was explaining the situation, Rebecca excused herself. "I need to go to the bathroom," she said—and ran off.

She bounced from one friend's house to another's before running into one of her mom's drug suppliers. That's when Rebecca became a drug runner and a user. Rebecca visited Joyce in prison on weekends, and slowly their relationship became stronger. Then Rebecca revealed a secret to her mother. When Rebecca had been five or six years old and they were living in the projects, she would play outside on her own. An elderly man, probably in his late sixties, would sit outside and give her popsicles and candy. One day, he lured her into his apartment and started kissing her. Then the man started touching her inappropriately and making her touch him.

"I knew it didn't feel right," she said. "But I'll tell you, the sick, twisted part is that he gave me a lot of attention that I was really needing.

"He told me that's what dads did with their daughters and that it was a secret," she recalled. "Because my dad had been in and out of my life, I thought maybe he was telling the truth, that that's really what dads did with daughters." It happened six or seven times. And then her dad came back from prison. Soon after, Rebecca tried to give her dad a long, deep kiss.

"My dad told me, 'You don't do that. I'm a grown-up, and you're a little girl, and I'm your daddy and that's not okay.'" Rebecca didn't tell her father about the man then, but now she did tell Joyce, who wept at the revelation.

One of Joyce's friends had taken Rebecca into her home and registered her in school again. Rebecca then found a job that enabled her to buy a car in which she could sleep, and while still homeless, she graduated from high school. As she turned eighteen, Rebecca was at a fork in the road. She had demonstrated extraordinary initiative and resilience to graduate from high school, and now she took a job as a cashier and cook at Arby's, allowing her to rent her first apartment. But Rebecca ultimately took the wrong fork. She continued to use and sell drugs, and she had a child, Chloe, at the age of twenty, and then another, Nate, a year later, with a different father. Nate's dad disapproved of drugs and tried to get her to stop, but she wouldn't listen.

"I don't think there's anything anybody ever could have said to make me stop," said Rebecca. She was haunted by the shame of sexual abuse and had no feelings of self-worth. Rebecca was sinking deeper into drugs and was repeatedly thrown into jail. Then Nate's dad left Rebecca, went to court and took custody of their son, while Chloe went to Joyce. "I really lost it at that point," Rebecca said. "When the kids got taken from me, I really went wild." Rebecca embarked on a crime spree that sent her to federal prison for three years for money laundering, bank fraud and identity theft. When she was released, she took out a loan on her mother's good credit, bought a small two-bedroom apartment with no money down and enrolled in school for an associate's degree in criminal justice—a field in which she did, after all, have expertise.

Increasingly, Rebecca wanted to start over. She called up her probation officers and said she wanted to go into drug treatment but lacked the money for it (she had no insurance). They said that they couldn't help unless she was arrested again on state charges.

"What you're telling me is I have to get in more trouble in order to get help?" Rebecca asked.

"Pretty much."

Soon Rebecca succumbed again to drugs and crime and landed back in jail, this time facing twenty-eight felony charges. In the booking room, she was handed two sets of orange jail uniforms.

At this point, Rebecca was fairly typical of women in prisons and jails in the United States. Look at their records and you see hardened career criminals who seem to have decisively chosen this course. But dig deeper and most were on a trajectory toward prison from childhood. One study found that 81 percent of delinquent girls in South Carolina had experienced sexual violence, while another in Oregon found that 93 percent of girls in the juvenile justice system there had experienced sexual or physical violence. Imprisoning them risks replicating this trajectory in the next generation, for 79 percent of women in jails have children under the age of eighteen.

Now dressed in her orange scrubs, Rebecca went through the dope sickness of withdrawal, but her outlook slowly changed. She read the Bible every day and prayed a lot. "When you get clean and you have a minute to reflect on your life, you realize what you've been doing to the people that you love the most," she said.

Chloe then was thirteen years old and refused to speak to her mom when she phoned from jail. That hurt Rebecca and helped push her to make a decisive change: "I was so tired of that life and being away from my children. I'm just repeating that same sick cycle." That's when she found out about Women in Recovery and became desperate to get in, telling everyone that she wanted to join the program. "If they had told me that I had to do handstands and walk that way for the rest of my life to stay sober," she told us, "I would have done it."

BACK IN NEW YORK CITY, Tani participated in his first tournament in 2018 with the lowest chess rating, 105, of any participant. He worked hard and attended a free summer chess program in New York City schools, and soon he began to win. Chess trophies began to stack up in the homeless shelter. He won chessboards as well, making it easier to practice. "He is so driven," Coach Martinez told us. "He does ten times more chess puzzles than the average kid. He just wants to be better."

Still, it was hard for Tani. He came home from school crying one day when classmates teased him about being homeless. At an immigration hearing, he misunderstood the judge and burst into tears when he thought he was about to be deported back to Nigeria. On the plus side, Tani had an enormously hardworking and supportive family. His dad, Kayode Adewumi, held two jobs: he worked long hours as an Uber driver using a car he rented and also passed a real estate exam and became a licensed real estate salesman. His mom took a course to become a home health-care aide. It was easy to see where the boy's diligence and ambition came from. Likewise, the family was enormously nurturing and proud of Tani's achievements. Every Saturday, his mom took him to a three-hour free chess clinic in Harlem, and his dad let him use his laptop computer with chess software that the school provided free of charge. Even Tani's older brother, fifteen-year-old Austin, who aims to become an engineer, regularly took time off to accompany Tani to chess events. The family is very religious but, a bit reluctantly, allowed Tani to miss Sunday church services to attend chess tournaments.

"Tani is rich beyond measure," Russell Makofsky, who oversees the chess program, told us—for what the boy lacked in family financial resources he received in family love and support. In 2019, with a rating that had swelled to 1587, Tani went to the state tournament. It had been only a year since he had started playing chess, but he had evolved into an aggressive, intuitive player. In one round, he boldly exchanged a bishop for a much less valuable pawn, and the school coaches worried that he had made a foolish move. But they fed the move into a computer simulator, and it declared that Tani's chances of winning had just increased: it saw, as Tani had, that the gambit improved his position several moves later. At this level, Tani was competing mostly against kids from elite private schools with their own $100-an-hour chess tutors, but in the end, Tani won that game and was undefeated in the entire tournament. He won the state championship for his age group.

"It's an inspiring example of how life's challenges do not define a person," Jane Hsu, the principal of his school, told us. Makofsky, the chess administrator, just shook his head wonderingly. "One year to get to this level, to climb a mountain and be the best of the best, without family resources," he told us. "I've never seen it."

MOST PEOPLE WHO HAVE an addiction need outside resources, though, especially as adults. Diversion programs have become more popular as many Republicans and Democrats alike have called for criminal justice reform and a greater response to drug addiction. There is broad agreement that prison terms are expensive and often accomplish little other than keeping inmates temporarily out of circulation and breaking up families, while initiatives like Women in Recovery have an excellent record of helping people transform their lives. The three-year recidivism rate for graduates of Women in Recovery is just 4.5 percent, far below prison recidivism rates.

Women in Recovery is built around intensive psychosocial counseling, which we discovered was the secret sauce of successful programs that are sprouting up around the country. Women in Recovery became our window into how these programs work. The women spend most of the day on-site and share housing, so they are surrounded on a daily basis by therapists, counselors and many professionals whose main objective is for the women to make it to the next phase and then graduate. They build camaraderie and sometimes use group voting to pass students to the next level.

"They can't pass the curriculum without saying, 'I'm responsible for this. I'm not a victim,'" said Catherine Claybrook, clinical director at the program. We remembered that Daniel McDowell at the Baltimore Station was also taught this principle. That's the paradox: individual offenders need to embrace the narrative of personal responsibility more fully, while American politics and society should be more skeptical of it.

Another well-validated therapy employed by Women in Recovery teaches women how to make decisions that keep them out of prison and guides them in developing the moral compass they didn't acquire while growing up. The counselors help the women resist temptation and explain why they are better off taking a dreary job at $8 an hour as opposed to accepting $150 for sex or $800 for transporting drugs. The Women in Recovery program lasts about eighteen months, far longer than most rehabilitation programs, and the length and intensity are crucial to its success. If the women fail periodic drug tests, they go back to prison, and that's a powerful incentive to make the do-over succeed.

The women pay nothing. They are housed and fed, schooled and counseled. The cost over eighteen months is $28,000 per person, contributed by the George Kaiser Family Foundation. That may seem expensive, but it's far less than a prison term would cost. Just as important, it includes children in the programing and aims to break the intergenerational cycle of drugs and poverty so that those kids are less likely to be arrested themselves in their teens or twenties.

Women in Recovery is a model of how a program can be humane while at the same time saving taxpayer money. It offers a proven tool-box to help people who are struggling, if only we will use it. And it's replicable and scalable. Indeed, in 2017 Oklahoma's Republican governor made Women in Recovery the centerpiece of a "Pay for Success" program to allow it to serve more women. Essentially, the expansion was paid for out of savings from money that would otherwise have been spent incarcerating the women.

REBECCA WASN'T INTERESTED in the abstract policy, though. She just wanted a life raft. The day of her preliminary hearing, Rebecca heard her name called at four a.m. from her jail cell. She was taken down the hall to be searched, then shackled and handcuffed. With other women, she was led to a small van that took them to a holding cell in the courthouse. Rebecca closed her eyes.

"Lord, please give me this opportunity," she prayed. "I'm tired of doing the same old thing over and over. Please open the door for me to go in this program."

When Rebecca's case was summoned, she saw the district attorney step up. At the previous hearing, he had terrified her: "They were pissed," she recalled. "They were like, She has multiple felony accounts. With this large number of counts, she's a menace to society." Then Rachel Delcour, a liaison at Women in Recovery who works closely with officials from the local courts and jails, interviewed Rebecca, who made a point of showing her determination to work hard and turn her life around. This time when Rebecca's case was heard, the DA announced, "We've gone over her records, and we've decided that she is eligible for Women in Recovery and has been accepted."

Rebecca had won the new start she had been dreaming of.

"I think it's God," she said. "My mom was praying, I was praying. Even my daughter was going down front in church every Sunday."

Rebecca devoted herself to Women in Recovery. She attended all classes, baring her soul in therapy sessions. She took a deep and emotional look at her past—the trauma, abuse, neglect and drugs. Therapists helped her assess her past decision-making and advised how she could avoid bad decisions in the future.

"We really studied the pathways that bring women into the criminal justice system," said Mimi Tarrasch, an energetic, passionate social worker who developed and runs Women in Recovery. "First thing on that pathway is family dysfunction." Tarrasch said that when women have been traumatized, abused, pimped by a mom or dad, then a rehab program for just one, two or three months isn't going to be enough to overcome a long-term addiction. Yet most rehab programs last only three months, if that long. In contrast, the default prison sentence for a repeat felony conviction is measured in years. Shedding an old way of life takes time.

Rebecca learned how to set goals, and then how to meet them. It's a basic discipline that these programs—like the military—inculcate in their people. She and her classmates received coaching on decision-making and taking responsibility, budgeting and conflict resolution, nutrition, relapse prevention, résumé writing, plus help getting GEDs, housing and jobs.

After Rebecca completed the program, she searched for employment through Women in Recovery's network of business partners who are willing to hire the program's graduates. Rebecca took a job at an air-conditioning company, handling billing and customer service, and on the side she enrolled in classes to learn the technical side of heating, ventilation and cooling. If customers become annoyed with her, she applies lessons about calming and anger management from Women in Recovery. Anyone looking at Rebecca's rap sheet might have come to the conclusion she was a hopeless recidivist, while anyone now working with her on an air-conditioning issue would encounter a happy, well-adjusted employee and solid citizen.

For the first time, Rebecca, at the age of thirty-seven, is not on any government assistance, but she does struggle to pay the bills, including mortgage and student loan payments as well as installments on $20,000 in debt built up in the local courts. It is not lost on Rebecca that some of her new work colleagues have saved for the past twenty years in the company's 401(k) and earned profit sharing, while she is just getting started. "Because I chose to go a different way," she said, "I'm just now starting in the last four years to rebuild my life and to prepare for the future. It's really challenging."

ONE OF THE IMPEDIMENTS to scaling up programs like Women in Recovery is that this intensive treatment is expensive, at least compared to traditional one-month programs, which are much less effective. Another impediment is the perception that drug treatment is a Sisyphean task that usually fails, and that even after enormous investments of time and money, most people will relapse. Yes, relapses are often part of recovery. But remember that astonishing recidivism rate for Women in Recovery: only 4.5 percent of those completing the program reoffend within three years. That's a stunning success and a sign of what is possible. It's true that this is partly because of self-selection and because the threat of prison hangs over anyone who fails a urine test, and not every program would be able to replicate it. But it underscores that with intensive long-term programs we could turn around the lives of countless people struggling with addiction, along with the lives of their children, and that far too many aren't getting the help that could be transformative.

Moreover, while the expense is real, the corollary of success is that it brings huge cost savings. Treatment is expensive, but so are crime, incarceration and foster care. One study found that if offenders in state prisons received needed drug treatment, the country would enjoy $36 billion in savings and benefits.

If quality treatment programs can be significantly expanded and replicated in many more cities and counties, these initiatives offer a way for America to move away from mass incarceration, while helping drug offenders get treatment, counseling and jobs. Judge Musseman told us that the majority of his cases were drug related. And when women with

Rebecca Hale, right, in her home, now has a much better relationship with her teenage daughter, Chloe. *(Photo by Lynsey Addario)*

children are jailed, the kids' lives are often ruined, too, sending them on a terrible life journey. "We're all about the two-generation model," said Tarrasch.

While Rebecca Hale was lucky to be in Tulsa to take advantage of Women in Recovery, vast numbers of drug users remain locked in cells because there is no such program available in their areas. We need Women in Recovery, and Men in Recovery, programs all across the country, creating hope where devastation has prevailed. But let's also acknowledge that charitable local solutions are not enough. More important, we need scalable, institutional macro-solutions—with initiatives like job training and job placement—to get earnings growing again.

The impact of Women in Recovery's two-generation model can be seen in Rebecca's children. Chloe, seventeen, with a round face, blue-gray eyes and brown hair, is a junior in high school, and while she still has the same homework and boyfriend troubles as her girlfriends, she has issues that most teenage girls don't have. Not only is her mom on probation, but the man she calls Dad is in prison three hours away. He is serving a five-year sentence for drugs and for adult kidnapping with a baseball bat, she told us rather matter-of-factly. As for her real father, she doesn't have contact with him now.

"We talked on the phone," Chloe said. "And then apparently he got drunk and said that I wasn't his daughter and that my mom was a whore, and that he wants nothing to do with me and that I should just go and kill myself."

The kids have undergone their own counseling, for their traumas make them vulnerable to substance abuse and health problems later in life. Once, when Chloe and Nate were home, an angry boyfriend started beating their mom. The boyfriend cut Rebecca's throat and face badly. Another time, he took a hammer and shattered her arm and hand and threatened to smash her head. Whenever violence flared, Chloe and Nate would rush to their bedroom, crawl out the window, run down the street to their grandmother's house and summon help.

"I already knew he was a bad guy," said Chloe. "He told me that he would take my mom from us if I said anything."

Asked about drugs, Chloe is firm. "Not for me," she said, and she has stuck with this so far. When her best friend of six years started using drugs at age fourteen, Chloe severed the tie. "She already has a kid," she told us.

Chloe works as a cashier at a Carl's Jr. hamburger restaurant, honing her customer-service skills with people angry about the food for one reason or another. She has had customers throw drinks at her, spit on her, curse her, but she tries to remain patient. "You have to try and calm them down," she said. "Be like, We'll get it out as fast as we possibly can. We're doing the best we can."

Chloe says she wasn't bullied or stigmatized at school about her parents being in prison, partly because she and Nate didn't tell people. "We'd make stuff up," she said. "Like, I live with Grandma because Mom is out of state. I said we had a perfect life." Chloe also wants to focus on improving her grades. She had a 3.89 GPA in ninth grade, but it slipped when she was breaking up with her boyfriend. Both she and

Nate are enrolled in Oklahoma's Promise, a state program that allows them to attend state college with free tuition as long as they keep their grade point average above 2.5. Chloe wants to volunteer at the local animal shelter, and for her birthday she got a pet potbellied pig named Dexter that stayed in her bedroom until she realized how much work a pig is. Dexter was then dispatched to her cousin's farm.

For a career, Chloe aspires to do something with art. And although she quips that lunch is her favorite class, she is deeply engaged in high school. She is joining the school's theater club and told us that she had recently read *The Secret Life of Bees*, and also a play that she described as "the classic with those characters, Brutus and Caesar."

"*Et tu, Brute?*" piped up Nate, an avid reader.

A sturdy high-school sophomore and football player, Nate is a playful jokester, poking and tickling his sister frequently. One vestige of childhood trauma may be his fear of loud noises. When he was young and arguments and beatings were exploding around the home, Chloe would run to the bedroom and cover Nate's ears with her hands or a pillow and sing him to sleep.

Nate is particularly enthusiastic about school, both academics and activities. He has tried multiple sports—tennis, soccer, track, wrestling and football—and he is also committed to doing well in school to get into a good college. He says he plans to apply to Stanford University or Yale University, and is also thinking about the navy or air force. After living for years on a tightrope, Nate and Chloe seem safer and happier now. Nate acknowledges that he's "spoiled" by his mom and his sister. And Chloe said, "I like my life now; it's really good."

So a story that began with drugs, sexual abuse and homelessness has been transformed into a tale of resilience and the coming together of a family—because Rebecca happened to be a woman in Tulsa, where Women in Recovery offers this lifesaving intervention. Almost anywhere else, Rebecca acknowledges, she would be in prison and the family would be a mess, but she focuses on the triumph of what has happened here. "We still struggle," she said. "But the cycle stops with us. It's not going past me."

Nate agrees. "I'm very confident we will break it," he said. His sister nodded and added, "We'll break it, keep going on with life like nothing happened!"

WE ARE HOPEFUL that grit will triumph over vulnerability. In Manhattan, we walked with Tani back to his homeless shelter as he lugged his huge trophy. An elderly white woman on the street looked at this scrawny black boy with an oversize trophy and asked him, "What's that for?" Without stopping, he said matter-of-factly, "Chess. I won the state chess tournament." The woman's eyes opened wider. "Chess?" she repeated. "Wow!"

Tani's triumph reflects his brilliance and diligence, but also a combination of circumstances that too rarely come together. It helped, of course, that Tani's family is strong and was committed to getting him into the chess club and to every practice and tournament. It was also crucial that the chess club was willing to waive all fees and admit him. None of this would have happened if PS 116 hadn't taught chess and employed a first-rate chess teacher devoted to helping Tani improve his game. Most homeless kids don't have Tani's talent, but they also don't have his opportunity or drive. "I want to be the youngest grand master," he told us.

Nick wrote about Tani in his *Times* column, and the resulting outpouring of goodwill was staggering. Within hours, a handful of families had offered housing to the family. One woman had an empty furnished home that she was prepared to let them live in, another had extra space in her apartment overlooking Central Park, and another said she would help rent the family an apartment near Tani's school. Several others offered to buy Tani's dad a car so he would not have to rent the car that he drives for Uber. A company offered jobs to Tani's parents. A couple of private schools offered full scholarships. Lawyers offered immigration advice. President Bill Clinton invited Tani and his family to visit him in his Harlem office, so the boy took the morning off from school for that. And hundreds of readers contributed to a GoFundMe page that quickly raised more than $250,000 for Tani and his family.

A few days later, we helped the Adewumis move into their new home, a pleasant two-bedroom apartment in Manhattan, not far from his school. A generous reader had paid the rent for the first year, and another family had furnished it. "I have a home," Tani told us giddily, as he raced around the empty rooms. "I have a home!" He said he was particularly excited about eating a home-cooked meal for the first time in a year. "I want my mom's cooking again," he explained.

The Adewumis were overwhelmed but grounded. They politely declined the scholarship offers from elite private schools, while saying that they might reconsider when Tani reached middle school. For now, he would remain loyal to the elementary school that had given him a chance and welcomed him onto its chess team even when he could not pay fees. "This school showed confidence in Tanitoluwa, so we return the confidence," his mom told Principal Hsu. And then, fighting tears, they hugged.

The challenge is that when we highlight an inspiring story like Tani's, readers invariably want to support that particular child rather than the class of people similarly affected. Humans are moved to help individuals, not to address structural problems. But the solution to child homelessness is not winning the state chess championship. That's not scalable. So what the Adewumis did next was particularly meaningful. They decided not to touch the quarter-million dollars in the GoFundMe account, aside from 10 percent that they would give to their church as a tithe. The rest went into a new Tanitoluwa Adewumi Foundation to be used to help struggling immigrants like the ones they had been a week earlier. "God has already blessed me," Tani's dad explained. "I want to release my blessing to others."

We asked Tani what he thought about handing over this vast sum rather than, say, keeping a few dollars to buy a bicycle or a video game, or simply going out for a celebratory dinner. "I want to help other kids," he said, but just a trace of wistfulness crossed his face when we mentioned the other options. So we pressed him: Wasn't there anything he wanted? After a long silence, he confessed: "Well, maybe a computer," he said. "That would be nice." As soon as Nick reported that, of course, Tani was deluged with offers of computers.

Exactly a month after the first article appeared, Tani's parents had a Nigerian-style dinner in their home for all the people who had helped them, from the chess coach to the donor of the new car parked outside. Philip Falayi, a Nigerian pastor who had let the Adewumis sleep in his church for their first few days in New York, blessed the food, and Tani played chess in the corner with one of his school buddies. A bookshelf of donated chess books, the towering state chess trophy and a practice schedule to prepare for the national tournament completed the scene. "We are so thankful to everyone," Tani's dad told those present. "This happened because of all of you."

To see Tani with his trophy was to sense the possibilities when needy kids are supported. It's the same sensation we had cheering the graduation for Women in Recovery, and the right policies can replicate both kinds of opportunities. We say "policies" because there's a risk that recounting such a heartwarming tale may leave the impression that charity can solve social ills entirely rather than fill gaps. The outpouring of help for Tani's family was moving, but kids should have housing even if they are not chess prodigies. What we need is not just the dazzling generosity that people showed Tani's family, although that was transformative here, but systemic solutions to help children even when they don't know a bishop from a pawn. So we should be inspired, yes, but inspired to try to build comprehensive systems to replicate that web of support as much as possible for *all* kids, and that requires Americans to show generosity not only in private charity but also in public policy.

11

Universal Health Care:
One Day, One Town

America's health care system is neither healthy, caring, nor a system.
—WALTER CRONKITE, former anchor for *CBS Evening News*

Once a year in Wise, Virginia, a small town in the rolling hills of Appalachia, people begin lining up outside the gate of the county fairgrounds days in advance. They camp out in sleeping bags, drink coffee out of thermoses and watch videos as trucks bring circus-sized tents, dental equipment and medical cots past them into the fairgrounds. On the night before the big opening, the crowd swells hugely into a serpentine line on the grass beside the road, the parking lots fill up, and parents and children doze together as doctors, dentists and technicians arrive in the wee hours to set up. The time we were there, at five a.m., still in a predawn inky darkness, the fairgrounds gate swung open, and a tall man with a British accent welcomed everyone and ushered in the first few hundred people in line.

They shuffled past him, nodding appreciatively, delighted that the wait was over. The tall man greeted them each with a cheery "Good morning!" They smiled and thanked him. Many recognized him as the founder of the organization running this health fair, offering free medical and dental care for three days. "Thank you, oh, so much," one woman said, and she began applauding him. Others paused and started clapping, too. "You're the best!" shouted another. One woman looked at him gratefully and choked up, tears rolling down her face. The tall man, betraying his British reserve, looked horrified but nodded politely and wished her well.

"The health of these people is appalling," mused the tall man, Stan Brock, eighty-two years old, gray hair brushed back over a lined face. Stan, a black belt in tae kwon do, ramrod straight without an ounce of fat visible on his body, seemed in better shape than most of those arriving. Stan had a long line of wheelchairs and volunteers behind him for those who needed help, and many did.

Stan seemed to have stepped out of colonial Kenya; you expected him at any moment to put on a pith helmet and suggest a game of cricket. Yet he acquired his eccentricity honestly. He had managed fifty thousand cows on one of the largest ranches in the world, in the British colony of Guyana in South America. One day, a wild horse knocked him down and rolled on him, leaving him badly injured and fighting for his life. It was a twenty-six-day hike to the nearest hospital, so Stan relied on local tribespeople to patch him up—and then he began to think how he could repay them. He started an aid group, Remote Area Medical, to bring doctors and dentists to isolated areas of Guyana, and then expanded to other poor countries, including Haiti and Uganda. Sleeping on the floor of the office to save money, Stan traveled constantly from his base in Rockford, Tennessee, to the poorest countries in the world.

Out of the blue, he received a phone call from the nearby town of Sneedville, Tennessee, where there was no dentist. A little embarrassed, the caller explained that he had heard that Remote Area Medical provided dental services in places like Haiti. "Any chance," the caller asked, "you can come here to Sneedville? We need help, too."

Stan loaded a dental chair on the back of a pickup truck and brought a dentist with him to Sneedville. To his astonishment 150 people lined up. Stan began to realize that in terms of health care, parts of America were profoundly needy, too. He held a few events in the United States offering free health or dental care and was overwhelmed by the response. He expanded his mission to include not just the poorest parts of the globe but also the richest and most powerful country in the history of the world. These days, Remote Area Medical holds seventy health fairs across America annually, especially in poorer areas of states including Tennessee, Alabama, Missouri, Kentucky, South Dakota and Nebraska. One of the biggest weekend clinics is in California. Volunteers come from nearby and from other states. We sought out the health fair in Wise to explore more deeply and viscerally why America does poorly in international health comparisons, to understand how it is that the most powerful country in the world is suffering declining life expectancy.

"Someone who's in a position to fix health care needs to see this," Stan mused, as people in Wise filed past him for care. "It's not a right-wing or left-wing issue. We just need something to cover health, dental, vision." He noted that dental care in particular tends to be neglected in America. Some 74 million people have no dental insurance, more than

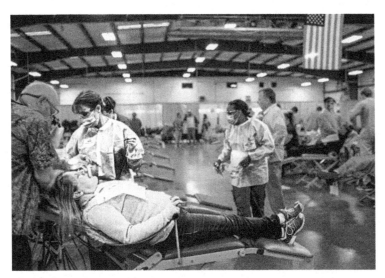

Volunteers provide free dental services at a Remote Area Medical health fair in Gray, Tennessee. Even in the richest country in the world, some people line up for days to get free care. *(Photo by Lynsey Addario)*

twice as many as lack health insurance. "Bad teeth lead to diabetes, to heart disease, to death," Stan noted. "People die from bad teeth in this country."

We left Stan at the gate and wandered over to the dental area, a huge tent with scores of dental chairs lined up in rows.* It looked like a factory floor: dozens of volunteer dentists were working on their patients, each a few feet from the next person. More patients were in the waiting area on folding chairs, mercifully facing the other direction so that they didn't have to see teeth being pulled as they awaited their own extractions. The first person we met in the waiting area was Daniel Smith, thirty years old, a contractor, lean and wiry with a long face from which his ears jutted out. He had short hair, a scraggly beard and was happy to talk to pass the time—better, he joked, than thinking about his teeth being pulled.

"Oh, how many teeth will you have pulled today?"

Daniel looked down at the paper he was clutching, given to him by the dentist he had just seen. "Hmm. Eighteen. I'm having eighteen teeth pulled today."

We must have gasped, because Daniel smiled grimly and explained, "I've always worked, since I was fourteen, but I've never had dental insurance."

"When did you last see a dentist?"

"Maybe it's been twenty years. My mom took me when I was little one time, and that was about it." He had once gotten an infected tooth and his mouth swelled grotesquely, so he went to a hospital emergency room, where a doctor pulled the tooth, told him that it could have killed him and sent him home again.

A volunteer interrupted our chat to say that a dental chair was free and then ushered Daniel toward it. Nora Hermes, a young dentist in residency, with brown hair and a long ponytail, was waiting, as was her volunteer aide, a college student thinking about a career in dentistry. Nora took Daniel's medical history, examined his mouth and reviewed

---

* Stan died unexpectedly in August 2018 of complications from a stroke and was mourned in communities across America that he had served. Remote Area Medical continues to hold health fairs in the United States almost every weekend.

the paper calling for eighteen extractions. She shook her head. "A young guy like this, it breaks my heart a little," she told us. Daniel, sitting in the chair as he was being talked about, looked at her anxiously.

We asked Daniel if he was apprehensive about facing the forceps, eighteen times over. Of course, he said, smiling wryly, but he added that he was in pain already—a chronic, never-ending ache in his mouth—and at least this way it would soon be over. He paused, looked down, and, a little shyly, looked up. "I want to look good, too," he said. "The only thing I'm self-conscious about is my smile. My teeth are messed up. I've got to figure out dentures next. I'd like to have a straight smile. I've never had one in my life."

"Dentures?" Nora looked up from the dental chart. "We can get you into a program to get cheap dentures. They'll be about two hundred dollars, which is a bargain."

Daniel beamed. "I'd love that," he said earnestly. "That's something I can afford."

Then Nora adjusted the lamp, asked Daniel to open wide, injected him with local anesthetic and got started. Her volunteer aide gamely handed her tools as requested but began to look increasingly green. All around Daniel, dozens of other people were getting extractions or fillings or other treatments. Two chairs away, Dr. Daniel Laskin, a ninety-two-year-old retired professor of oral surgery, was beaming. He had just pulled nine teeth from a thirty-seven-year-old man, and everything had gone smoothly.

From the dental tent we wandered to the vision tents, where, with the help of the local Lions Club, patients were being screened for glaucoma and other vision problems—including a desperate need for glasses. A nearby trailer was a mobile lens-making lab with special equipment to grind, shape and size prescription lenses in an hour, so patients could get a new pair in one visit.

"There are people who can't see the biggest letter on the chart," Jennifer Jolliffe, a volunteer screener, told us in wonderment. "And you ask them how they came here, and they say, 'I drove.'"

"It's an absolute indictment of our health-care system," Dr. John Watters, an ophthalmologist working nearby, told us. "It shows the need is there and is not being satisfied in this country." The solution, Dr. Watters said: a universal health coverage system like that found in most other advanced countries. Indeed, even some poor countries like Rwanda are moving toward universal health care, and the World Health Organization under an Ethiopian doctor, Tedros Adhanom, is helping other developing countries do the same.

In all, some 2,300 men, women and children received free medical or dental care during the three-day fair in Wise, served by 1,400 volunteers. Later we visited a similar three-day clinic in Gray, Tennessee, where Remote Area Medical had a trailer for making eyeglass lenses, alongside one providing mammograms and pap smears. Ashley Edwards, a thirty-two-year-old factory worker who needs sharp eyesight to inspect rubber window seals for cars, was there for glasses. She came to Gray at midnight the night before to wait on line and secure a ticket for a free vision checkup. Ashley had health insurance through her minimum-wage job, but vision and dental were extra, so she had been going without.

These health needs underscore a larger truth: medical care is another field where the United States has become an outlier, with tragic results. In the 1960s and 1970s, American health statistics were in line with those of other advanced countries, with life expectancy in 1970 a bit better than the average among OECD nations. Likewise, child survival was a bit better than average.

Since then, most other countries have built universal health-care systems, so that today the United States is the only major country in the advanced world without one. The health fairs that we saw in Virginia and Tennessee would be unimaginable in Canada or France, because they would be unnecessary. Those countries have their own problems, of course, and they arguably piggyback on research and pharmaceutical development in the United States, but their citizens don't slip through the cracks the way they routinely do in America.

The upshot is that since 1970, life expectancy has improved in the United States, but much less than in other countries. From a bit above the middle of the pack, we've tumbled to number 27 out of 35 OECD countries. We're now behind Chile in life expectancy and just ahead of the Czech Republic and Turkey. Life expectancy in the state of Mississippi, were it a country, would rank second to last, tied with Mexico. Children in America today are 55 percent more likely to die than kids in other affluent countries, according to a peer-reviewed study in *Health Affairs*.

"The U.S. is the most dangerous of wealthy, democratic countries in the world for children," said Dr. Ashish Thakrar of the Johns Hopkins Hospital, the lead author of the study. If the United States had simply improved at the same rate as other advanced countries, 600,000 children's lives would have been saved, Thakrar calculates. If America had the same mortality rates as the average in the rest of the rich world, 21,000 kids' lives would be saved each year. Because we failed to modernize our health system the way our peer countries did, we lose fifty-eight children a day.

We think of worm infestations in people as a problem that affects impoverished villagers in Africa or South Asia. But a few years ago, Catherine Flowers, a woman from Lowndes County, Alabama, read an article by Dr. Peter Hotez, an expert on tropical diseases, and contacted him to say that many families in her area didn't have modern plumbing. She wondered if they could have parasites, too. So researchers took stool samples from Lowndes County, and 34 percent tested positive for hookworms. "It's probably in many other places, too, but nobody tests for it," Hotez told us. "We can't get the money to test."

The gaps in health coverage lead to painful disparities among neighbors. In Philadelphia, a baby born in the mostly white and affluent Liberty Bell area, zip code 19106, has a life expectancy twenty years longer than a baby born four miles away in the mostly black North Philadelphia zip code of 19132. When life expectancy rests so heavily on where a child is born, we can't pin it just on the person's bad choices.

Dreadful health statistics are a consequence not only of lack of insurance but also of poverty, stress and hopelessness that lead people to engage in all kinds of risky behaviors, including neglect of preventive care. At the clinic in Gray, Tennessee, Joseph Gambacorta, clinical dean of the School of Dental Medicine at the State University of New York at Buffalo, said that many people who can't afford dental insurance don't take care of their teeth, and that is why they end up with tooth decay at an early age. Dr. Gambacorta had examined Megan Reed, a twenty-seven-year-old certified nursing assistant who had only twenty-five teeth left and needed all of them extracted because of severe decay. Megan had been short on money for dental care, so some of the teeth had hollowed out and were causing severe pain. The day before, a man in his midforties had wanted all his teeth pulled because he already had his front teeth missing and he wanted dentures to give him nicer teeth, without having to keep up with any dental hygiene.

"It's a whole-person issue, a social dynamic," Dr. Gambacorta said. "You have to look at the social determinants of health—poverty and education."

Gambacorta's colleague at SUNY Buffalo, Robert Cronyn, a professor of oral and maxillofacial surgery who was overseeing Megan's teeth extraction, said that over the years, he has observed that many poor and less-educated people believe there are three sets of teeth: your baby teeth, which are replaced by your adult teeth, which are replaced by

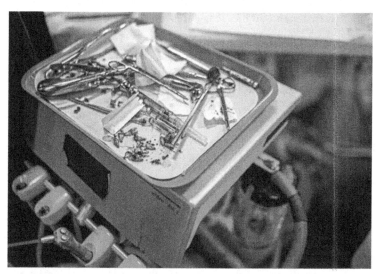

Megan Reed, twenty-seven, had fifteen teeth pulled at a health fair in Gray, Tennessee. Afterward, they lay in a dental tray for disposal.
(*Photo by Lynsey Addario*)

your grown-up teeth, which are plastic, or dentures. He once fought with a woman who had perfectly good teeth but now, at age twenty-one, she said it was time for her to get her dentures, as her mother and grandmother had done.

"Since I won't extract your teeth, you're going to go around dentist to dentist until you find one who will pull out your teeth, right?" Dr. Cronyn asked her.

"Yes," she said.

"If you find one, he's going to be a crook. You don't need your teeth pulled."

On a dental tray a little later, fifteen of Megan's teeth lay in a cluster, as she looked relieved both that the extraction was over and that her top teeth were out.

Presidents since Harry Truman have been pushing for universal health coverage, but it has never quite come to pass. Lyndon Johnson extended the umbrella to older Americans with Medicare, and Barack Obama widened the safety net further with the Affordable Care Act, but there are still huge gaps. The number of Americans without health insurance dropped steadily through 2016 but has since stalled because of assaults on Obama's legacy by President Trump and congressional Republicans.

Every other advanced country solves this problem, so the United States can, too. Medicaid expansion is a no-brainer, yet the states in the South and the middle of the country with the worst health metrics have refused to join in, condemning their own citizens to more unnecessary deaths. Researchers find that lack of insurance coverage kills tens of thousands of Americans annually. For every 830 people who gain insurance, at least one life is saved each year, according to a peer-reviewed paper by Professor Katherine Baicker of the University of Chicago.

One way to improve the current health-care system would be to expand Medicare to fill some of the gaps, and there are a number of proposals to do just that. Paul Starr, a leading health scholar, proposes opening up Medicare to Americans at the age of fifty rather than sixty-five, at least for those who do not have other insurance through their jobs. Likewise, the creation of a public option would provide a mechanism for expansion of coverage over time. Members of Congress opposed to a public option don't seem to object to the government covering the cost of medical services for themselves: in addition to receiving a 72 percent subsidy—paid by taxpayers—on premiums for a gold-level ACA plan, they can use the navy-run Office of the Attending Physician and get free outpatient services at military facilities in the Washington area.

The reason we have a single-payer health-care system for the elderly (Medicare) but not for children is simple: seniors vote, and children don't. So while American children die at 55 percent higher rates than children in other advanced countries, Americans who make it to age sixty-five and qualify for Medicare then have a remaining life expectancy similar to that of our peer countries.

Opponents of universal coverage for all ages protest that it is unaffordable. But we already provide coverage for the most expensive demographic (the elderly) while not for the cheapest (kids); instead of directing money to children, we shower it on drug companies and hospital companies. Xarelto, a drug used to prevent or treat blood clots, costs $292 in the United States for a thirty-day supply; in Switzerland, the figure is $102. Tecfidera, used to treat relapsing multiple sclerosis, costs $5,089 for a thirty-day supply in the United States; in the United Kingdom, it's $663. An appendectomy averages $15,930 in the United States; in Spain, it's $2,003. Overall, America actually spends much more on health care than any other country, roughly $10,000 per person per year, nearly one-fifth of national income. That's almost twice as much as in Europe.

The American health-care system is expensive and performs poorly in part because pathologies of inequality and poverty are so widespread. Obesity in the United States is a marker of poverty and the working class, and it's no coincidence that Cindy, Kevin and Clayton Green were obese. Americans are more likely to be overweight than citizens in other advanced countries, and this costs everyone. The annual medical costs for an obese person are $1,900 more than for a person of normal weight, and by one estimate, weight-related issues account for 9 percent of U.S. health-care spending.

The system is also simply irrational at times. Consider Drew Calver, a forty-four-year-old high-school history teacher and swim coach. A fit swimmer who had completed an Ironman triathlon five months earlier, he had just taken out the garbage when he collapsed from a heart attack. A neighbor rushed him to the emergency room of a nearby hospital, St. David's Medical Center in Austin, Texas. Doctors there inserted stents in his clogged coronary artery during a four-day stay. Calver asked the hospital if insurance would cover the procedures and he was told not to worry, that the hospital would take his insurance. The hospital did indeed take an insurance payment of $55,840, but it also charged him an additional $108,951.

"They're going to give me another heart attack stressing over this bill," Calver told *Kaiser Health News*. "I can't pay this bill on my teacher salary, and I don't want this to go to a debt collector."

St. David's did indeed send the bill to a debt collector, who sent Calver a letter demanding immediate payment. Meanwhile, experts said the billing was hugely inflated. For example, St. David's charged $19,700 for a stent that costs hospitals about $1,150. After *Kaiser Health News* published a story reporting that, St. David's abruptly suspended debt collection efforts and agreed to reduce its fee from $108,951 to $332.

Such a farce could not have occurred in other countries. One study published in *The American Journal of Medicine* found that 42 percent of Americans diagnosed with cancer between 1998 and 2014 drained all their life assets over the next two years. That, too, doesn't happen in other countries. The bottom line is that since 1970 we have seen American exceptionalism in health care in multiple ways: we lack universal care, we spend more on health and we get worse results.

Actually, there's a fourth area where we are exceptional as well: the United States is squeamish about sex and reproductive health, partly as a spillover from the abortion wars, so Americans are particularly bad at providing contraception and reproductive health care. President Trump compounded this gap by cutting back on reproductive health programs like Planned Parenthood and Title X—and no, it's not that he didn't want to pay for abortions. The United States already bars the use of federal funds to pay for abortions. The Planned Parenthood money was instead being used for cervical cancer screenings, breast exams, family planning programs and treatment of sexually transmitted infections. The impact is that moms die.

We say in America that we love motherhood, but that's a cruel joke. A woman is about twice as likely to die in pregnancy or childbirth in America as in Britain—because the British make a real effort to save moms' lives, and we don't. Indeed, the maternal mortality rate actually began rising again in the United States around the year 2000, even as it was falling in the rest of the world. Today one of the most dangerous places in the advanced world to become pregnant is the American South, where women die in childbirth at far higher rates than, say, Spain or Sweden. So we traveled to Houston to shadow Dr. Lisa Hollier, the president of the American College of Obstetricians and Gynecologists, at her Center for Children and Women, part of the Texas Children's Health Plan, a health maintenance organization just for children. Dr. Hollier explained that she is on a mission to reduce maternal mortality because of an experience she had in Dallas as a young doctor.

A patient called Amy, twenty-three years old, expecting a baby for the first time, seemed healthy as she approached the end of an uncomplicated pregnancy. Amy and her husband were thrilled to be starting a family. When she was expecting to go into labor at any time, she suffered a painful headache and showed up with her husband at the hospital to have it checked. She was brought into a room to be examined, a fetal monitor was attached—and then Amy abruptly collapsed and lost consciousness. Doctors and nurses rushed to her bedside, and her husband was shooed away. The fetal monitor showed the baby was in distress, with a slowing heartbeat, so doctors hurried Amy into the operating theater to perform an emergency C-section and save the baby. As the surgeon removed a healthy baby girl and sewed up Amy's uterus, the staff made arrangements to get imaging on her brain. The results showed that Amy had suffered a massive stroke. This is a well-known risk during pregnancy. Dr. Hollier huddled around Amy's bedside with neurologists and a group of nurses. Amy was declared dead late that afternoon. Dr. Hollier will never forget the scene at the nursery later, as the baby was discharged and given to the newly widowed dad. He stood alone, holding his baby daughter, ready to leave the hospital—devastated.

"Here's this dad," Dr. Hollier said, and she wiped her eyes at the memory. "It's supposed to be the happiest day of his life, and there's this look on his face. He's just so lost." Dr. Hollier paused to manage her emotions. "We need a commitment as a country," she said. "Let's set a goal of no preventable maternal deaths."

A pregnancy-related death occurs in the United States on average twice a day, with black women at particular risk. The toll is magnified because many young women aren't insured, don't have primary physicians or gynecologists and don't have ready access to contraception. American and European kids have sex at about the same rates, according to surveys, but American kids have babies about three times as often. That's because American kids are less likely to receive comprehensive sex education, and because Americans don't have as good access to free family planning, especially to long-acting reversible contraceptives like implants or IUDs. "You can't die from a pregnancy when you're not pregnant," Dr. Hollier said, noting that almost half of pregnancies in America are unintended. Only half of Texas women get prenatal care in the first trimester, she told us, and only 60 percent return after birth for a postpartum checkup.

Something about reproductive health makes politicians and local officials lose their reasoning faculties. State education officials and local school board members know that teen pregnancy is a huge problem, yet they often refuse to allow teaching to avoid it. Just eighteen states require schools to teach birth control, and only about half of American kids receive any classroom instruction in contraception before the first time they have sex, according to the Guttmacher Institute. Only 35 percent of high-school students learn how to use a condom correctly, according to the Centers for Disease Control and Prevention.

Astonishingly, the share of students who don't get education in contraceptives is going up, not down. The Trump administration even tried to cut off funding for a teen pregnancy prevention program (lawsuits forced it to continue that funding). What's confounding is that these same officials are often anti-abortion, yet they don't seem to understand that preventing unplanned pregnancies will reduce abortions. They believe that condoms will promote promiscuity, when condoms no more cause sex than umbrellas cause rain. These same officials then thunder about the irresponsibility of girls who get pregnant, oblivious to their own irresponsibility.

A nurse told Dr. Hollier that her patient was ready for her, and we tagged along with the permission of the patient, Monica Leija. A Latina in her twenties, Monica was eight months pregnant—and had a huge tattoo of a skull on her belly. Dr. Hollier examined Monica, measured her abdomen and chatted idly with her.

"I notice this pregnancy wasn't something you planned for," she said.

"No!" Monica said, shaking her head firmly. "Definitely not."

"What happened?"

Monica explained that she had been taking the pill but then switched jobs and in the process had a three-month period when her contraception wasn't covered. "So I skipped taking the pill," she explained. "It was forty dollars a month. I just didn't think that it would happen." She paused, then looked at Dr. Hollier and added, "And you know what's really crazy? I work for an insurance company."

After Monica had left, Dr. Hollier sighed in frustration. "Contraception is the most powerful anti-poverty measure we have," she said. "Contraception allows a woman to finish school, plan a family, pursue her life goals."

Other countries have managed such challenges in family planning and reproductive health. Some parts of America have as well. California made a determined effort to save women's lives in pregnancy and childbirth, monitoring every death and trying to understand what went wrong, and the upshot is that California cut its maternal mortality rate almost in half. It is now about as safe to have a baby in California as in Europe.

Dr. Hollier's Center for Children and Women, funded with state and federal money, shows that even in Texas it's possible to have a transformative impact. The center is attractive and welcoming and provides childcare while mothers are being seen. It even boasts a dental clinic. The staff walk women and girls through the process of signing up for

Medicaid so they get covered and then helps them choose the right kind of contraception. The doctors give them Pap smears to potentially save their lives from cervical cancer (which still kills one woman every two hours in America) and breast exams. They treat their infections. When patients are pregnant, the staff coach them on breastfeeding and looking after infants. And while in the center, they can get free dental care, free eyeglasses and prescriptions filled at the pharmacy.

Dr. Hollier's clinic and Remote Area Medical show what is possible. For that matter, so does Medicare. So do Canada, Britain and just about every other advanced country. Why is it that in the richest country in the history of the world, so many Americans die because they don't have access to health care like that?

12

Homeless in a Rich Nation

Keep your coins. I want change.
—Sign held by a homeless man as a social protest
    in a painting by Australian street artist Meek

The man's straggly hair and white bushy beard hung from a tired, wrinkly face as he stood by his shopping cart filled with clothes, shoes and empty cans, his only belongings after living on the streets for years. When Americans approach such a homeless person, the natural response is to avert their eyes and hurry past, pretending not to notice. That's impossible when you suddenly realize, with a stab in the heart, that the homeless person is an old friend and neighbor, Mike Stepp. He was in the park by the library in McMinnville, the county seat of Yamhill County, and our reunion was warm, poignant and unsettling.

"It's good to see you," he greeted us warmly, and we exchanged hugs. "We used to walk up and down that hill! Too many times!"

Mike and his brother, Bobby, were Nick's closest neighbors when he was growing up, and the three of them walked each day up and down a hill to and from the school bus. Bobby, good natured and eager, made some money trapping animals for their fur, while Mike, a few years younger, was funny and excitable and something of a ham.

The Stepps were much like the Knapps and the Greens: solid working-class people whose lives had improved dramatically over recent generations and who looked forward to further gains. The dad, Robert Stepp, had lied about his age to join the Marines as a sixteen-year-old at the outbreak of the Korean War, and then he regularly volunteered for reconnaissance patrols. One of them was ambushed by a North Korean unit and Stepp was shot twenty-two times. Before he blacked out, he remembered the North Koreans going from body to body, stabbing each American to make sure he was dead. Unsure how he survived, he woke up in a military hospital and spent the next eighteen months recovering from grievous injuries. As a nineteen-year-old injured war hero, he married Lorena Dockery and found work at a lumber mill north of Yamhill.

Robert became an alcoholic, drunk at night but functional, hard-working and law-abiding by day. He was deeply proud of his military service and active in the local American Legion. When Bobby struggled

Mike Stepp, Nick's closest neighbor growing up, is now homeless and living on the streets of McMinnville, Oregon.
(Photo by Lynsey Addario)

in high school, Robert and Lorena, who also drank heavily, sent him off to the Marines to toughen him up, but Bobby failed boot camp and soon returned. Likewise, Robert nudged Mike into the military when he dropped out in the eleventh grade, but Mike settled for the Army Reserve and was then pushed out as unreliable. By the time Robert died at age fifty-six, he was deeply disappointed in his offspring.

Bobby is now in a prison in Colorado, serving a life sentence for sexual assaults on three children, including an eleven-year-old stepdaughter who said she had been raped by him for three years. It's a reflection of the disintegration of the social fabric that Bobby was one of two boys on the old Number 6 school bus later imprisoned for sexually assaulting a child. Bobby told us that if he eventually gets out of prison, he would like to return to Yamhill but doesn't know if he will be accepted or if he will end up jobless and homeless—like his little brother.

Friends had told us that alcohol and meth, plus a bad bicycle accident, had left Mike's brain cloudy, but he excavated clear memories of our old farm dog, a giant white Kuvasz that had terrified him. "Just an old hillbilly," he called himself. He said that he had followed our careers and occasionally read our articles in the library.

Mike said he began with drugs in high school, smoking marijuana in the parking lot. "I never really quit," he explained. He said that he had purchased meth periodically from Clayton Green and helped water Clayton's marijuana plants. He and his ex-wife, Stephanie Ross, had argued about everything, he said, including her nagging him to quit drinking. So eventually he just walked out. Most of all, though, Mike wanted to brag about his kids, Brandie and Mike Jr. For starters, he talked about how Brandie got her name.

"I was in the labor room with my ex-wife; she was in there forever, ever, ever, trying to have that baby," he began. He went out for a smoke and a swig of brandy, he said, and a nurse surprised him by telling him that the baby was born and asking what her name would be. "I thought, 'Brandie!'" Mike told us, laughing. "Oh, yeah. I can still taste it. Brandy."

He proudly told how he had supported his kids financially as they both went through college, with Brandie planning on teaching art and

Mike Stepp with his shopping cart and all of his belongings at a street corner in McMinnville. We're accustomed to averting our eyes from the homeless, but that doesn't work when a homeless man is one of your oldest friends. *(Photo by Lynsey Addario)*

Mike Jr. aiming to be an engineer. "I went through hell putting them kids through college," he said. "I'm so proud they didn't end up like me."

On Christmas every year, he said, his kids come and "hunt me down like a pack of wild dogs" for a reunion to wish him well.

We asked if he had any mental-health issues. "I ain't crazy," he replied. "Sometimes I get kind of lost in my own head, you know. My mind kind of wanders. I can never remember what day it is." He said he earns about $10 a day by collecting cans and bottles for deposits and eats meals at church soup kitchens (including one that Nick's mom volunteers at). He supplements this by dumpster diving for food: "If I'm hungry, hungry, hungry, I'll eat it." He had food stamps but was suspended for a year when he let a friend, while shopping for both of them, use his card.

Ebullient just as he had been as a boy, Mike regaled us with stories about heroic military deployments, about a Purple Heart and "Medal of Valor," about a bullet wound in the stomach from combat in Central

America. When we expressed awe, he humbly said that there were others who never made it back at all.

BY EVEN A CONSERVATIVE COUNT, there are more than half a million homeless people in America at any one time, including nearly two hundred thousand living on the streets rather than in shelters. Homelessness has increased in the last forty years even as America has become much wealthier, because of a confluence of factors. After World War II, new rent controls and land-use zoning rules discouraged new affordable housing. Then President John F. Kennedy had a vision of moving the mentally ill and physically disabled out of specialty institutions into community centers closer to family. But not enough centers have been created, so vulnerable people end up homeless. As a philosophy of personal responsibility took hold in the 1980s, President Reagan cut the federal housing budget in half, and housing subsidies have never recovered. The Great Recession of 2008–09 also meant that millions of homeowners lost their jobs and then their homes when they couldn't make mortgage payments.

"We have an affordable housing crisis and, in fact, it's reached historic heights," Diane Yentel, chief executive officer of the National Low Income Housing Coalition, told us. "Today we have a shortage of over seven million homes affordable and available to the lowest-income people." Research suggests that when families are decently housed, children do better in school and, probably as a result, earn more as adults and even live longer. Conversely, when children are homeless, health and other outcomes are worse—and that's expensive. One analysis found that in 2016, homelessness resulted in $8 billion in additional costs for children's health and education and for mothers' mental and physical health.

"We're paying for this as a society one way or another," Yentel told us. "If we were to direct those avoidable costs into affordable housing, we'd all be better off for it."

Homelessness detracts from the well-being of an entire community. It can also affect public health, as in the comeback of the ancient scourge of murine typhus, a variety of typhoid fever. The disease, long associated with poverty, is spreading in the southern United States because of homelessness.

We tend to think of the homeless as people with mental-health or addiction issues, and that's often true. But increasingly, the lack of affordable housing has forced into homelessness people who are sober, holding jobs that simply don't pay enough for them to rent an apartment. That's why the top states for homelessness are not in the most depressed parts of the country but include some fast-growing economies. Indeed, the highest rate of homelessness in America is in Washington, D.C., followed by Hawaii, New York and California. These are areas lacking adequate affordable housing.

Two people each working full-time at the federal minimum wage of $7.25 per hour would be unable to afford a two-bedroom apartment anywhere in the United States without breaching the rule of thumb that one shouldn't spend more than 30 percent of one's income on housing. Since 1960, the share of renters paying more than 30 percent of incomes on rent has more than doubled to 49 percent.

"This is touching people it hasn't touched before," Matthew Desmond, a sociology professor at Princeton University, told us. "It's touching nurses and police officers. It's touching parents with older children who have to move back in because the housing market is so brutal." In San Jose, California, at least a dozen police officers reportedly live in RVs in a parking lot near police headquarters. Others spend up to four hours a day commuting, a burden on them and their families.

"When we think about our housing policy, we have to confront the problem that all the families that are trying to get help that qualify for help will never be given help because there's just not enough aid to go around," Desmond added. "That's a big decision we've made as a country."

Marquita Abbott, a thirty-year-old African-American woman living in Washington, D.C., with her very bright six-year-old son, Mason, reflects this crisis in affordable housing. Marquita has no mental-health or addiction problems, she graduated from high school and she had a full-time job—but that didn't prevent her from becoming homeless.

A single mom, Marquita was working full-time in the hotel business but earning just $27,000 a year. Since Mason's father was absent and not helping with child support, Marquita was barely able to afford an $850-a-month two-bedroom basement apartment. Then in the summer of 2017 she came home one day from work and found the apartment flooded with two inches of sewage on the floors. The apartment owners did nothing to address the situation except offer her a more expensive apartment that she could not afford.

The sewage had ruined many of Marquita's possessions, including clothing, shoes, photo albums and toys and books belonging to Mason, as well as a brand-new carpet. Frustrated, she threw out more than she needed to, and buying new clothes set her back financially. Marquita and Mason moved in with her grandmother for a time, as she frantically tried to save money and find alternative accommodations. Then the landlord took Marquita to housing court for not paying rent after

Marquita Abbott playing with her son, Mason, at the D.C. General shelter for the homeless in Washington, D.C. Marquita has a job working for an upscale condominium but still can't afford rent for herself and Mason. (*Photo by Nicholas Kristof*)

the flood. Marquita appeared without a lawyer and was ordered by the judge to continue paying rent at a reduced rate of $450 per month for an uninhabitable apartment. It was difficult to imagine that this would have happened if Marquita had had a lawyer or had been more adept at managing the system. Eventually, Marquita was able to end the lease, but it was infuriating for her to be paying rent to a landlord who had allowed her apartment to flood and her belongings to be ruined.

When her grandmother moved away in the fall of 2017, Marquita and Mason showed up dejected at D.C. General, a former hospital that had been converted into a homeless shelter. It was clean and guarded, with shared bathrooms, and near the subway so that Marquita could easily take Mason to school each morning. But the aging elevators broke down regularly, and there had been a notorious disappearance from the shelter of an eight-year-old girl, Relisha Rudd, presumed murdered by a janitor who killed himself as police searched for him. That added a sinister backdrop, and Mason was afraid of using the bathrooms.

"He's wetting his bed again," Marquita told us fretfully. "That hadn't happened for years, and now he's wetting his bed three or four times a week." At school, she said, Mason's first-grade teacher reported that he was "a little off," while in the shelter he began bullying other children. "It's rough being in here, it's really rough," Marquita told us.

Mason is a sweet child and an enthusiastic reader—he's two grades ahead of his class in reading level—who understands that his mom is depressed by the homelessness. "Sometimes I tell her funny jokes," he told us. "Sometimes I do funny things to make her laugh." She grabbed him and hugged him.

Paradoxically, homelessness meant that Marquita was less able to work. Curfews and the need to escort Mason forty minutes to and from his elementary school on the subway limited what jobs she could take, so she lost her hotel job. However, she did find a part-time job as a concierge at an upscale condominium in Washington, where her charm and social skills made her a valued employee. This job was rich with ironies: a homeless woman working in an upscale housing unit of the kind that made Washington more desirable for many, but that made affordable housing more scarce. There was also a racial dimension: almost all the residents of the condos were white, while virtually all those living in the homeless shelter were black.

On the political left, some people have advocated rent controls for people like Marquita, but these haven't worked well when they've been tried, for reasons of basic economics. Rent control doesn't increase the supply and tends to constrict it because people don't give up bargain apartments, and developers are wary of building if they think their returns will be held down. In some cities, owners can also convert rentals to unregulated condominiums. Meanwhile, rent control tends to increase demand, so you have more people competing for fewer apartments.

There's also a growing consensus among economists that zoning rules—such as limiting many areas for single-family dwellings—reduce the supply of affordable housing and thus increase homelessness. Builders often find it more lucrative to supply housing for the top end while neglecting the low end. In some areas, the economists Edward L. Glaeser and Joseph Gyourko concluded, "our evidence suggests that zoning and other land use controls play the dominant role in making housing expensive." Liberal economists in the Obama administration agreed, declaring in a White House report in 2016, "In areas with high-cost housing such as California, zoning and other land-use controls contribute significantly to recent sharp cost increases." Another problem was that housing programs historically tended to concentrate poor people in blighted neighborhoods that often replicate poverty from generation to generation. In that sense, some housing initiatives may have undermined upward mobility. Instead, experiments have shown that we can help families with young children use vouchers to move up to better neighborhoods and schools.

We've learned more in the last decade about how to solve housing problems. It's tricky to address only locally, however, because a community that provides good services tends to attract homeless people from other areas that ignore the problem. So, nationwide and statewide strategies are more effective. One successful approach in Seattle and elsewhere has been rapidly and inexpensively building clusters of tiny homes of only one hundred to four hundred square feet each. Other areas have experimented with placing the more stable homeless in the homes of families who volunteer to help.

Invariably, the most successful approaches are also holistic. Salt Lake City's Housing First program sheltered homeless people regardless of whether they were addicted to drugs or alcohol. This is now widely regarded as a successful model, for people with mental-health issues and addictions make up a significant portion of the homeless population. Jim Vargas, who runs a large homeless program in San Diego called Father Joe's Villages, says that in one recent internal count, about 26 percent of adults with kids reported a mental illness, 14 percent reported alcohol abuse and 22 percent reported drug abuse. So requiring people to give up drugs or alcohol simply means that they remain on the streets.

Washington, D.C., has an effective, though underfunded, voucher program that ultimately offered Marquita and Mason a way out of homelessness. After a year in the D.C. General shelter, Marquita received a housing voucher that would help her afford an apartment rental. The vouchers would last a year to allow Marquita to get back on her feet economically and be able to afford to take over the rent payments herself. Frankly, we were skeptical. The new apartment was a two-bedroom for $1,300 per month—she was adamant about having an apartment of that size—and it was difficult to see Marquita making that rent after a year. To Marquita's credit, while homeless, she had been taking classes in using computers, and these skills would help her find better-paying work.

Housing problems underscore the need for financial literacy classes in high school. In our reporting, we've often seen that when renters have utilities cut off for nonpayment, it isn't only because of a sudden medical expense or a job crisis, but often due to weak budgeting. People moved into larger apartments than they could afford, and then something went wrong. When carefully studied, financial literacy programs have had a mixed record overall, but some seem effective in improving outcomes for at-risk young people.

Despite our reservations about whether Marquita will be able to keep her new apartment after the vouchers run out, the idea of giving vouchers to a mom and a child is a good one. Yes, housing programs can be expensive, but homelessness also has an extravagant price to society in health, policing, lost potential of children and the erosion of a community's soul. Everyone knows that there are government housing programs for the poor, like Section 8 (costing $30 billion annually), but few Americans realize that in recent years we have spent more than twice as much on subsidizing housing for mostly affluent homeowners ($71 billion annually through mortgage interest deductions and other benefits). In fact, the federal government has poured huge sums into mobile-home parks for low-income renters, yet the money went not to the renters but to private-equity firms. Fannie Mae, the government-sponsored lender, provided $1.3 billion to Stockbridge Capital, a huge private-equity firm, to buy existing parks—and Stockbridge then raised rents to achieve a 30 percent return, according to *The Washington Post*.

By some estimates, a rough doubling of the size of housing programs for the poor, to $60 billion a year, would solve much of the homelessness problem, and the total cost, as you can see, would still be less than subsidies for more affluent homeowners. The first task should be ending homelessness for children, and that is doable, if we make it a priority.

MIKE STEPP'S TALE of his life and homelessness—his military exploits and the Purple Heart, the naming of his daughter, how he had paid for his kids' college, how his kids visited him on Christmas every year—had left a deep impression on us. Then we went to speak with Stephanie, his ex-wife.

"None of that is true," she told us.

Mike had never seen combat or won medals, she said. Brandie, she said, was not named because of a covert swig at the hospital; her name had been picked out long before. The kids had gone to college, but without support from their dad, who hadn't seen them since 2001. "They can walk right by him on Third Street" in McMinnville, she said tartly, "and he doesn't recognize any of us." Stephanie still describes Mike as "the love of my life" and suggests that his brain may be so fogged that he may not realize that his stories aren't true.

There is a shelter in McMinnville that could take Mike in, but those using it have to give up drugs and alcohol—which he says he can't. He insists that he likes being outdoors on his own, but he wept when police evicted him from a covered county parking lot. At this point, though, there are no easy solutions to Mike's problems. He doesn't want a job and may not be capable of holding one. Still, he could be given space in a shelter if it did not require guests to be sober, and that would at least get him off the streets.

The best interventions to prevent his homelessness are those that would have occurred decades ago, particularly when he was a child. He could have received early childhood education, allowing him to do better in school; a major effort could have been made to help him remain in high school and graduate instead of dropping out; a vocational education would have prepared him for a particular career such as plumber or carpenter—all those might have reduced the risk of his ending up as he is.

We asked Stephanie what might have made a difference for Mike, whom she began to date when she was fifteen years old. His big problem, she said, was that in Yamhill he was surrounded by friends and relatives who thought it was cool to get drunk and smoke meth. If he had been plucked from that crowd—perhaps if he had followed his dad's urgings and enlisted in the military as a teenager—then things might have worked out, she said, but at home the pressures to stray were inescapable. The common thread of the Mike Stepps, the Farlan Knapps, the Ricochet Goffs, the Rebecca Hales is that they grew up in chaotic circumstances, buffeted by drugs, alcohol, crime and other temptations and without much of a lifeline from extended family, the school or government. They were set up to make poor choices, and they indeed made poor choices, with nary a safety net to be seen.

13

The Escape Artists

I don't run away from a challenge because I am afraid. Instead, I run toward it because the only way to escape fear is to trample it beneath your feet.

—NADIA COMANECI, Olympic gold medal gymnast

Clearly, not everyone in Yamhill staggered through an inferno—far from it. We were struck while looking through Nick's old high-school yearbooks that almost every single person in the National Honor Society did just fine, as did many others. Brad Larsen became a pilot. Brett Peloquin a banker. Bob Bansen a successful organic dairyman and his sister Lisa a professor of French. Barry McNabb a dancer and choreographer on Broadway. Joni Marten a silverware dealer with her sisters, and a pillar of local charities. Then there were the Jernstedt girls, five sisters who were stars in high school and thrived afterward, with two earning PhDs.

We were puzzled: Why did some kids avoid peril? And how could we re-create that success? Most of the kids who thrived came from stable, nurturing families attentive to education, while, as research would suggest, those who struggled came from homes with chaos, substance abuse and an indifference to schooling. The Jernstedts farmed grass seed and planted in their daughters an expectation that they would go to university; today, one is a professor of botany at the University of California, Davis. We asked the Jernstedt girls where their PhDs and success had come from, and their answer was immediate: "We won the lottery with our parents," as Lisa put it.

Some rural working-class families, especially where the wage earner had a good union job, established middle-class status, values and aspirations. Joni Marten's dad worked in a sawmill, then a foundry that swallowed up most of his retirement account when it went bust, and finally for many years as a janitor at the elementary school, while her mom worked as a waitress and later at JCPenney in McMinnville. They raised six kids on those wages.

"It never really occurred to me that we were the working poor," Joni told us. "My parents had friends in the community from all walks of life and incomes."

Money was tight, and Joni's family kept a cow for milk and a few beef cattle for meat, supplemented by deer they shot and fish they caught. Her mom made dresses for the girls and canned fruits and vegetables for the winter, while the kids found jobs of their own, with Joni getting her first job at fifteen. Her parents made her save part of each paycheck in a bank account, to build a habit of savings. "Every Saturday night, Mom would make sure our hair was washed and put it in pin curls or rollers for church in the morning," Joni recalled. "There was always a parent available," she said. "They never missed a play, a music program, any activity that we were involved in. One or both were always there." And that involvement made school pretty much the center of Joni's young life.

"Dropping out was not an option, and neither was getting a C," Joni told us. "It was the work ethic. We weren't allowed to skip school. We weren't allowed to miss work."

For those parents who were deeply embedded in the community, there were also multiple eyes on each child, reducing the opportunities for mischief. "If I did something out of line, my parents knew before I got home," Joni recalled. "There was no getting away with much. Our neighbor was the chief of police here in town, so he'd say, 'Oh, you know I saw Joni with that so-and-so boy. She shouldn't be hanging around with him.' People looked out for each other's kids. No parent was afraid to correct another person's child." Joni summed up what made the difference for her: "Looking back, we were quite poor, but rich in family love and support." Joni not only inherited that social capital but also transmits it, for she's a constant weaver of social fabric in the area. She helped run a food pantry, and when Nick's dad died she was the best of neighbors, arriving with home-cooked meals that lasted us weeks.

Those kids who threw themselves into school activities mostly did well afterward. Those who participated on several sports teams did fine, and the same is true of those who were passionate about FFA, Future Farmers of America, or other clubs. Peer groups mattered enormously as well. Brad, Brett and Nick grew up as very close friends, pushing one another academically, and they were the first Yamhill kids in memory to go out of state to university: Brad to the Air Force Academy, Brett to the Naval Academy and Nick to Harvard.

The Mormon Church, which has after-school activities and strong social support for its families, had a very strong protective influence: Mormon kids just didn't end up in trouble or in poverty. That seems true of engagement in church more broadly. A 2018 Harvard study published in a peer-reviewed journal, the *American Journal of Epidemiology*, found that children raised in religious households were less likely to suffer what it called the "big three dangers of adolescence": depression, substance abuse and risky behaviors. They were 12 percent less likely to suffer depression, 33 percent less likely to use illicit drugs and 40 percent less likely to have a sexually transmitted disease. Conversely, they were more likely to volunteer and to report that they were happy.

Yet in Yamhill, some people with all the risk factors, individuals who should have ended up prematurely in the cemetery, survived unscathed, even in good humor. We dubbed them the "escape artists," and we wondered what lessons we could draw from them.

One escape artist was Dale Braden, a classmate of Nick and Farlan Knapp's who lived near the Knapps in the former Cove Orchard schoolhouse and considered them buddies. Dale seemed every bit as much

at risk as Farlan. He was the middle child of seven, the son of an itinerant construction worker, and the family felt considerable economic
pressures—which Dale's dad addressed by drinking in the bars with his
buddy Gary Knapp. They were both alcoholics with a propensity for
violence.

"He would often come home drunk out of his mind and whip us for
no apparent reason," Dale told us. "I can still hear the screams of my
siblings and the voice of my mother pleading with him to stop." Dale
also remembered a fistfight among his father's drunken friends just
below his window as he tried to sleep. "The drunkenness scared me,"
he said, "mostly because of the sense that these people had absolutely
no control over themselves." He has vivid memories of his father passed
out drunk in the home or in the yard, or of the time his father's shirttails
caught fire on the stove.

"I must have been thirteen or fourteen at the time, and I was slapping
him with a towel trying to get the fire out," Dale recalled. "He looked
at me as if he was going to knock me out. Fortunately, he wasn't hurt
and probably had no recollection of the event."

Yet Dale said that his dad, when not drunk, was loving and caring
(and he eventually gave up drinking after a health crisis) in a way that
Gary Knapp never was. "I remember being scared of Mr. Knapp, unlike
any other parent I knew at that time," he said. "There was always something about him that was sinister and dark." He knew of Gary's abuse
of his spouse and children. But while the Knapp kids seemed drawn to
trouble, Dale was risk averse.

"I was too afraid of getting in trouble to try something dangerous,"
he recalled. "I'm sure that helped me tremendously." Zealan was the
first to convince him to try marijuana, he said, but even as a teenager,
Dale was uncomfortable with it.

Dale's parents had both dropped out before reaching high school,
and he was a mediocre student in his teens. He attributes that to "flat-
out laziness," but also to lack of guidance from his parents. "They just
didn't know any better," he said. Teachers didn't take much notice of
Dale, with the exception of an art teacher in Yamhill, Lucita Duke, who
saw in him artistic talents that she nurtured. Introverted, just trying to

fit in, dodging bullies, Dale mostly glided precariously through school. "I never thought about college, nor did anyone steer me in that direction," he said. "Honestly, I was probably fortunate to graduate."

Dale didn't want to spend the rest of his life in a family of nine crushed into a single-wide trailer. His place to sleep each night was on the floor under the dining table, and he was ambitious for a bed of his own. He also knew that he was very good at art, so his self-esteem was intact. "I always felt I could make something of my life despite all that was going on around me," he said.

After high school, casting about for something to do, Dale enlisted in the army. It may have saved his life.

"The army was the best thing that ever happened to me," Dale told us. "It taught me something I had never learned previously. I learned about self-discipline, respect and responsibility." He also saw something of the world, going to Georgia for basic training and then serving for three years in northern Germany. In the army, Dale studied technology and afterward earned a college degree in information technology with a 3.8 GPA.

"I wanted to prove to myself that I am so much more than that skinny little kid from such a poor and depressing upbringing," he said. Dale found a job at Nike and married a woman with whom he has been together for thirty-four years. They have two daughters, both of whom went to college. Now Dale is a project director for a health-care company in Nashville, Tennessee, managing a multimillion-dollar clinical system conversion and earning an MBA on the side.

"I'm glad I did not travel down the same path as the Knapps, but I was so precariously close," Dale said. Indeed, some of his siblings have struggled, and Dale is unsparing in his description of them: "They have migrated toward a life of poverty, living off the government while swindling my parents out of every dime they had. They've taken zero responsibility for their lives, and their kids are heading down the same identical path. Drugs have not been as prevalent but alcohol certainly has played a role with some of them."

Dale is conservative, partly a legacy of his military experience and partly a reaction to what he sees in his siblings. He has scolded them for their financial recklessness: a brother bought a truck on installments that he couldn't afford, and a sister purchased the latest iPhone knowing that she probably wouldn't be able to afford payments on it.

"What happens then?" Dale challenged her.

"Oh, it's okay. They'll just repossess it."

"But think what that does to your credit!" Dale told her. "You'll ruin your credit rating."

She shrugged, he says, and returned to her phone.

The American military performs an indispensable role in creating opportunity for working-class kids. It is particularly good at building discipline and teamwork, at inculcating basic social skills and technical training and especially at creating career paths without discrimination for African Americans and Latinos. It invests in the human capital of young people, with an emphasis on learning, management and leadership. The military has become a lifeline for kids seeking to escape troubled families and communities and has enabled them to acquire skills and university degrees and get traction in the professional world. A 2018 study found that the military particularly helped black men, substantially raising the likelihood that they would reach the middle class. The United States historically has been reluctant to invest in social-service organizations, but the military manages to play just that role for those teenagers who graduate from high school (or earn a GED instead).

America's military also is remarkable as a bureaucracy that offers much more support for those at the bottom than is typical in, say, large companies. The pay ratio between a general and a private is about ten-fold, compared to three-hundred-fold between a bank CEO and a bank teller—and in the military both have access to the same insurance benefits. Because the military is focused on achieving missions and getting results, recruits learn how to plan and implement to achieve goals, a very useful life skill. And it basically treats people equitably. Even offspring are taken care of in its outstanding childcare program for service members that should be a model for the country. Wes Clark, the former four-star general, told us that the military is "the purest application of socialism there is," and he was only partly joking.

A number of studies have documented the benefits to disadvantaged kids from serving in the military, by gaining discipline and the kind of soft skills that enable them to thrive in a company afterward. But the military cannot, of course, be reconceived as an organization to turn young lives around; it has its own mission. Moreover, many of the young people who would most benefit from military life would not qualify because they did not complete high school or cannot pass a drug test. So one alternative approach is to expand successful national service options that take at-risk young people and teach them skills, teamwork and military-style discipline while employing them for public projects. Among the best are City Year, YouthBuild and National Guard Youth Challenge, and we should expand these initiatives—while rigorously testing outcomes—to see if we can offer one more exit ramp for young Americans headed for trouble.

14

A Shot in the Face

Poverty is the mother of crime.

—MARCUS AURELIUS

It was a muggy July evening, and Debbie Baigrie was out with friends for the first time since the birth of her second child. Blond and slender, twenty-eight years old, a cantor's daughter raised in an Orthodox Jewish home, she was a stay-at-home housewife who relished the chance to escape the house for a happy hour with two girlfriends in Tampa, her hometown. They partied and gossiped, and Debbie was feeling good as she left the restaurant.

"You know this is a dangerous neighborhood?" asked a man from her gym whom she'd run into in the restaurant. "You shouldn't be walking to your car by yourself." He offered to escort her to her car, which was parked on the street, and as they walked a handful of boys approached. A scrawny black kid pulled out a gun and pointed it at Debbie's face.

"Give it up!" he shouted, demanding her purse. "I'm serious!"

Before she could react, the boy pulled the trigger and fired a bullet into her mouth. It tore apart her jaw and exited her cheek. Debbie turned and ran, still clutching her purse, blood pouring down her face and drenching her blouse as she tottered on her pumps back toward the restaurant. The gunman fired several times at her back but missed, and then ran off. At the restaurant door, Debbie plowed past the bouncer.

"Help me!" she shouted. "I've been shot! Is my face gone?"

Debbie's face was still there, albeit permanently scarred, and she would require years of painful reconstructive oral surgery. "My dentist wept when he saw my mouth," she recalled. Surgeons had to remove flesh from her palate to rebuild her gums, and then insert tooth implants. The shooting happened on July 27, 1990, yet all these years later Debbie still can't eat an apple; her latest repair surgery was in 2018.

Police didn't have any clues to the perpetrator, but several days later they pulled a few teenagers out of a stolen car. One of the backseat passengers, a small boy named Ian Manuel, thirteen years old, waiting for his mom to pick him up at the police station, idly spoke up to a police officer. "You know that woman who was shot in the face the other day?" he asked. "I did that." Manuel still isn't sure why he admitted to the crime.

This was a case guaranteed to inflame the public. Debbie, a pretty white mom shot in a brutal way, was a sympathetic victim. Ian, a black boy who grew up in the projects and already had a dozen convictions in juvenile court, fit Tampa's stereotype of a cold-blooded monster.

Ian, round faced, slight of build, all arms and legs, was widely recognized as bright. In elementary school, he had received awards as the best reader and writer in his class. But he never much tried to make it academically—and his school seemed to give up on the kids anyway. Ian never knew his dad, like so many other boys in his neighborhood. His mom, Peggye, who had no problems with the law, was working all day to cover the bills, so he grew up on the streets. Drugs and crime were everywhere, and toughness was the currency to get ahead, as well as compensation for his modest size. Ian regularly missed school and, to Peggye's despair, fell in with a rough crowd of somewhat older boys. He began shoplifting, accumulating his arrest record, and to the authorities he seemed incorrigible. While Ian was widely seen as a poster child for sociopaths, the truth was that he should have been seen as a poster child for neglect. Where a community allows children to go wild, and doesn't invest adequately in school programs or outreach efforts, the costs aren't borne only by those kids but also by the innocent victims they lash out at.

Ian was tried in the headlines for the shooting and judged a guilty brute, and the prosecutor quickly determined that Ian, even though he was barely a teenager, would be charged as an adult with attempted murder. A public defender advised him to plead guilty, saying his sentence would be reduced as a result, so Ian did so. The judge had other ideas. "We're going to make an example of you, Mr. Manuel," he told the thirteen-year-old, sentencing him to life without the possibility of parole. Ian stood there dry-eyed, Peggye sobbing nearby, as the magnitude of the sentence seeped into his consciousness. *I'm going to die in prison*, he thought.

"Baby, we're going to get you out of here," Peggye told him through her tears, as she hugged him. It would be the last time she was able to touch him. In the holding cell, Ian realized that his freedom was gone forever. He began crying. Paradoxically, because of quirks in the sentencing system, if Ian had killed Debbie, his sentence would have been shorter, a maximum of twenty-five years. So at thirteen Ian became the youngest and scrawniest prisoner in the Florida state penitentiary system. There was only one way he wasn't treated as an adult: he wasn't allowed to buy cigarettes in the prison canteen, because he was too young.

In prison, Ian was bullied by inmates and guards alike, and he didn't handle it well. "He rebelled," recalled a fellow inmate, Victor Jory. "He acted out. He was bound to prove that he was a man, the adult that courts had declared him to be." Ian was repeatedly punished with stints in solitary confinement, a cell seven feet by nine feet, with meals handed through a slot in the door and no regular contact with anyone. Shouting meant removal of the mattress and being forced to sleep on the concrete floor and having time in solitary extended. Ian protested by trying to commit suicide and by cutting himself; each time, his period in solitary was extended. He was teargassed when uncooperative and injected against his will with psychotropic drugs.

FOR HALF A CENTURY until 1970, America's incarceration rate held steady and was in line with the norm for other advanced countries. Beginning in the early 1970s, our incarceration rate soared fivefold, peaking about a decade ago before dropping somewhat. The United States had fewer than 200,000 people in federal or state prison in 1970; now it has 1.4 million, not even counting those in local jails. Democrats and Republicans alike embraced tougher prison sentences, although Republican politicians often appeared particularly enthusiastic. Among the intellectual authors of this policy was Attorney General William Barr in his previous stint in that office, under the first President George Bush; at that time, Barr issued a report entitled "The Case for More Incarceration." The upshot is that one in seven Americans in prison today is serving a life sentence, nearly half of them people of color. Total spending on them while incarcerated is about $1 million per person.

The United States now accounts for almost one-quarter of the world's incarcerated people. Its national incarceration rate is six times that of Canada or France, twelve times that of Sweden. In the United States, 70 percent of criminal sanctions involve incarceration; in Germany, it's 6 percent. In Germany, the sanction is more likely to be a fine, community service or obligatory job training. There is an emphasis on supervised work that helps the criminal compensate the victim.

Policing in America is harsher than in other democracies. In Grand Rapids, Michigan, police officers pointed a gun at and handcuffed a shrieking eleven-year-old girl who wasn't suspected of any offense but happened to be at a home being searched. Video of that encounter left even the police chief shaken. "You listen to the eleven-year-old's response, it makes my stomach turn," said the chief, David Rahinsky. "It makes me physically nauseous." At about the same time in Eustis, Florida, police arrested a ninety-three-year-old woman accused of trespassing because the old age home in which she had been living for six years said she was behind in rent.

American incarceration often involves private for-profit prisons, an idea other countries find unthinkable because it gives corporations substantial control over individuals. Texas was the first state to introduce for-profit prisons, in 1985, and now about half the states have them.

At the federal level, a scathing Justice Department report found that private prisons had glaring security lapses, and President Obama began phasing out their use at the federal level. President Trump reversed that and expanded the use of for-profit prisons to house people in immigration custody.

For-profit prisons save money by cutting costs, even if it means reduced security that endangers both inmates and corrections officers. A Mississippi private prison had an assault rate at least double that of similar public facilities, while in Florida a juvenile detention center was accused of physical and sexual abuse, including forcing youths to fight one another like gladiators. "It's the *Lord of the Flies*," one investigator said. In Michigan, a private contractor was accused of serving inmates rotten food with rat-bite marks on cakes camouflaged by frosting. Just as alarming, private prisons lobby for harsher sentences to increase their occupancy rates and improve their profitability. The two largest for-profit prison companies have devoted $25 million to lobbying.

In Pennsylvania, the corruption was explicit: the owner of private juvenile detention centers paid hundreds of thousands of dollars in bribes to two judges who then found youths guilty and sentenced them to his centers. This "kids for cash" arrangement led to children being unjustly detained, including one boy, Edward Kenzakoski, who had no previous record but was held for months for supposedly possessing drug paraphernalia. That started Edward on a downward slide, and he later committed suicide.

"Do you remember my son?" Edward's mom, Sandy Fonzo, screamed at one of the judges, Mark Ciavarella, who had put her son in detention, after the judge was convicted. "He's gone. He shot himself in the heart, you scumbag."

America should remember Dostoyevsky's observation: "The degree of civilization in a society can be judged by entering its prisons." The United States needs not just more humane prisons and shorter sentences, but also, as we've made clear, more interventions to help at-risk children before they end up facing judges. If social workers had reached Ian Manuel when he was a young boy, and if there had been some after-school program for him other than the streets, he might not have found himself pulling a gun on Debbie Baigrie. We know that when children are randomly assigned to home visitation programs like Nurse-Family Partnership or to good preschool initiatives, they are less likely to have trouble with the law years later. Likewise, school programs like Citizen Schools, Becoming a Man or Communities in Schools, and gang outreach initiatives like Cure Violence, seem to reduce crime rates. Yet these programs are starved of funds: home visitation reaches less than 2 percent of the households that would benefit from it.

Also inspiring are some of the efforts to help prisoners readjust to society, programs like Women in Recovery, which was successful in turning Rebecca Hale's life around. Recidivism rates are high partly because we don't do enough to support people as they emerge from prison. There are already some signs of a shift, though. We see agreement among many on both left and right that mass incarceration has gone too far, and red states such as Texas have been leaders in reducing the number of prisoners. Overall incarceration rates in America have finally started coming down, and politicians and experts alike are talking about reforming the bail system—which has fueled the sharp rise of people in jails around the country and imposed enormous burdens on the poor. After Harvey Weinstein was arrested for sexual assault following accusations by more than eighty women, he was freed on bail. In contrast, a young adult caught smoking marijuana may be unable to afford bail and thus be stuck indefinitely in jail, losing his job and, unable to make payments, perhaps his home and car as well.

There's belatedly a broader rethinking under way of the harshness of the "justice" system. Leann Bertsch, the head of the North Dakota prison system, visited a prison in Norway and was startled by how humane it was. The mission of prisons in Norway is to prepare inmates for reintegration into society, so facilities are well-kept and inmates are usually housed in prisons near family, for officials discovered that frequent family visits reduce the likelihood of recidivism. The maximum sentence for most crimes is twenty-one years. After the prison visit, Bertsch retreated to her Radisson Hotel room and wept at the misery she oversaw in America's penal system. "We're hurting people," she realized. Bertsch, who is also past president of the Association of State

Correctional Administrators, told *Mother Jones.* "I had always thought that we run a good system. We're decent. We don't abuse people. We run safe facilities with good programs." But after seeing Norway's prisons, she wondered, "How did we think it was okay to put human beings in cagelike settings?"

Conservative Republicans like Governor Phil Bryant of Mississippi have introduced reforms that shorten sentences, and Bryant told us that the political climate has changed so that voters like this stance and appreciate the money saved. Mark Holden, a senior vice president of Koch Industries, agrees with us on almost nothing but told us that he believes the justice system is such a mess that "it needs to be blown up"—here he smiled—"in a nonviolent way."

IAN MANUEL, growing up in prison, soon found the most unusual of allies. He was allowed one phone call a month, and on Christmas Eve 1992 he asked the operator to place a collect call to Debbie Baigrie in Tampa. When Debbie answered the phone, the operator asked if she would accept a collect call from Ian.

"Ian who?" she asked.

"Ian Manuel," he told the operator.

Out of morbid curiosity, Debbie accepted the charges.

"I just wanted to wish you a Merry Christmas," he said, a bit sheepishly.

"Ian," she asked, "why did you shoot me?"

"I didn't know what I was doing," he said heavily, and there was a long pause. "It was a mistake. It just happened so quickly. I'm sorry."

Debbie was moved by Ian's youth and contrition. "I felt guilty," she recalled. "I felt I had taken his life away. He didn't kill me but I killed him." Debbie was also acutely aware that Ian had grown up in a neighborhood saturated with drugs, crime and violence, without ever getting serious counseling and support or a way out. Debbie remembered her own teenage misbehavior in a nice Jewish neighborhood; if she had had Ian's upbringing, she couldn't say what she would have been like.

Thus began a seemingly bizarre friendship and correspondence that buoyed Ian's spirits, giving him hope—if his victim could forgive him, perhaps others could. Ian followed up his phone call with a card he'd drawn showing a hand reaching through prison bars to offer her a rose. He began writing more frequently. Debbie herself went back and forth about how she felt. Sometimes she would be in pain, unable to eat and facing another surgery, and she would be livid at Ian and unforgiving. Then another day she would think, *He's just a kid. When you're thirteen, you do stupid stuff.* On balance, even when she was gritting her teeth and crying in frustration, she reflected that Ian was in as much pain as she was.

Debbie posted some of Ian's notes on her Facebook page, and her friends and family were repulsed. "He's manipulating you," her husband protested. "He's using you." Debbie and her husband had increasingly bitter arguments about Ian, and other friends warned that she was a victim of Stockholm syndrome. Debbie resented the paternalism, and she credited Ian for giving her a sense of mission.

"He woke me up," she told us. "My life became so much more enriched by forgiving him." Then Debbie took a further step. She wrote to the court asking for a reduced sentence for Ian. "No one knows more than I do how destructive and reckless Ian's crime was," she wrote. "But what we're currently doing to him is mean and irresponsible. When this crime was committed, he was a child, a thirteen-year-old boy with a lot of problems, no supervision, and no help available." The court ignored the letter. Debbie's empathy for Ian did have one concrete result: it led to her divorce.

IF YOU'RE EVER ARRESTED for a felony and go to trial, be sure your lawyer makes key motions right after lunch. Judges are more likely to rule against defendants when they are hungry and apparently grouchy, either shortly before lunch or late in the afternoon, a 2011 study found. Judges also issued longer sentences the day after their college football team unexpectedly lost a game, according to a 2018 study, and these longer sentences disproportionately applied to black defendants. In fact, blacks routinely get the worst of it in the judicial process, particularly when they are poor. The issues of race and poverty seem to have been hanging over Ian's sentence. "If he'd been a cute white boy at thirteen, with little dimples and blue eyes, there's no way this would have happened," Debbie told us.

The United States Sentencing Commission found that blacks get sentences 19 percent longer than whites do for the same offense, even after controlling for criminal history and other variables. The darker an African American's complexion, the longer the sentence, researchers found. Blacks are also more likely to be found guilty and to be sentenced to death: in Louisiana, a black person is 97 percent more likely to receive the death penalty than a white person, researchers have shown. So on top of the other problems with mass incarceration, the fundamental truth is that our justice system acts in racist ways.

The bias in the judicial system is only one facet of discrimination that is baked into many aspects of society. One way researchers measure bias is to send out the same résumé in response to help-wanted posts, in some versions with a name that "sounds black" (like Lakisha Washington or Jamal Jones) and in others with a name that sounds white (like Emily Walsh or Greg Baker). The same résumé with a white name gets 50 percent more responses. Whites are often unaware of the scale of past discrimination and how much it affects race gaps today. After one column Nick wrote about race, many whites responded earnestly that of course slavery and Jim Crow were terrible, but that today they're simply being used as excuses. "As whites, are we doomed to an eternity of apology?" Neil asked. "When does individual responsibility kick in?"

As we hope we've made clear, we believe wholeheartedly that personal responsibility is important. This is indeed accepted in the black community. A survey found that 92 percent of black youths agreed that black males are "not taking education seriously enough," and 88 percent agreed that too often they are "not being responsible fathers." In a 2015 CNN poll, 61 percent of blacks said family breakdown was a reason for the difficulties of African Americans today, and 42 percent cited "lack of motivation and unwillingness to work hard." President Obama led the way on this front by starting My Brother's Keeper, an initiative to support more responsible behavior by men and boys of color.

After World War II, the GI Bill of Rights made it easy for vast numbers of veterans to attend college, and the Federal Housing Administration and other initiatives enormously expanded homeownership. These efforts ushered white workers into the middle class, but blacks were commonly excluded. That's one reason the median black family has only 10 percent as much wealth as the median white household.

Remedies for past inequity are complicated. But the least we can do is provide disadvantaged black kids today an equal shot at education. Instead, educational discrimination continues: the average white or Asian-American child attends a school at the 60th percentile in test results; the average black child attends one at the 37th percentile. The political system is unresponsive. Researchers found that white state legislators, both Democrats and Republicans, were less likely to respond to a constituent letter when it was signed with a name that sounded African American. It didn't help when President Trump said to blacks, "You live in your poverty, your schools are no good. You have no jobs. What the hell do you have to lose?" One element of white advantage today is obliviousness to that advantage.

A highly successful black friend who has held senior roles in government told us how shocked he was when his white fiancée threw away her receipt as they left a New York City department store. "What are you doing?" our friend asked her. He would never toss a receipt for fear of being accused of shoplifting. She didn't understand what he was upset about, for she couldn't imagine herself being accused in that way.

"In the jewelry store, they lock the case when I walk in," a twenty-three-year-old black man wrote in May 1992 in *The Stanford Daily*. "In the shoe store, they help the white man who walks in after me. In the shopping mall, they follow me." He described being stopped by six police officers who detained him for thirty minutes, guns at the ready, as a dangerous suspect when he was simply driving his car. The young man was Stanford University's senior class president, a newly selected Rhodes Scholar named Cory Booker.

White Americans sometimes used to blame race gaps on "black culture," diagnosing the problem as irresponsible black men fathering babies outside of marriage, or as a predilection for dropping out of school and using drugs. But increasingly it looks as if the great black sociologist William Julius Wilson was right when he argued, in books like *When Work Disappears*, that the fundamental problem is a lack of jobs, and in particular the disappearance of good blue-collar jobs. At the time, Professor Wilson was commenting on urban African-American communities in the inner city, but that tide of joblessness has now reached rural white America—and "white culture" has reacted in pretty much the same ways. It turns out that when communities of any race lose jobs and self-esteem, people are more likely to soothe themselves with narcotics, drift into crime and suffer family breakdown. And it doesn't much help to hear Horatio Alger pieties about personal responsibility from those who have made it.

"I hear a lot of, 'I grew up poor, and I turned out fine,'" noted Sean Reardon, a sociology professor at Stanford University. "Everyone can tell a story of someone who grew up poor and pulled himself up by his bootstraps." But Reardon observed that outcomes are largely shaped by beginnings. Children growing up in affluent homes or middle-class security see role models all around them. "So it seems clear to them that there is a payoff to making the right choices," Reardon said. In addition, affluent kids benefit from a safety net that protects them from bad choices. "Rich kids make a lot of bad choices. They just don't come with the same sort of consequences."

Beto O'Rourke has made this point about himself. As a young adult, he was arrested twice, once for trespassing and once, at age twenty-six, for drunken driving. In both cases, he was able to avoid serious consequences and soon was active in El Paso politics, running for office and serving in Congress. Speaking in 2019 as a presidential candidate, O'Rourke noted how he had overcome the challenge posed by his arrest record. "It's not because I'm a great person, or I'm a genius, or I've figured anything out," he acknowledged while campaigning in Iowa. "A lot of that has to do with the fact that I'm a white man, that I had parents who had the cash to post bail at the time. A lot of people don't have that."

Progress arrives in part by illuminating the problems. When a group of researchers found that professional baseball umpires and basketball referees were more likely to call outs and fouls against players of a different race, the NBA strongly protested and commissioned its own (flawed) study purportedly showing no bias. The controversy generated much debate within the professional basketball community, and a few years later the original scholars did a follow-up study of referee calls. This time, they found that the bias had disappeared: it seemed that once referees were aware of their unconscious bias, they could overcome it.*

HOPE EMERGES in unexpected places. As Ian Manuel matured, he used his decades in prison to read and get an education. He turned out to have a first-rate intellect, earning perfect marks for much of his work.

The worst day of his life, he says, wasn't the day he was sentenced but June 8, 1996, when he was in solitary and was informed that his mother had died of complications of AIDS contracted from an old boyfriend. His only real connection with the outside world, other than Debbie Baigrie, had been severed. He received only three personal visits while he was incarcerated.

The guards once punished the prisoners by tuning their television in the dayroom to PBS—the prisoners wanted to watch sports—and it happened to be airing a documentary called *To Be Heard*, about a poetry class in the Bronx. Ian was mesmerized. When he returned to his cell, he began writing poetry: stern, image-laden poems about prison life, a bit like rap, expressing his feelings and frustrations. "Poetry saved my life," he told us.

When he was sitting in his prison cell one day, he received a letter from Bryan Stevenson, the legendary lawyer who runs the Equal Justice Initiative. Stevenson was looking for a juvenile serving a life sentence without parole to be the centerpiece of a lawsuit arguing that such

---

* Any discussion of race should also acknowledge that some of the greatest racial disadvantage and inequity in America involves Native Americans, especially those living on reservations in the West. Life expectancy for Native Americans in South Dakota and Montana is in the sixties, less than in Bangladesh. The graduation rate at high schools run by the Bureau of Indian Education is only 53 percent. The Indian Health Service, which provides health care on reservations, is shamefully underfunded, getting only $3,900 per person it serves—less than half what the Bureau of Prisons spends ($8,600) on health care for each inmate in federal prisons.

punishment was unconstitutional. Ian was delighted to figure in such a suit, and in 2010 the Supreme Court ruled in his favor. Ian would have to be resentenced, and Baigrie testified at his sentencing hearing to urge leniency.

Through Stevenson, we came to know Ian while he was waiting for his resentencing, and he soon became our pen pal. Regularly an envelope would arrive with a thick letter from Ian, and occasionally a poem that he had written. No sooner would we write back than another would arrive. In 2016, after twenty-six years behind bars, Ian was released for time served—and celebrated with Debbie Baigrie. They exchanged bear hugs. Nobody watching would think that Ian had once shot Debbie; he called her his "guardian angel" and "second mom." They moved on to an Italian restaurant for a dinner of pizza and soda not far from where he had shot her in 1990.

After his release from prison, Ian moved to New York, found a job

Debbie Baigrie and Ian Manuel sharing a pizza dinner the night he was freed after twenty-six years for shooting her in the face when he was thirteen years old *(Photo courtesy Debbie Baigrie)*

in a restaurant, then at a health club, then at a program working with at-risk kids. He had never held a mobile phone, but now he became an Instagram devotee, posting constantly. He was poignant and funny, seemingly unscathed from twenty-six years behind bars.

Here was someone who had committed a truly savage act and had suffered for it, but the victim had chosen to forgive her assailant. If America since the 1970s has often approached crime, drugs and poverty with an unforgiving ethic of harsh punishment, Debbie's actions represent an alternative: an ethic of grace. She knows better than anyone that someone who shoots another in the face deserves punishment, but her belief in second chances and redemption should inspire us all to imagine a world in which America is leavened by a politics of grace. Partly because of her, and partly because of a great public-interest lawyer, a boy who had once been seen by the courts and the news media as a symbol of incorrigible violence instead became a symbol of redemption and resilience. A tragedy ended up a tale of hope.

15

God Save the Family

You are the bows from which your children
As living arrows are sent forth.
—KHALIL GIBRAN, Lebanese-American poet

I rene Green still ruled as matriarch of the Green household outside
Yamhill, a fit and clear-minded octogenarian who had survived two
husbands and three children, Kevin, Cindy and Thomas Jr. She
came across as middle class, and the walls of her home were decorated
with her panoramic oil paintings of waterfalls and landscapes. But her
children, grandchildren and great-grandchildren were more troubled,
and her role now seemed to be mostly as chauffeur to those who had
lost their driver's licenses for one offense or another. She no longer had
time for painting.

For us, the most painful aspect of our visits back home has been seeing how easily adversity was transmitted from one generation to the
next, partly through the mechanism of family breakdown, which has
become symptomatic of the crisis in America's working class. Cindy,
Kevin and Clayton had each had one or more children but did not replicate the kind of strong two-parent family that they had grown up in.

In 1965, Daniel Patrick Moynihan wrote a famous report warning about family breakdown, particularly in African-American communities. He cautioned that the rise of single-parent households would make poverty more intractable, and in a follow-up he declared, "From the wild Irish slums of the 19th-century Eastern seaboard, to the riot-torn suburbs of Los Angeles, there is one unmistakable lesson in American history: a community that allows a large number of young men to grow up in broken families . . . never acquiring any stable relationship to male authority, never acquiring any set of rational expectations about the future—that community asks for and gets chaos."

Some liberals denounced Moynihan as an out-of-touch racist. Moynihan had grown up as the child of a single mother and worked as a shoeshine boy, but he was chided for blaming victims. Moynihan had emphasized that "three centuries of injustice," including slavery and discrimination, had helped create the family breakdown, and he was farsighted in recognizing the importance of jobs. However, the denunciations of Moynihan led President Lyndon Johnson to distance himself from the report. Scholars avoided studying the relevance of family for a generation.

That began to change only when William Julius Wilson praised the Moynihan Report as a "prophetic document," and it became increasingly clear that Moynihan had been prescient, as problems with family structure spread into the white community. Today a greater share of white children are born outside marriage than black children were when Moynihan wrote his report. A majority of American children now live at some point before they turn eighteen with a single mom. There's still debate about the issue, but a growing share of poverty experts agree that family structure matters considerably, for black and white kids alike.

One reason progressives are sometimes reluctant to acknowledge the importance of family is that conservative champions of family values regularly turn out to be hypocrites. Newt Gingrich rose to become Speaker of the House as a "moral values" man, even as he worked his way through three wives. Cheerleaders of family values embraced Donald Trump despite his philandering, divorces and payoff to a porn actress. Trump in turn initially chose for the Federal Reserve Board (and later dropped) Stephen Moore, a conservative commentator who had called for a "personal and national commitment to sturdy families" as part of a "culture of virtue." Moore's wife had won a divorce after alleging that he committed adultery and abused her emotionally so that she had to flee the house; in a court filing, he admitted the charges against him. After the divorce went through, the judge scolded Moore for failing to pay his ex-wife more than $300,000 in alimony, child support and other payments owed (the IRS said that he also owed $75,000 in back taxes). When people like Moore talk about the need for strong families, it's understandable that skeptics roll their eyes.

WITH CLAYTON GREEN AILING and spending most of his time on the couch, the torch was being passed to the next generation. The most salient figure in this generation was Clayton's son, Eathan. Tall, thin, dark haired, voluble and gregarious with a sense of humor, he seemed the opposite of his father. While Clayton was now more than four hundred pounds and had such difficulty walking around that he drove from

Clayton Green starting his pickup truck as his son, Eathan, looks on
(Photo by Lynsey Addario)

his house to his workshop one hundred feet away, Eathan was limber and athletic. It was hard to get Clayton to say much; it was difficult to get Eathan to stop talking. What they had in common was intelligence, wit, rowdiness and a tendency to get into trouble—and on the other's nerves.

Eathan's parents hadn't stayed together long, so he had bounced between them. Mostly he grew up in Yamhill, never finishing high school, although like his dad and uncle Kevin he is gifted at fixing things. He left home after he got into a fistfight with Clayton when he was eighteen, moving to Payette, Idaho, where his mother lived, to work in the construction industry there for the next thirteen years. Working his way up, Eathan eventually earned $3,000 a month, purchased a home and began paying off his mortgage.

He married and had three children (he believes the middle one isn't actually his). After the Great Recession, construction dried up and he couldn't get steady employment. His problems were compounded by an opioid addiction; he says he spent about eight of those years in Idaho addicted to opioids but eventually quit, cold turkey. Without his job, Eathan and his wife got behind on the mortgage and lost the house. He ended up working at a cupcake shop and then scrubbed floors at a senior center, but relations worsened with his wife. "Nothing I did was ever good enough," Eathan recalled. "So I was like, 'Lady, find somebody else to frickin' try to mooch off of for the rest of your life.'" After five years, the couple divorced and his wife kept the kids.

Eathan dropped by one day to visit his children. "I was trying to be a good guy, you know?" he explained to us. "And she was sitting on the back porch; we had a tandem swing in the back. This dude was sitting there, who was my friend . . . she was straddling him. . . . I spun around and punched the door and caved it in." Eathan went on a rampage through the house, destroying pretty much everything he could.

We pointed out that after a divorce, a woman is free to find a new boyfriend, but Eathan offered his temper to explain: "I'm known as a hothead. I'm fine, cool and collected right now talking to you just like anybody else, but you start pushing my buttons, you hit that switch, dynamite! I don't think anymore; it's attack."

It was after a jailhouse fight that he first determined that he is a bit crazy, he said. That, plus the fact that he found himself talking to walls when he was by himself. He's not sure where this came from, he added, but possibly because he was kicked in the head by a horse when he was twenty-four.

PEOPLE ARE COMPLICATED. But it's certainly true that individuals like Eathan growing up in chaotic single-parent households—especially boys, just as Moynihan had predicted—don't do as well on average, and then the cycle is often repeated with their children as well. Forty percent of American kids are now born outside of marriage, and four out of five of them will experience the stress of a parent forming new relationships and raising half-siblings. Eathan faced particularly long odds because he didn't just come from a low-income single-parent family but from one with felony convictions, a history of drugs and violence and a lack of education, compounded by his own decision to drop out of high school.

There's a growing amount of data that underscores that, on average, outcomes are better for kids growing up in two-parent households. One challenge is simply mathematical: a single parent has only one income to support the family, not two incomes. The economist Isabel Sawhill calculates that the rise in single parenting since 1970 has increased the child poverty rate by about 25 percent. Growing up with just one biological parent on average is also associated with a 40 percent lower chance that a child will graduate from high school. Kids raised by single moms on average get lower grades, have more behavioral problems in school and are more likely to drift to crime and drugs, according to a large number of studies.

"A father's absence increases antisocial behavior, such as aggression, rule-breaking, delinquency and illegal drug use," with the effects greater for boys than for girls, Sara McLanahan of Princeton University and Christopher Jencks of Harvard University concluded after assessing the evidence. Yet there's a danger of drawing too sweeping a conclusion here, for it's difficult to untangle correlation from causation, and in any case many single moms do brilliantly. In addition, most of the data is driven by low-income households, where a single parent means a constant financial struggle; more affluent single-parent households are much more likely to succeed.

In any case, what matters isn't a traditional family structure so much as stability. In principle, it probably doesn't matter to the child whether the parents are formally married, but there is a difference in practice. Three-quarters of married parents are still together when their child turns twelve; fewer than one-third of unmarried couples are. Yet only about half of American households are headed by a married couple. Same-sex couples seem to have slightly better outcomes for their kids than heterosexual couples, perhaps because no gay couple ever had a child by mistake.

If Eathan's family demonstrates the challenges of working-class family breakdown, the Davis family in Pine Bluff, Arkansas, shows how a strong family can create a protective cocoon for kids even in a difficult environment. Pine Bluff is poor, overwhelmingly African American and riven by gangs and crime, and the Davises didn't have much going for them economically. They are working-class African Americans with seventeen children in the family, all from the same mom and dad. Yet all graduated from high school and studied in college or went into the military. One daughter was high-school valedictorian, a couple of kids were salutatorians and another daughter graduated with a 4.0 grade point average.

The mother, Mary Davis, a vigorous sixty-year-old who works at a nonprofit that coaches families with preschool kids, says she always emphasized school to her young children. She went to the parent meetings, her kids' school events and parent-teacher conferences.

"I'm not going to deal with your foolishness," Mary remembers telling her children bluntly. "When I send you to school, I'm sending you there to learn. Not to go be the class clown."

At home, Mary was almost like a drill sergeant. When kids returned from school, she made sure they did their homework while the "mind is still fresh" and then they did their chores—washing dishes, tidying their rooms, making their beds, cleaning the bathrooms, washing clothes, cooking dinner. If there was time left over, along with some daylight, then they could go outside and play.

Her husband, Edward Davis, now sixty-five, always had a steady job, first in construction, then as a security guard and finally at Union Pacific Railroad, fixing tracks and trains. His income immediately went to pay for food, clothes and the mortgage on a four-bedroom, three-bathroom redbrick home, the nicest one on a block of many simple white or gray aging houses. To reduce the household bills for nineteen people, Mary scoured the newspapers for coupons; she bought food in bulk and clothes and shoes only on sale. Nothing was wasted. The kids found work as soon as they could and often handed down jobs to their next sibling, and the older working children pitched in to buy school clothes for the younger ones. All but two of the kids are out of the house now, either in school or in jobs across the country.

"Once you crossed the river, you can't just look out there and tell where the deepest part is," Edward said with a smile. "You can look back and say, 'I wonder why I didn't drown.'"

Edward Davis was eventually injured on the job at Union Pacific Railroad and had to leave work, and Mary then became the sole bread-winner. She is clear about where help came from: "I serve a true and living God and He is my source. He is my provider and if I didn't serve Him, if I didn't believe in God, I wouldn't have made it." The family typically went to services at a Pentecostal church three days each week when the kids were young, often two or three times on Sunday.

Edward says his kids seemed to listen to his advice. "They were taught to work," he said. "And I always taught them that you have to be careful what you do because you don't represent only yourself but you represent your family. When you embarrass yourself, you embarrass your family, too."

Lakesha Thomas, thirty-four years old, is the seventh-oldest child. She studied business management at college for one semester and then dropped out. "I was already making the starting pay of a graduate, so I said ain't no point in me continuing on and getting caught up in student loans," she said. She is a saleswoman at Frito-Lay, Inc., and bought a house recently, so she will stay in Pine Bluff for now.

Lakesha has a strong sense of initiative and got a job as a cashier as soon as she could, while in high school. When she was young, she didn't get birthday parties, so when she earned some money, she gave her younger siblings birthday celebrations. She even helped pick out the name for her youngest sibling, Ke'Niya. As the youngest of seventeen, Ke'Niya has benefited from the love and help of her older siblings, but she has also had a bumpy ride. Ke'Niya became a teenage mom when she was in her junior year of high school and is struggling to find her way through college. Now eighteen and unmarried, with a two-year-old son, Ke'Niya attended a high school that started with a freshman class of about a hundred and ended with just sixty-six seniors.

Overall, in line with Moynihan's writing, Richard Reeves of the Brookings Institution has shown that when children are born in the bottom wealth quintile to parents who stay married throughout their childhood, they do well: only 17 percent remain at the bottom, while 19 percent achieve the top wealth quintile in adulthood. But for kids born in the bottom quintile to parents who never marry, 50 percent remain at the bottom as adults, and only 5 percent rise to the top quintile. In short, one of the greatest kinds of privilege is to grow up in a loving, stable two-parent household.

There are also perfectly good reasons for couples not to marry or for parents to split up: a loving single mom may do much better for her kids if she ejects an abusive husband, for example. But the evidence has been gathering that Moynihan had a point and that family structure truly matters, especially for boys.

One paradox is that on matters of sex and family, working-class Americans tend to believe in traditional values even as they don't necessarily adhere to them. Frustrated and overwhelmed by difficulties, they sometimes don't show the discipline that they believe in. In contrast, educated liberals are less judgmental and say in polls that they accept premarital sex and various living arrangements, but they have relatively few lifetime sexual partners and are less likely to divorce. In short, while the educated don't profess traditional values, they are more likely to live them and to try to get their children to live them. Bradford Wilcox, a sociology professor at the University of Virginia who runs the National

Marriage Project, calls this "talking left, walking right." In contrast, young working-class conservatives disapprove of hookups even as they engage in them. Effectively, they talk right and walk left.

AFTER THE FAILURE of his marriage, Eathan Green found a new girlfriend, Ginnetta, a sweet and stocky woman with a wide face and long hair; to complicate things, she had been the girlfriend of the man who moved in with Eathan's ex-wife. A blonde with her own painful history of trauma, including being kidnapped and buried alive as an infant, Ginnetta filled a vacuum in Eathan's life. "I wasn't by myself anymore," he told us. "I didn't feel like a lone soldier trying to fight a war by myself. I had help! Sweet!"

Ginnetta had had five children by the time she was twenty-five, including two with Eathan, and in addition there were Eathan's three children with his ex-wife. All eight children had been removed by the authorities, apparently because of concerns about drugs and allegations

Eathan Green practices target shooting on the Green farm in Yamhill as his girlfriend, Ginnetta, observes. *(Photo by Lynsey Addario)*

of abuse, which Eathan and Ginnetta both deny. Growing up, Eathan says, he was beaten with a belt, a rake or a board when he misbehaved, and he insisted that he has been far more restrained to avoid hurting his own children. "I barely go past one swat on the butt," he said.

Eathan and Ginnetta were frantically trying to get back their youngest child, Lilly, born in Yamhill County in 2018 and put in foster care. They made regular trips to visit her and to meet a lawyer whom they are paying to advocate for them. Many child-welfare advocates agree with them that the authorities are too hasty to take children from low-income families and put them into foster care, saying that kids do best with parents or other relatives, sometimes with intensive coaching, supervision or support. Foster care costs about $26,000 per child per year, yet outcomes tend to be poor: only 58 percent graduate from high school. One-quarter are incarcerated within two years of graduating from foster care at age eighteen, and they are about six times more likely to end up homeless as to end up with a college degree.

Why did neither Eathan nor Ginnetta have a job at a time of a booming economy when Help Wanted signs were everywhere? Eathan is smart and has a much-valued skill as a construction worker, while Ginnetta is pleasant and diligent and struck us as dependable. Eathan, like some others in Yamhill, blamed immigrants from Mexico. "I do resent them for the fact that it makes it harder for me to get a job," he told us. It's true that in places like Yamhill, immigrants may have taken some jobs from low-skilled workers. Several employers made the point to us that they would be crazy to hire a white high-school dropout who was often high on meth, wasn't terribly interested in difficult outdoor work and would not show up reliably. One employer told us that he had tried to hire local people but ended up with an all-Mexican work crew because the immigrants are approximately twice as productive as local white residents.

Another challenge was that Eathan's driver's license was suspended for nonpayment of a fine, and Ginnetta doesn't drive either. Eathan also said that he had injured his back and couldn't do heavy lifting, and they had many appointments with lawyers and with Lilly, making it difficult to hold a job. But Clayton told us that Eathan is just lazy: "I guess he's not as mature as I thought he was."

Eathan was sometimes even more dismissive of his father. By the fall of 2018, Clayton had had a series of health crises, including several hospital stays. He had water in his lungs, a failing heart, diabetes and 420 pounds on his five-foot ten-inch frame, and when he was released from the hospital he sometimes needed help getting his clothes or shoes on. Sometimes he fell off his bed and became wedged between the bed and the wall so that it was nearly impossible for the family to pull him up. When he toppled outside, a tractor bucket had to be used to lift him. Irene, sleeping in the next room, would listen through the thin wall to his rough breathing and periodically go check on him; as a result, she had trouble sleeping. We were deeply worried that we might lose our old friend, but Eathan seemed less concerned.

"I'm just like, Wow, Dad, you can't even walk. You can't even get out of bed," he told us. "You used to be all this and now you're not nothing."

Eathan was mostly reconciled to losing his four older children, but he deeply wanted to build a family around Ginnetta and Lilly. He asked our mutual friend Rev. Rhonda Kroeker to marry him and Ginnetta, and Rhonda struggled to answer. "I love that boy with all my heart," she told us. Gently, she put it this way to him: "Eathan, if this was my daughter, I'd want to know that you were going to be able to provide for her. I'd want to know that you were going to provide a life for her that was wholesome and that she was going to be able to be all that she could be. And that you were going to be a good father to your baby. And I don't think I would give you my blessing."

There was a pause, and then she added, "So, no, I'm not ready to marry you."

Ginnetta was listening, and she spoke up, too: "Eathan, I'm not sure that I want to do that right now. I don't think I'm ready."

It has been more than half a century since Tom Green, a mason earning a good living with just a fifth-grade education, bought the farm in Yamhill as part of his family's upward progression during much of the twentieth century. He and Irene raised a strong family, for Cindy, Kevin and Clayton were smart and good workers, yet each of them cratered in their jobs, in their health and in their personal lives. In the next generation, Eathan has a better education than his grandfather did. He should be better equipped to thrive and find a job, yet today it's painful for old friends to see the Green family stalled in a way that it never was before. When a strong economy leaves behind Americans, who then aren't able to contribute to America reaching its peak competitiveness, there's a risk of collective anger surfacing. "History always repeats itself, so we had a revolution once, it's going to happen again, but how long is it going to take to get there?" Eathan said, standing outside the farmhouse. When we asked if he would join in, he exclaimed, "Yes, I am! I'm not going to watch it."

"They say that I have a problem with control?" Eathan seethed to us. "Look, dude, I have ten guns, and I can't control myself?"

IN PINE BLUFF, ARKANSAS, Ke'Niya may be a single mom, but she has drive instilled by her parents and sixteen older role models. She won accolades from kindergarten through high-school honor roll. Her mother preserved her children's awards to signal that this was what the family cared about. Ke'Niya completed high school with a GPA of 3.8, making her fifth in her class. She was also elected homecoming queen, served on student council and volunteered with a mentoring group for younger girls. She was determined to attend college, and she received college guidance from a local nonprofit called TOPPS—for Targeting Our People's Priorities with Service—which took her on college tours and helped her with her entrance exams. "Education is important to me," Ke'Niya said. "And especially when I had my son, it's like, okay, now you don't have a choice but to make something out of yourself."

So three months after her son was born, Ke'Niya got a job, even as she stayed in high school: she started as a cashier at a grocery store, and four months later she became the office's main cashier, balancing the books of the entire store.

"I basically set up a system for myself," said Ke'Niya. "School was school and then when I got home it was all about my son. On the days

I had to work, I worked." Ke'Niya soon found a better job with health benefits at a local bank, while living at home with her parents and her older sister to save money. Her boyfriend, who has a job in construction, picks up their two-year-old son each day from day care. The child has learned most of the alphabet, his colors and basic numbers, so the teacher is recommending him for an advanced program for toddlers. Ke'Niya won a Pell Grant and is starting a college degree online while continuing to work at the bank.

As for parenting, Ke'Niya says she is pulling through with a lot of help—thanks to her rather experienced mother and father, who dote on their grandson. "I definitely had a lot of support and a lot of help, which is really what kept me going," she said. "My whole family helps."

If the Greens started on an upward trajectory and then floundered, for reasons that included a fragmented family, Ke'Niya took an opposite path. She wasn't born with any of society's advantages, but with a strong family behind her, she is managing her young family, holding a job and starting college. She has many people betting that she'll succeed.

16

The Marriage of True Minds

Love alters not with his brief hours and weeks,
But bears it out even to the edge of doom.
If this be error and upon me prov'd,
I never writ, nor no man ever lov'd.
—WILLIAM SHAKESPEARE, Sonnet 116

Dave Peper, our pistol-packing neighbor in Yamhill who had been homeless seven times in his life, started drinking at the age of twelve and dropped out of high school, much like the Greens and the Knapps. After being kicked out of the house at age seventeen by his disciplinarian father, he enlisted in the navy but was expelled for cocaine use. He worked for a company making dynamite, partying on the side, but soon he ran out of money and lost his car and home. One stormy night, he showed up soaking wet at his parents' door, hungry and forlorn.

"Can I stay the night?" he asked when his mom answered the door.

His dad, hearing his voice, bellowed from the other room: "Tell the little son of a bitch no. He made his bed, and now let him lie in it!"

Before putting Dave out, his mom handed him $50 and told him to go to the YMCA, where he found a cheap bed. He continued to struggle

Dave Peper tends to the chores at the dog kennel he runs in Yamhill, Oregon. Dave has overcome struggles with alcohol and drugs, with the supreme help of his wife, and now runs a very successful business. *(Photo by Lynsey Addario)*

with alcohol and drugs, including cocaine, heroin and meth. Dave married at twenty-four and had a daughter, Tara, but continued to drink too much and abuse drugs. When the marriage collapsed, he started up a new romance with April Simmons, a teenager who had some success checking his bad habits. Dave started his own dog kennel, Ramshorn Boarding Kennel, just down from the Kristof farm, and this kept him working seven days a week. Dave had a strong work ethic and an excellent way with dogs, and was equally charming with their owners, so the kennel business showed promise.

WE GROW UP THINKING that marriage is about roses, Valentine chocolates and growing old together—but it's also a social and economic institution that benefits not just children but also the parents themselves. There's evidence that this is particularly important for men, and that wives sometimes act almost as probation officers, steering their husbands away from risky behaviors and toward jobs and childcare. This may seem saccharine or traditionalist, but researchers find that one of the factors that most reduces recidivism in male convicts is a solid marriage. Likewise, a 2018 study found that one of the factors correlating most strongly with success for black men was marriage: 70 percent of married black men are in the middle class, compared to 20 percent of never-married black men.

Married families turn out to be good for a community as well. A major research project called the Opportunity Atlas by Raj Chetty, an economist at Harvard University, and others looked at neighborhoods and which factors were associated with upward mobility. Not surprisingly, the richer the area, the better the kids did, and the same was true of neighborhoods with more university graduates, with higher employment rates, and with better school test scores. But one of the highest correlations with upward mobility was the percentage of two-parent households in the neighborhood. That may be because areas with two-parent households have more social capital and stronger role models for boys.

DAVE AND APRIL HAD a daughter, Breanna, but April resisted marrying Dave because of his ongoing alcohol problems and her concerns that his debt would undermine her credit rating. Meanwhile, Dave struggled to balance his work with his alcoholism. He accumulated four convictions for driving under the influence and for a time had a breathalyzer on his truck, requiring him to blow (nonalcoholic) breath to start the vehicle. Dave figured out how to outwit the device: he blew through a fifteen-foot hose, pushing all the clean air into the machine so that he could start the car (the government has improved its devices so that this would no longer work today). Dave and April had all their money invested in the property and the dog kennel, were heavily in debt, and everything depended on Dave devoting himself to the dogs rather than to drink.

Then in 2003, Dave received the worst phone call any parent can get: Tara, just eighteen years old, had been killed in a car crash when her boyfriend lost control of the vehicle and swerved into oncoming traffic, killing both instantly. She had just graduated from high school and was preparing to attend college in the fall. "She had everything freaking going for her," Dave told us, his voice cracking, as we sat in his home by the dog kennel.

Tara's death devastated Dave. "I can't even describe the despair, but I really went to drinking hard," he recalled. "I just didn't give a shit at that point really about anything." When drunk, Dave sometimes exploded, pounding his fist through the walls. When April saw him losing control, she would take Breanna and drive to a friend's house to stay the night, for she didn't want the girl to see her dad drunk or violent. Three or four nights a week, April was fleeing the house, and Dave's dog kennel was also suffering. It looked as if he might lose his business, his home, his girlfriend and his remaining daughter.

The couple underwent family counseling, but it didn't seem to help much. Desperate to keep him from buying alcohol, April kept all the family cash with her, along with the checkbook. After Dave began returning cans and bottles to stores for cash to buy liquor, she made sure that there were no returnables in the house. She even made sure there were no odd pennies or nickels lying around.

Dave started a line of credit at the Cove Orchard grocery store to buy liquor, even though April visited the store and begged the owner not to let Dave purchase alcohol. Several times Dave dropped by our farm and asked Nick's mom or dad if he could borrow a bit of cash; they gave him the money, guiltily, fearing it would go for liquor.

Then one day in November 2005, Dave had been drinking all day and was "stump drunk," as he described it. After running out of alcohol, he drove into Yamhill to buy more beer at T&E, the town grocery, and then dropped by the gas station to fill up. When he tried to drive off, he hit another car. That driver called the police, who arrested Dave and took him to the county jail.

"You're ruining my life," Dave shouted at the police officer from the backseat of the squad car. Even in his haze, he knew that under tightened drunken driving laws, this fifth DUI could mean a felony conviction and up to eighteen months in the state penitentiary, plus lifetime loss of his driver's license.

"Mr. Peper, your life is not ruined," the officer responded calmly. "Everything is going to be okay, you just can't see it right now."

Dave screamed at the officer: "I want to bring you to my house and tie each one of your appendages to one of my horses and whip those sons of bitches until my arms fall off."

April received a phone call from the police about Dave's arrest. Furious, she let Dave stew in jail overnight rather than bail him out immediately. The next morning, sobered up and sitting in his blue jail uniform, Dave was terrified and remorseful. *I'm going to lose everything*, he thought to himself. *What's April going to do? Is she going to be gone for good this time?* That was when Dave decided that he had to give up alcohol to try to save his marriage and business and keep his daughter.

The next morning, April went to the jail and bailed out Dave, and then they had a tough conversation. His lawyer had recommended that Dave enroll in an inpatient rehab program to show the court his determination to become sober, but these programs were extremely expensive and he had no health insurance. April had health coverage through her job, but because she had never married Dave, he didn't benefit from her policy. It wasn't clear how he would get treatment.

That's when April did something extraordinary. Three weeks after Dave's arrest, she married him—so that he could get on her Kaiser health insurance. Then he enrolled in a $30,000 one-month inpatient rehab program, and she took a leave of absence from work to run the dog kennel while he was away. With an act of faith in a partner who didn't really merit it, she stepped in to save him.

By the time Dave's court date rolled around in 2006, he had successfully graduated from rehab, was sober and had committed to never touching alcohol again. The judge put him on work release, letting him stay out of jail but keeping him on four years of probation with an ankle bracelet, plus a lifetime revocation of his driver's license. The judge also ordered him to apologize to the police officer he had threatened with his horses.

WE'VE ARGUED THAT, in retrospect, conservatives had a point in emphasizing the importance of family structure. But conservatives in the George W. Bush years tested various strategies to strengthen marriage and families—such as marriage promotion—and they didn't move the needle. It seems the conservatives also neglected two critical factors that have undermined families in America, particularly in low-income communities.

The first of these damaging factors is mass incarceration and the sevenfold increase in the number of people in jail or prison since 1970. The strain on families has been compounded by the prison system's practice of sending inmates far from home where family members can't easily visit. It then charges extortionate rates for phone calls from prisons, creating another barrier between inmates and families.

A second harmful force has been the decline of well-paying blue-collar jobs, exacerbated by the erosion of unions and the failure of the minimum wage to keep pace. Marriage is in many ways an economic institution, and when American men without a college degree experienced a decline in earnings in real terms after 1970, they became less marriageable. Indeed, the MIT economist David Autor and his colleagues found that when Chinese trade competition badly affected certain areas of the country and lowered male employment, marriage rates also fell—and out-of-wedlock children increased, as did the share of children living in poverty. The labor market shaped the marriage market. The decline in marriage is not because working-class men and women disdain marriage. It's that social and economic policies have made low-income men less attractive as marriage partners.

Families are also undermined in America by the lack of paid parental leave, which only seven other countries worldwide do not provide. Some evidence shows that those leaves may increase breastfeeding rates, reduce infant mortality, reduce postpartum depression and get dads more involved in their kids' lives.

Even if marriage promotion doesn't work, a few alternate strategies have been shown to strengthen family structure. Lifting the minimum wage or providing pay subsidies such as the Earned Income Tax Credit results in men who marry at higher rates. Helping young men get jobs through the Career Academies program, which trains high-school students for vocational occupations, raises the marriage rates of participants. Programs that move low-income children to better neighborhoods also raise their marriage rates.

Perhaps the most effective strategy to promote marriage is simply family planning. When girls avoid getting pregnant at seventeen, they are more likely to marry in their twenties and raise children in a two-parent household. Some 70 percent of pregnancies among single women under thirty are unplanned, and by helping those women plan childbearing, we can improve their outcomes and their children's.

Yet, partly because of abortion politics, family planning is toxic. Even a bipartisan program like Title X that provides contraception and has nothing to do with abortion has lost two-thirds of its inflation-adjusted funding since 1980.

DAVE PEPER'S LIFE HAS BEEN transformed since his rehab. He hasn't touched alcohol and he also quit his two-pack-a-day cigarette habit after thirty-five years. He threw his energy into his dog kennel, even expanding it, working hard to win new customers. Dog owners, some of whom came from far away to drop off their pets, noticed. He began earning a nice income to support April and Breanna and used some of the profits to renovate their house and add a patio and hot tub in the back.

Ten years after his conviction, in 2018, Dave successfully petitioned the court to get his driver's license back. Now he and April drive with their new boat for weekend jaunts on nearby Hagg Lake. He has added a pool in front of their home. Breanna graduated from high school and now has a good job working as a dog groomer; she is a pal of our daughter. When Breanna began dating a black man from Portland, we wondered what Dave, a conservative Trump supporter, would think. "I admit, it took a little getting used to at first," Dave told us. "But he's a great guy, and he's good to Breanna. I really like him."

Dave was lucky to get arrested, he says: "That night saved my life. Had I kept drinking I'd be dead right now." He also deserves credit for his work ethic and great determination to overcome his alcoholism. But he was even luckier to be with April and to be embedded in a family that saved him.

17

We Eat Our Young

America is going to hell if we don't use her vast resources to end poverty and make it possible for all of God's children to have the basic necessities of life.

—MARTIN LUTHER KING JR.

G ary Knapp is no longer shooting at Dee, for he is long dead, along with all of his children except the youngest, Keylan. The challenge now is Gary's grandchildren, for they are having their own run-ins with drugs, alcohol and the law. Keylan muses about a family curse, but it's more that each generation inherits disadvantage.

We like to think young children are malleable and resilient, but they can also be as fragile as spring blossoms in a hurricane. As a society, we denounce "delinquents," "hoodlums" and "hooligans," but the truth is that we routinely fail troubled kids before they fail us. More children die each year in the United States from abuse and neglect than from cancer. For every child who dies, thousands are injured, raped or brutally abused. We shrug as millions of children undergo trauma in ways that harm them and unravel our social fabric—and then we blame the kids when things go wrong. Some species eat their young; it turns out that we are one of them.

Keylan's son avoided drugs because of his own family's experience and went to college for a time with money that Keylan had sent him. All seemed promising. A big, strong man, the son found good work as an electrician. Unfortunately, he had a predilection for impulsiveness and violence, like so many in his circle. "The girlfriend he was with, she kept screwing around with some Mexican drug dealer," Keylan explained. This inflamed his son. "He got drunk, took his forty-five, went down there and shot the damned cars up in the driveway and told them, 'Get the fuck out of town and leave my girlfriend alone.'" The police arrived and arrested the young man, who is still in prison.

Evidence from neuroscience, psychology and economics underscores that a crucial window for helping American children is the first five years, partly because they often suffer lifelong brain damage when raised in chaos and deprivation during those years. In these circumstances, they are exposed to "toxic stress" and their brains are flooded with cortisol, a stress hormone that changes brain anatomy. Peer-reviewed studies have found that five-year-olds who have experienced serious adversity have thinner frontal cortexes on average, and as a result less impulse control, less emotional regulation and less working memory.

Given the scale of substance abuse in America, it's also inevitable that large numbers of children are exposed prenatally. Almost one-fifth of children born in West Virginia have been exposed in the womb to drugs or alcohol, and research, while not conclusive, suggests that later in life they will be much more susceptible to substance abuse. We now have a term for these childhood traumas and toxic stresses: adverse childhood experiences, or ACEs. An ACE can be physical abuse, a parental divorce or living with an alcoholic. Many adults have one, and one in eight has four or more. Even though the ACEs occur in childhood, they correlate to problems in adulthood: with four ACEs, a person has a 460 percent increased risk of adult depression and a 1,220 percent increased chance of adult suicide.

One of the most infuriating elements of American myopia about investing in at-risk kids is that politicians often insist that they don't have the funds to pay for social services—but they somehow find the resources to pay for prisons later on. Republican lawmakers don't want to pay for $500 IUDs for low-income women, so they pay $17,000 for Medicaid births. They don't want to pay to reduce lead poisoning, even though that means paying for special-education classes for years to come; one study by the Pew Research Center found that every dollar invested in large-scale efforts to reduce lead poisoning saves $17 in public money later on.

Indeed, some of our most successful national policies have been those that targeted at-risk children. We've reduced teen pregnancies by 67 percent since the modern peak in 1991. We've raised high-school graduation rates by 5 percentage points since 2011. But too often, we underinvest in proven strategies. The cost of this myopia is that dysfunction is transmitted to another generation, at enormous human cost and public expense—and then we blame the victims.

One of the most important advocates for troubled children in America is George B. Kaiser, a Tulsa billionaire whose family escaped Nazi Germany and made money first in the oil business and then in banking. Kaiser, a lean and graying septuagenarian, told us that he was moved by the evidence that early interventions could break the cycle of poverty and concluded that creating opportunities for children was essential to provide basic fairness in life.

"No newborn child bears responsibility for the circumstances of her birth, and yet those circumstances to a very large degree determine her," he says. "And that seems fundamentally unfair." Kaiser has used his wealth to finance experimental programs that have made Tulsa a surprising red-state laboratory for evidence-driven initiatives to break the cycle of poverty. His George Kaiser Family Foundation nurtured the Women in Recovery program in Tulsa that helped Rebecca Hale break out of drugs, and a big focus has been on helping children—because that's where the greatest impact is. He adds that it's "absolutely, fundamentally unfair" that wealthy American kids have enormous advantages over children born in more dire circumstances.

"Successful people tend to believe or want to believe that they got where they got by initiative and discipline and intelligence, which they developed on their own," Kaiser says. "I tend to believe that we got where we got largely by dumb luck and by what Warren Buffett calls winning the ovarian lottery."

FARLAN KNAPP, Nick's classmate, tried to be the loving dad that he had never had. He did much of the cooking and cleaning in the house. "I'd call him on holidays where I'd ask him what he was doing," said Dee. He would reply, "I'm trying to stuff this turkey, Mom. And it's sliding down the sink!" He had long, honest conversations with his daughters, Amber and Andrea, and spent time joking with them or taking them fishing. He teased Andrea for being "wimpy" when she would fuss at being woken at four a.m. to go steelhead fishing. While Farlan had detested his father and plotted to kill him, the girls idolized their dad.

Still, the girls grew up surrounded by the temptations of alcohol and drugs; in one of Amber's baby pictures, there's a plate of cocaine in the background. And for all Farlan's affection for his daughters, the home had the same bleak atmosphere as the one he had grown up in a generation earlier, for he and his wife battled furiously.

"Part of the reason that my sister and I knew that he was dying from AIDS or HIV or hep C was because she would tell him, 'Go dig your grave and die, AIDS boy,'" Amber recalled. In fact, although he had AIDS and hepatitis C, he ended up dying of alcohol-related liver failure. Farlan sometimes retreated from such verbal abuse, Amber said, and other times struck back physically. During these fights, Amber emerged as a protective big sister: she would cover Andrea's ears so she wouldn't hear the fighting.

When Amber was in seventh grade, she became friends with a hand-some eighth-grade boy named Nicholas Baughman, a son of a single mom. The most common version in the Knapp family of what happened next is that Amber and Nicholas fell into each other's arms and, during a hookup, began talking about their families.

"My dad is named Farlan," Amber began.

"No, my dad is named Farlan," Nicholas interrupted.

Confused, they resolved to each bring a photo of their father to school the next day—and that's how they found out that they were siblings. In fact, as both Nicholas and Amber tell it, they were good friends but not romantic partners. Nicholas says that he had never met his dad but knew that he was named Farlan Knapp—and knew that Amber's last name was Knapp but didn't think much of it until, one day, he heard that Amber's father's first name was Farlan. The next day, Nicholas pulled Amber aside at school and showed her the only photo he had of his dad, taken at age eighteen.

"Do you recognize the guy in this picture?" he asked.

"No," Amber replied flatly.

"Look closely," Nicholas urged. "Do you recognize this guy?"

"It looks like my uncle Keylan," she replied doubtfully. Then she flipped the photo over and saw a scrawl: "Farlan." Her jaw dropped.

"Did your dad ever tell you that you have an older brother?" Nicholas asked.

Amber became close friends for a time with her half-brother, and Farlan worked on building a relationship with his teenage son. Nicholas Baughman ended up joining the navy, then earning a college degree and getting a good job in the private sector. He represents a successful path that the Knapps had been capable of but that none of them managed.

As for Amber, she graduated from high school, rented her own apartment and then took in Andrea, who was fifteen, to give her a more stable life and encourage her to stay in high school. Years passed, and for a time the girls seemed to have made it. After high school, Andrea married and started her own real estate business. Gorgeous, smart, talented and entrepreneurial, Andrea seemed to be thriving. But Farlan's death devastated both his daughters, and Andrea accelerated her binge drinking and steadily declined.

"She drank herself to death," Keylan said. She was buried in 2013 at the age of twenty-nine.

Amber seemed the member of the young generation of the Knapp family most poised for success. She was the first Knapp ever to graduate from high school and then took a job at a telecommunications company, managing databases and training staff to use the computer systems. Amber projects a firm intelligence and competence. In speaking to her, we were struck by her intellect and her interpersonal skills. She was self-possessed and articulate, and it was easy to imagine her as a lawyer or business manager. Amber took community college classes in computing that helped her get jobs in information technology, and she was soon thriving in the field.

"PowerPoint presentations and Excel and pivot charts and matrix analytics, that's what I like to do," she told us. "Exporting and importing data and putting it on slides and showing the executive staff how your company is running in what areas, and how much money is past due or not invoiced.

"I made a lot of money, had a really good job, really good benefits, everything," she added. She married and had two children, and she was that rarity, a Knapp not on drugs. She was also making progress in the corporate world. For a time, she seemed to have escaped the Knapp curse.

However, when stressed, old patterns revived and childhood traumas resurfaced. In grief after her father died, Amber turned to anti-anxiety medications like Xanax, prescribed by her doctor. They helped, but she became dependent on them. After running out of them, she cast around for an alternative, and that's when she smoked meth for the first time in her life, at the age of thirty-two.

"I was dead set against it my whole life," she remembered. "I hated it. I'd seen what it did to everybody. My dad was a junkie who cooked meth and lost everything. You would think that that was enough." Yet Amber found herself physically sick, anxious and depressed by her withdrawal from anti-anxiety medications, unable to sleep and desperate for relief. Meth helped temporarily: "It made me feel better, it pulled me out of my depression, it made me able to be a supermom." Amber thought she had it figured out.

"In the back of my mind, and this is what most addicts will tell you, is that you don't think you will be the one to lose control," Amber said resignedly. "You don't think that it's going to consume your life. You think that you're going to be able to be a functional drug user."

Instead, Amber found herself hooked. She was soon in and out of jail, and eventually she pled guilty to felony charges of possession of heroin and meth. She lost her job, lost her health coverage and couldn't get access to the drug treatment programs she needed. Even when out of jail, Amber was unable to find work because of her felony drug convictions. She lost her driver's license, her marriage and her two kids, who were put into foster care. After one stint in jail, Amber stayed drug-free for a while and had a third child, a son, with her old high-school sweetheart; she thought the baby would help keep her off drugs. It didn't work, and this son was taken away as well.

"I lost everything," she told us. "It happened quickly."

How did Amber let it happen? Surely, part of the answer is that she made awful choices, but research also suggests that addictive behavior is heritable, either through genetics or epigenetics, so that as the daughter and granddaughter of people with substance abuse issues, Amber was exceptionally vulnerable. Children like Amber and Andrea in chaotic households grow up with dysfunction, abuse, divorce, mental illness, neglect, economic hardship or parenting by people with addictions—all classic ACEs. Researchers have found that toxic stress impairs development of a child's brain and leads to lower levels of education and, even decades later as adults, to higher unemployment, greater poverty and higher rates of cardiovascular, lung and liver disease, addiction and psychiatric disorders, even early death. The overall cost to society from child trauma and ACEs for medical care, special education, social welfare and criminal justice, not to mention loss of productivity, was $125 billion in 2008, according to the Centers for Disease Control and Prevention.

AS THE KNAPP FAMILY STORY suggests, there is a real cost to the failure of policies to support at-risk children. The kids pay a price, but so does the entire country. Several studies have found that child poverty costs the United States about $1 trillion each year in increased health, crime, prison and welfare spending as well as in reduced earnings. That's about $8,000 per household annually. Most researchers find that each dollar invested in reducing child disadvantage would save the country at least $7. Crime is a particularly expensive consequence of child neglect: researchers calculate that the economic cost of a single murder is $3 million or more. Half of America's crime is caused by 5 percent of the population, so a small number of dysfunctional and neglected youth impose a large financial and emotional cost on society—and for now kids in disadvantaged families are often steered more toward crime than college.

"Inequality affects the vast majority of the population, not only a poor minority," argue Richard Wilkinson and Kate Pickett, a husband-wife team of epidemiologists in Great Britain who have studied precisely this issue. Skeptics disagree, saying that what matters in a society is not the inequality but the absolute income level of the poor, and that this is what we should focus on improving. Yet inequality in and of itself seems to be associated with damage to the social fabric—and not just for people who are poor. Wilkinson and Pickett found that even middle-class or affluent people are better off in a society that is more egalitarian, like Japan's, and live a bit longer there, face less violence and have kids more likely to thrive. Violent crime and imprisonment are higher, economic output is lower and discontent is greater in unequal societies. Mental illness and infant mortality are two or three times higher in unequal societies. Teenage births, incarceration rates and homicide rates are up to ten times greater, and those, too, diminish the well-being of an entire society.

The Centers for Disease Control and Prevention found that in 2017, almost 32 percent of high-school students reported persistent feelings of sadness or hopelessness in the past year. In addition, 17 percent of high-school students said that they had contemplated suicide in the last year. Many people think we can't prevent suicide, for if people want to kill themselves they'll eventually succeed, but that's incorrect. The American military has conducted rigorous research on strategies that reduce suicide risk by about half. Other researchers have found that suicide prevention programs for troubled teens reduce suicides by an even greater proportion. Successful strategies include helping people make crisis plans to turn to a particular person for help when they are thinking of suicide, and also therapy to help young people work through their issues. When Connecticut introduced an anti-suicide program called SOS, ninth graders in schools assigned to participate in the program were 64 percent less likely to attempt suicide than those in a control group.

There are no guarantees for success, but Amber and Andrea might have had a better chance with professional intervention in early childhood, when the brain can more easily create positive neural connections for healthy development. The aim is to work with parents and kids alike to make homes less chaotic or violent and more nurturing, to coach parents on reading to their children, to instill in children skills like patience, cooperation, self-denial and conflict resolution. These interventions have a good record of effectiveness.

Eight years ago in Richmond, Virginia, a study found that a high number of preschoolers who had been expelled from school had previously suffered early trauma. It was ACEs that likely led to disruptive behavior, so educators in Richmond turned to Kathy Ryan, a trained clinical child psychologist, to create Circle Preschool to address therapeutic needs of kids with ACEs. Teachers are specially trained to heal trauma using play-based therapy, and they also conduct weekly coaching sessions with parents. Now, Ryan is helping set up a teacher-training institute, as a first step toward scaling the approach. During our visit, the kids in the classroom were playing quietly. "We have a way of talking with them that is much calmer than typically you would hear in a school," said Ryan. "We want to help them to develop a voice to talk about what's going on for them inside."

Circle Preschool can afford to take on only eight children at a time, so it's an expensive intervention. But the results have been impressive. We watched a boy named Jay, who is now in the custody of his uncle, Timothy, playing quietly with a large train set. When Timothy and his wife, Rebecca, took in the boy a couple of years ago, Jay was an angry child, frequently screaming and yelling. He knocked over chairs and threw things at teachers and at elderly women who visited his day-care center; he threw toys in restaurants so it was hard to take him out with their other two sons. Then Jay entered Circle Preschool in September 2018, and four months later he had become a fun-loving, playful and charming child. "I've seen a big difference just in his behavior in everything, it's amazing," Rebecca told us. Timothy is more emphatic. "It was a total one-eighty."

Some of the most-studied interventions for troubled children have been early childhood programs like Perry Preschool Project and Family Connects Durham, which turned out to have far-reaching beneficial effects. One simple program is Reach Out and Read, in which pediatricians "prescribe" reading during doctor visits and hand out free children's books. It's exceptionally cheap, at $20 per child per year, and many parents end up reading significantly more to their children. Unfortunately, while other countries are building up their early childhood initiatives, America is a laggard. Of thirty-six advanced OECD countries, the United States ranks thirty-fourth in the share of four-year-olds in early childhood programs.

It's common for children to have one ACE, maybe two, and those who have three or more ACEs are at very significant risk for educational failure, mental-health problems and substance abuse; Amber and Andrea were both walking collections of ACEs. Yet only 4 percent of pediatricians screen for ACEs in children.

Dr. Nadine Burke Harris is trying to change that. California's first surgeon general, she is leading development of nationwide, evidence-based protocols for interventions, including some that involve sensors for biofeedback to measure the biological stress response and neurofeedback to monitor brain electrical activity. Dr. Burke Harris, who has found that California's highest prevalence of ACEs is in rural counties, has initiated a public education campaign that has so far reached 31 million families with messages about childhood adversity, how it impairs health and how to heal. Even *Sesame Street* is in on the act. It has a series on coping strategies for kids who have suffered traumatic experiences, with the Cookie Monster learning breathing exercises to calm down. A new law in California provides for statewide screening for ACEs, a model that all states should adopt.

"I'm not trying to wrap our kids in bubble wrap and baby them from every outcome . . . but to help our little people go through the world and understand how to take on challenges," said Dr. Burke Harris. "The big question that we're facing as a nation is whether or not there will continue to be opportunity for everyone in America."

The United States has about 13 million children living in poverty. Of those, about 2 million may live in "extreme poverty" by global definitions (in households earning less than about $2 per person per day), when looking at their cash incomes. These kids would be considered extremely poor if they lived in Congo or Bangladesh, yet they're here in the United States. We don't want to overstate the comparison— Congolese kids can't typically access food stamps, hospital emergency rooms or church pantries and soup kitchens—but it is still staggering that by formal definitions some American children count as extremely poor even by Bangladeshi standards. The presence of extremely poor children in America, far more often than in other advanced countries (Germany has virtually none), is partly a consequence of the 1994 welfare reform that eventually cut off benefits for some families: it was meant to hit deadbeat adults but has been devastating for their children as well.

Welfare policy is complicated, with good intentions sometimes having unintended consequences. But there are effective ways to help children, from home visits to early childhood education programs. Anti-poverty efforts for the elderly have been a huge success, with the share of seniors below the poverty line plunging by two-thirds since the mid-1960s. But we sometimes spend more in public money on hospitalizations for an octogenarian than on a child's entire education. Let's be blunt: America as a nation is guilty of child neglect. We have punished children, mainly because they don't vote. Meanwhile, other countries offer home visitation, paid family leaves and monthly cash allowances for families with children to reduce disadvantage.

Angus Deaton, the Nobel Prize winner in economics who with fellow Princeton professor Anne Case did the critical work on "deaths of despair" in America, says that the revelations of extreme poverty in America have led him to recalibrate his personal giving to donate more at home: "There are millions of Americans whose suffering, through material poverty and poor health, is as bad or worse than that of the people in Africa or in Asia."

It's perhaps telling that the United States for years was, embarrassingly, the only country in the world besides Somalia and South Sudan that had not ratified the Convention on the Rights of the Child. That has now changed: the United States is the *only* nation that hasn't bothered to ratify it. Maybe that's a symbolic matter, but here's something profoundly real: children make up almost one-third of Americans living in poverty, and on any given night some 115,000 children are homeless in the world's most powerful country.

SINCE AMBER AND ANDREA MISSED that childhood window to get help—as so many like them do—were there ways to assist them as adults? Employers usually fire workers who are in trouble, costing them their health insurance, rather than send them into treatment. But employer attitudes may be changing, partly as addiction encroaches more into the workplace. In a 2017 survey of five hundred mid-to-large employers across the country, 70 percent said they had been affected by prescription drug use, for example, through employees missing work, testing positive for drugs or using pain relievers at work. In an indication of their willingness to help, a similar percentage also said they would like to help employees return to work after treatment.

At age thirty-nine, Amber Knapp was trying to start over. We met her at a park near the halfway house she was living in, and she brought a breathalyzer that could detect the scent of alcohol; midway through our conversation, on schedule, she had to breathe into it. She explained that if she failed a drug test or a breath test, she would return to prison for twenty-six months.

After having worked as a corporate manager, Amber found it mortifying to be a felon struggling with addictions. She said that her goal was to build a five-year track record of being sober: no drugs, no alcohol, no run-ins with the law. That would give her more job options, including a return to information technology.

As part of her probation, Amber Knapp had to use a breathalyzer at regular intervals to show she had not been drinking. Her daughter looks on.
(Photo by Lynsey Addario)

When Amber reflected on her roller-coaster life, she attributed it to the shadow of her childhood. "When you're raised in chaos and you're around chaos a lot, your body adapts to the chaos," she said. "I was actually creating the chaos to feel normal."

Amber turned to her daughter, a strikingly beautiful fourteen-year-old, and shook her head. "Don't do it," she said somberly. "You're more prone than somebody who doesn't have addicts as parents."

We left Amber feeling hopeful. She was so smart and self-aware that she seemed to have a fighting chance to put her problems behind her, return to the corporate world and become the mom she aimed to be. We messaged a few times about photos and other issues, and then she stopped responding. Finally, her daughter answered our texts: Amber had been arrested for failing a drug test and was back in prison for another couple of years. The kids were back on the tightrope. They weren't quite sure what would happen to them, and the world around them had just reverted to chaos.

18

Raising Troubled Kids

Act in such a way that you treat humanity, whether in your own person
or in the person of any other, never merely as a means to an end,
but always at the same time as an end.

—IMMANUEL KANT

If America has a Mother Teresa, it's Annette Dove, a sixty-four-year-old woman in the struggling town of Pine Bluff, Arkansas. Once called "the most dangerous little town in America," Pine Bluff is mostly black and poor. Annette, an African American, stout and bustling with purpose, didn't always have a sense of mission. She fell in love in high school—and then she was pregnant. She dropped out at sixteen to marry her seventeen-year-old beau, who drove an ice-cream truck.

"I was head over heels," she remembers, but it didn't last long. Her husband had come from a tough background and used drugs, and he struggled to hold on to jobs. He was domineering and became physically abusive, she says. One day, when Annette was pregnant with her second child, he stayed out all night partying, returning in the morning to take a bath. "Where've you been?" she asked. They argued. In a rage, he threw her against a wall. Fearing for herself and her unborn baby, Annette grabbed a heavy lamp and hit him over the head with it. He toppled, bleeding, onto the floor, and Annette's heart stopped. *I've killed him*, she thought. In fact, he rose woozily, but that was it for her. As he reeled, she walked out on him and took the baby with her.

Annette earned a degree in special education and took a job as a teacher of disadvantaged kids in a public school, winning renown for her success in turning children's lives around. Entry into her special-education classes went from stigmatized to prized, and education officials took note. Annette married a much-loved parole officer, William Dove Jr., and they began helping kids in the community, even taking homeless kids into their own home.

Then one day, Annette couldn't find her husband in the house. She walked through the rooms, calling his name—and found him dead in the bathroom, of a heart attack. She was devastated, emotionally and financially, but also reminded of her own mortality and life goals. So with three kids still in school, Annette quit her well-paying day job, found an old rotting house built in the 1800s that she gutted, and with

Annette Dove, right, meets with a family in her program after bringing groceries to help the kids. Thirteen people live in the house.
(Photo by Lynsey Addario)

the help of a man who donated lumber, windows and doors, together with her savings and some donated funds, she opened a nonprofit called TOPPS, for Targeting Our People's Priorities with Service. Annette gets a bit of funding from foundations and the local government, but TOPPS has always operated hand to mouth; once Annette had to file for personal bankruptcy to keep it open.

In part, TOPPS is an after-school program for teenagers who don't have anywhere else to go, whose lives are chaotic and needy. They drift to TOPPS each afternoon, looking for fun and for food. It was TOPPS that helped Ke'Niya Davis, the youngest of the seventeen children in the Davis family, learn more about college. And it was in the food line at TOPPS that Annette met a sweet boy of nine named Emmanuel Laster.

A lithe black boy with a trim haircut, cherub cheeks and sparkling eyes, Emmanuel would pounce on any food available. Annette visited his home and found that his mom, Christine, was consumed by drugs and that Emmanuel often fell through the cracks. So Annette gave him odd jobs—taking the garbage out, sweeping up, trimming the bushes— and paid him, as a way of letting him earn money to pay for food. Over the years, though, Emmanuel and his family were constantly moving, then getting evicted, then moving again. He would disappear for months, then reappear—and he began to grow up into a gangly, awkward teenager, a perilous age for impoverished black boys in America.

Emmanuel was thirteen years old when Annette first took us to his home. It was an old white wooden clapboard house with a porch and a broken door that didn't lock or even fully close. Annette explained that the house was a drug crash pad, with people passing through to buy and use drugs; indeed, the entire house reeked of marijuana. The house was dark, with all the blinds and curtains closed, and the furniture and walls were decayed. The kitchen sink was full of dirty dishes that clearly hadn't been touched for days. There was no sign of food in the house.

"I just go hungry," Emmanuel explained to us.

Emmanuel, who was wearing a black T-shirt and looking customarily sunny, told us he earns A's and B's in school. We asked him what he wanted to do in life, and he paused and looked dreamy. "I'd like to go to college," he told us. "I'd be the first in my family. I want to be a police officer, or a fireman, or a judge." But, he acknowledged, there wasn't a single book in the house.

The gangs in the area are involved in the drug trade and begin to recruit boys when they are thirteen or fourteen. Emmanuel said he wasn't involved in gangs, but he was arrested once for shoplifting. "I'm not doing that again," he said, embarrassed. He told us his friends carry knives for protection but that he doesn't. Yet.

His mom, Christine, showed up then, and Annette Dove introduced us. Christine is disfigured—she has boils and bubbles on her skin. She said that she has struggled with drugs for many years. She hasn't had much schooling and had difficulty writing her name down for us. We asked about the utilities, and Christine said proudly that the electricity was working, even though she hasn't paid the bills.

"That's why I keep the pit bull there in the backyard," she said, pointing. "Mean critter. He's expensive to feed, but he keeps the utility people away, so they don't cut off our power."

The pit bull is also useful in keeping away the repossession teams who periodically come to take the furniture she buys with down payments. Christine likes to buy on installment plans—and then stops paying, daring the repo men to get by her dog.

Emmanuel led us to his bedroom, off a dark corridor at the side of the house, away from the front room where people sleep off their drugs, and a bit safer for that reason. The room has a nice bed and matching chest of drawers and isn't as filthy as the rest of the house, and it also has three televisions: two large-screen models and a smaller one. "That one doesn't work," Emmanuel explained when we asked about them. "And any day now they're going to repossess that one."

Here we had a window into the chaotic, contradictory world of American poverty: three televisions, a pit bull, no food, much chaos. While poor Americans may have a color TV and access to hospital emergency rooms, they also have a life expectancy similar to that of Mongolia, a homicide rate higher than in Rwanda and an incarceration rate that is the highest in the world. What we found everywhere in our journey, in white communities or black ones, in cities or rural areas,

Annette Dove works in Pine Bluff, Arkansas, which is largely African American, with few good jobs and many rundown homes like this one.
(Photo by Lynsey Addario)

was that the defining ethos of life in the homes of kids like Emmanuel is disorder, dysfunction, despair and danger.

Annette Dove's mission is to nurture kids like Emmanuel and keep them in school and away from gangs and drugs, providing at-risk kids with the kind of support that is routine in middle-class homes. She lures kids to her programs with food, games, youth clubs and field trips. In particular, she focuses on mentoring fatherless boys and offering them the kind of guidance that middle-class boys would often get from their dads. The mentoring clubs coach the boys on sitting straight, looking an interviewer in the eye, being punctual, knotting a tie and other skills that would help kids land good jobs. Birth control, alcohol and dating are discussed, and how to know whether a girl wants to be kissed—along with why it's not cool to kiss a girl who doesn't want to be kissed.

"We teach about holding hands with a lady instead of grabbing hold of her and touching her all over," explained Mike Dove, Annette's son, who oversees the boys' mentoring programs even though he commutes from Dallas, where he is a federal agent with the Department of Labor. When we visited, President Trump had just defended lewd comments about women as "locker room" talk, so we asked a few of the boys in the group what would happen if one of them made "locker room" comments about a girl. They looked aghast.

"That'd be push-ups," said Devonta Brown, shaking his head soberly. He made it clear that the boys had learned better manners than that. Devonta came into the program as a troubled fourth grader and was now senior class president at his high school, earning a 4.0 grade point average and headed for college.

Of course it doesn't always work that neatly. Annette coaxes Emmanuel Laster to come daily to the after-school sessions and offers him $5 for each book that he reads and writes a book report about. For a while the bribes worked and he was eager, but then he was diverted by fun-loving friends and was caught stealing a CD from a music store. Emmanuel seemed contrite and vowed never to steal again, and for a while he attended regularly—but then his family was evicted, and he disappeared again. Annette feels she's in a tug-of-war with Emmanuel over the street gangs, and it's not clear who's going to win.

Annette pours her soul into TOPPS, and she has moved it into a bigger space, but she works seven days a week, even drawing on her retirement savings to invest in the kids. The rest of her family is also involved. One daughter, Raychelle Grant, quit her job in the finance department at a hospital in Little Rock to help at TOPPS, where she now does the accounting and coordinates programs such as the breast cancer awareness effort each October. Annette's other daughter, Kasee Dove, a computer specialist, helps run a graphic arts training program at TOPPS. Every day during the school year, Annette provides dinner to some three hundred kids. In the summer, she serves breakfast and lunch to as many as seven hundred people as well. Most of them live in high-crime neighborhoods, with abandoned and burned houses.

Mike Dove took time before a recent Election Day to explain to the eighteen-year-olds how to register to vote and why they should

Emmanuel Laster and his mother speak with Annette Dove, who is in the foreground. Annette is trying desperately to keep Emmanuel out of gangs and headed for college. *(Photo by Lynsey Addario)*

participate in nonpresidential years. Mike stays in close touch with 150 TOPPS students, texting a different group of five of them each day of the month.

Two years after our first visit, when Emmanuel was fifteen, we caught up with him again. He had moved a few more times with his mother. Once their house had burned down and the family lost all its possessions: family pictures, school certificates, clothes and shoes. Emmanuel also had grown quieter, and he acknowledged having been to juvenile detention five times. He says he doesn't have a gun and hasn't used one, but he seems to be hanging out with a delinquent crowd, and he was on probation until his sixteenth birthday in the summer of 2019.

"He was getting in trouble being with the wrong group of people," his mother, Christine, explained.

"So did you learn from that experience?" Annette asked Emmanuel.

"Yes ma'am, I did," Emmanuel replied.

"Being locked up is not what you want to do," Christine warned.

"What did you do?" Annette asked.

"Shoplifted," Emmanuel said, sheepishly.

Emmanuel said he wants to try playing football, if he can get his medical checkup in time for the start of practice.

"If you need help with your work and stuff, you need to let us know, okay?" Annette says to Emmanuel. "'Cause you need to keep your grades up if you're going to play football. They're not going to let you play when your grades are bad."

"Yes ma'am."

Emmanuel mentioned that his dad, who is now living in Texas, was supposed to send him a pair of shoes for school, but that he hadn't received them yet. Annette asked for his shoe size, but shopping for him is tricky. Annette once visited Emmanuel soon after shopping for him, only to discover that he no longer had any of the new clothes she had given him. She suspected they had been returned for cash. Another time when the three went shopping for shoes, Annette paid and Christine went to grab the receipt; Annette explained she needed it. Still, Annette has kept trying to rebuild a rapport with Emmanuel, who had been giving lame excuses for not visiting her—he said he lost her number or he couldn't ride his bike through the glass on the streets near her. But Emmanuel continues to talk of going to college, perhaps through ROTC, to study computers, while Christine says that she wants to see her son "walk across the stage" and graduate from high school.

When Annette organized a trip to Florida for some of the students, she wanted Emmanuel to come. She told his mom months in advance that he needed some spending money to buy food for five days, and she repeatedly gave Emmanuel odd jobs so that he would have the money. On the day of departure, his mom brought Emmanuel to TOPPS at ten a.m., instead of the scheduled departure time of ten p.m. When Annette asked about spending money, Christine said that he had some: thirty-five cents. Exasperated, Annette told Christine to bring him back that evening and give him more spending money. That night, at ten p.m., an employee came into TOPPS and said a boy was outside in the pouring rain. It was Emmanuel, with no extra money.

"Ms. Dove," Emmanuel reassured her, "I'm not going to eat, I'm just going." During the trip, she noticed that his feet were on top of his shoes, not inside them, and she thought he was just being playful. It turned out that these were the only shoes he had, and he had outgrown them.

With increasing apprehension, Annette has watched Emmanuel straying from the path she had hoped to put him on. It was frustrating to give him so much attention, to try so hard to help him, and yet be rebuffed. Once Emmanuel stole a video game from TOPPS, and Annette found it in his backpack.

"Why would you do that?" she asked him. "You're taking from these kids."

"Ms. Dove," he promised, "I'm not ever going to do that again."

Annette has expanded TOPPS to thirteen programs, and the oldest and brightest kids in her program have graduated from TOPPS and are attending college, about forty of them so far, often from broken, chaotic homes like Emmanuel's.

"We take them on college tours so they can see different universities," Annette said. "We pay for their application fees to get in college, and then we're talking to them about why they're in college to make sure that they graduate."

Mike Dove runs the precollege program, called DREAMS, in which he gives students a glimpse of college and teaches them a variety of skills they don't learn in school or at home: how to apply for scholarships, how to maintain good credit scores, how to keep a budget so you don't go broke, what to expect when you live on your own, how to keep up in college. TOPPS helps defray expenses and offers tutoring for the college entrance exams. Many of the TOPPS graduates also return to help the new students: during our visit, a medical school student, poised and articulate, came over to lead a session on college preparation for high-schoolers.

Annette says there are times when she is at her wits' end trying to help a troubled child. One small boy was so violent that she told his mother that TOPPS just couldn't take him. When the mother broke down in tears, Annette took him back and worked with him, gradually winning him over. Now he works in the job-training center and says he wants to go into graphic design.

Martino Green benefited from mentoring by Annette and Mike. When he was eleven years old, his mother died during pregnancy, and he and his brothers effectively became orphans. Their school principal collected donations, and Martino and his brothers went to live with their grandmother, who sold candy and pickles to make a living. She was a heavy drinker who often got angry at the boys, telling them they'd amount to nothing and giving them "whoopings" with a curtain rod or a broomstick. From age eleven to fifteen, Martino moved home ten times, as his grandmother either couldn't afford rent or was worried about the boys getting dragged into gangs and drugs. It was during those years that Martino was introduced to Annette and TOPPS. This, he says, was transformational.

"She was like everybody's mom," he said. "That program, it's really helped me grow into who I am today. They've always been in my corner." He was able to join TOPPS trips to Georgia, Louisiana, Wisconsin and Minnesota. "If it wasn't for her and that program growing up, I probably would have never been outside of Pine Bluff, Arkansas," he said.

When Martino was fifteen, he and his brothers moved into a two-bedroom apartment. The older brothers got jobs and paid the rent and major bills, while dropping Martino off at school every day. Martino graduated from high school and tried college for a year while working on the side, but he was too exhausted to keep up and couldn't afford college without a job. Then he followed an older brother into the Army National Guard for four months, partly to pay for college, but his interest in college faded and he took a job at Lowe's, and then one at a state prison. Meanwhile, his brother had become a policeman, so Martino entered the police academy and now, at the age of twenty-two, Officer Martino Green has found his calling.

"I love my job," he told us. He rides patrol, trying to prevent robberies or other crime. When Martino returned to TOPPS for the first time in his police uniform, Annette cried with joy at seeing how far he had come. Martino now volunteers at TOPPS, helping Mike, while also coaching pee-wee football. He plans to earn a college degree, too, so he can join federal law enforcement and earn more than the $15 an hour he currently earns. He is now taking three classes toward a degree at the same community college where Ke'Niya is studying online.

"I don't like school, but I can tolerate it," he said, and he offers the same lesson to the students he mentors at TOPPS. "I know in order for me to get to my main goal that I'm trying to reach in life, I need school."

It's frustrating that it's so difficult for after-school programs like Annette's to raise funds, but governments are much more willing to pay for incarceration than for initiatives that would prevent crime. One young black man in Pine Bluff, Kenneth Reams, was born to a fifteen-year-old mom, struggled in school, ran away from home at thirteen and dabbled in juvenile crime. He desperately needed guidance of the kind that Annette offers, but he found outreach only from gangs. In 1993, at the age of eighteen, Reams helped a friend, Alford Goodwin, rob a man at an ATM, because Goodwin needed money to buy a cap and gown to graduate from high school. The robbery was botched, and Goodwin carried a .32 pistol that he used to shoot and kill a white man, Gary Turner. Goodwin pled guilty and was sentenced to life in prison, while Reams pled not guilty and was sentenced to death as an accomplice, even though he had not held the gun. The case went through endless appeals over twenty-five years before the Arkansas Supreme Court, in 2018, overturned the death penalty, finding that Reams had had ineffective counsel. Arkansas devoted more than $1 million to adjudicating the case and imprisoning Reams, even as it provided next to nothing to programs like Annette's that bring kids back from the brink of criminal careers. The Reams case is a tragic reminder of what can happen when kids in places like Pine Bluff get help only from gangs: in this case, Turner was murdered, Reams spent twenty-five years on death row and Arkansas devoted scarce tax dollars to prisons, police, lawyers and courts instead of educating children and directing them to become, say, police officers rather than criminals.

Because the cost of crime is so high, the evidence is that programs like Annette's targeting at-risk kids can generate huge returns. One randomized controlled trial looking at a similar program in Chicago,

Becoming a Man, found that the program reduced violent crime arrests by about half and increased high-school graduation rates by about 15 percent. The study showed that each dollar invested in the programs saved up to $30 over time. These programs should be replicated all across the country, so as to help young people and the country itself.

There's an ongoing debate about private initiatives like Annette's. Conservatives tend to love private charitable efforts like these, while some liberals see them as largely symbolic and taking on roles that should be filled by the state. Our view is that we need both state support and private charity.

Liberals are right that governments have to play a role in supporting kids, and we can't just leave the job to charities. Imagine if we had tried to rely on volunteers and charities to build the Interstate Highway System. We need highway departments and tax support to plan and invest in national infrastructure, even though not everyone uses the highways; we also need federal, state and local governments to invest in America's human capital and help at-risk kids get on the right path forward. But while we're waiting for governments to step up, conservatives are right to praise charities like Annette Dove's that are getting kids into college and extricating them from gangs. Grassroots safety nets run by churches or neighborhood leaders have a local knowledge and buy-in that goes a long way; local dynamos like Annette know who needs a handout, who needs a helping hand and who needs a kick in the pants.

Annette isn't going to solve America's poverty problem on her own, but she's Emmanuel Laster's best hope, and we should honor her for that—and appreciate all the other Annettes around the country who run food pantries and free clinics, homeless shelters and suicide hotlines. Whether we're talking about public or private money, the highest-return investments available in America aren't in hedge funds or private equity, they're in American children.

19

Creating More Escape Artists

If you're lucky enough to do well, send the elevator back down.

—CRAIG NEWMARK, founder of Craigslist

B y 2011, the Reverend Diane Reynolds was emotionally exhausted after performing funeral rites for one young person after another who had died a drug-related death. After presiding over one funeral in McMinnville, she was driving and listening to the saxophonist Kenny G on the radio when she started crying.

"You got to do something," she remembers saying aloud to God, "because my heart cannot handle not being a part of the solution and just putting these young people to rest."

She was so upset that she pulled her car over and parked on a quiet street. There was a For Rent sign for a small room, with a phone number. An idea started percolating. She dialed the number and asked about the space, which was about three hundred square feet in a basement. Diane's husband drove over to take a look, and they met with the landlord and rented the space for $200 a month.

Diane had lived with hardship all her life. She came from a family in which at least four generations had abused alcohol or drugs, and her dad had fled the home when she was three. She says her mom invited dozens of men into the home over the years—and some of those men then abused Diane, starting when she was four or five years old. As the oldest child, Diane endured the sexual assaults and looked after her siblings, washed dishes and cleaned the kitchen but almost never attended school. She says that when she was nine, she was planning suicide with her mom's pills when she heard a whisper in her ear that she attributes to God: "You could grow up and help people stuck like you are right now." She decided to live.

At fifteen, Diane married a much older man who frequently beat her. She had four kids with him but suffered broken ribs and other injuries over sixteen painful years. After he put a gun to her head, she packed up her things, put the kids and bags in a car and drove away. She divorced him.

Despite having had essentially no formal education, Diane found a job at Evergreen International Aviation, in McMinnville. There she fell for an aircraft mechanic, married him and started a new life in her thirties while raising four kids and her younger sister. She became an ordained minister, but she had always had a yearning to help troubled children like the one she had once been, and that's how she came to stop her car that day and rent that basement room in 2011.

"That was October seventeenth," Diane said. "We opened the doors October eighteenth with absolutely no plan, no business plan, just my heart knowing we needed to do something." She started by offering soup every day to people in trouble, then other food, then meals. Sometimes people just came to sit.

Eight years later, Diane has helped transform the treatment of addiction in Yamhill County with group therapy and peer counselors. Provoking Hope, the nonprofit born in that basement room, now has thirty-four employees serving 7,800 people each year, and it is expanding elsewhere in Oregon. Provoking Hope saves the county money by reducing jail expenses and the cost of emergency room visits for overdoses (each such visit costs $4,200). This is the collective impact model, a framework first described in 2011 by John Kania and Mark Kramer, who run FSG, a mission-focused consulting firm cofounded by Kramer and Michael E. Porter at Harvard Business School. Essentially, governmental and charitable organizations and even businesses in an area integrate their services around shared goals to solve a problem in local communities. Yamhill County Health and Human Services began partnering with specialty community organizations like Diane's to help the sick, including people with substance abuse disorders. The department works with organizations that reach out to people with addictions or to pregnant women for maternal care; nurses visit homes with new babies and young children to give support on parenting.

"It's harder for a government employee to go out and make that connection," said Silas Halloran-Steiner, who runs the department. So the county pays community workers such as nurses to do outreach, as well as peer counselors to help people overcome addictions. Many of these counselors have themselves recovered from addiction and therefore have street credibility with patients, and the aim is to remove barriers that keep people from getting help.

One day, we attended an affiliate program run by Provoking Hope

Drew Goff and his youngest child, Ashtyn, at a halfway house. Drew's older children had been taken from him, but he is trying very hard to stay off drugs and away from crime to give Ashtyn opportunities he didn't have. *(Photo by Lynsey Addario)*

for men recovering from addiction, and there was one young man who was the clear leader of the group: articulate, bright, ambitious and determined to succeed in a new drug-free life. He seemed to know us, but we hadn't caught his name; afterward, he rushed over and pumped our hands, saying, "It's me, Drew!"

It was Drew Goff, son of our late friend Ricochet, a close friend of Kevin and Clayton Green. The last we had heard, Drew was in prison, and we had exchanged letters with him when he was there. But now he was free, avoiding drugs and caring for his child, an infant named Ashtyn; he had lost custody of his first two children.

Drew is smart and charming when sober, but he falls apart when high and sometimes becomes violent. He said that his troubles began at the age of twelve or thirteen when a family member introduced him to alcohol, marijuana and a cheap variant of meth known as crank. It became a way of fitting in, of numbing pain.

"My family, we didn't have the nicest things at school," he recalled. "I'd get picked on. I didn't like it. I wasn't socially able to interact with the other kids really well and I started using drugs." Drew began running with a gang. For a time, one of his jobs was dropping off cash to pay for meth at a farm in Yamhill: that was how he first came in contact with Clayton Green. Looking back at that period of his life, Drew realizes he had been surrounded by risky circumstances and then made bad choices. "I had plenty of opportunities in life that I didn't choose to take," he told us. He was in and out of prison, and while in prison got into fights and was put in segregation, isolated for twenty-three hours a day for eighteen months. He told us that when he received our letter, after his dad died, he had cried in his cell.

Over time, he said, he grew weary of prison and the messy lifestyle and ashamed of what he was doing to his family. He was more aware after twenty or so convictions that he was going nowhere, and that there were alternatives that would help him and his kids. His young son, Ashtyn, who was born addicted to drugs because of his mother's use, is giving Drew additional motivation to stay drug-free, he said, so he signed up with Provoking Hope, and it has given him a stronger footing. These days, he surrounds himself with people who are living the way he aims to live. He hasn't touched drugs or alcohol since February 17, 2018—the longest he has been sober since he was twelve—and has a job at the front desk of a hotel, likewise for the longest period he has ever held a job. He is devoted to Ashtyn, making sure the boy is fed, clothed and changed. He has taken parenting classes and brings Ashtyn everywhere with him, wiping his nose and constantly talking to him.

"I try to stimulate him with voice, and touch, sound," Drew said. "We're shooting for two hundred words at eighteen months." On our visits, we sometimes saw Drew ready to take some rash step and then back off out of concern for losing Ashtyn. "I'm a work in progress," he told us ruefully after one such episode. "The old me wants to act out, and I will not allow that." He added, "It's a tightrope that I'm walking. And sometimes it seems to be made of fishing line."

Drew admired his dad but told us, "I don't want to follow in his footsteps. I mean, I love my dad, but I don't want to be like my dad." Still on probation, Drew lived for nearly a year in a halfway house, attending classes and becoming the kind of person the program hopes to nurture. He dreams of starting his own business. Ricochet would have approved: he didn't want his son to follow precisely in his footsteps either.

Ricochet had shared with us his worries about his grandchildren, and we think he was right to be anxious. Education theoretically should provide an escape route for at-risk children, but in reality, across the country, mostly it doesn't: poor children generally go to weak schools, don't have access to enough vocational training and often can't afford either community college or a four-year college. Ricochet was pushed out of school in the eighth grade by a principal annoyed at his truancy, and exactly the same thing happened a generation later to Drew, who was also pushed out of school in the eighth grade.

We asked Judge John L. Collins in Yamhill County, who deals with many of these troubling criminal cases, what he thinks works to break the cycles of intergenerational drug use and crime. He emphasized that mentors can make a huge difference, because at-risk young people often come from dysfunctional families without a good role model. Collins cited one promising mentoring initiative, Friends of the Children, which was started in 1993 by Duncan Campbell, an Oregonian with his own troubled history. Campbell's parents were alcoholics, and his dad was in and out of prison. Campbell later made money in logging and started the charity to work with the highest-risk children in a community, and it has since enjoyed great success, been much praised and is rapidly expanding around the country. The program seeks out the most disturbed, most vulnerable young children in kindergarten and provides a paid mentor who works four hours a week with that child all the way through high school. Friends of the Children seeks to provide stability in the child's life, someone to trust, and a coach who can help with schooling; evaluations have found that it has helped many children find a healthy path.

There's a welcome discussion among politicians about getting more young people through university, but America doesn't pay enough attention to the fact that even now, about 14 percent of Americans still don't complete high school. Those kids are typically destined to hold marginal jobs, endure difficult lives and die early; their entire lives will be a tightrope walk. The Department of Labor has seven pages of regulations about ladders, yet some states still allow children to drop out at sixteen (most have recently raised the age to seventeen or eighteen). America pretty much invented the public high school, but today Americans are more likely to drop out of high school than in most other advanced countries, and completion of high school doesn't necessarily signal mastery of basic skills. About one-fourth of those who graduate from high school cannot pass the American military's qualifying exam.

There has also been a growing appreciation that the United States could add skills training in high school and college to better prepare students for jobs. That's not to take anything away from a liberal arts education, which can be tremendously empowering for top students. But we have a mismatch between a labor market that is in desperate need of certain skilled workers and an education system that turns out young people who flounder and end up unemployed or underemployed. In Switzerland, 70 percent of students learn a marketable skill in the school system. We need coders, plumbers, electricians and a range of health workers, and European countries do a far better job of putting some students on a vocational track, sometimes including apprenticeship, that meets the needs of both the economy and the young people themselves.

There were almost 7 million job openings in early 2019. That is where job-retraining and skills-building programs need to play a stronger role. Job-training programs have had a mixed record, partly because many government-sponsored ones haven't been good at discerning employer needs in local areas and then matching them with worker training. Yet some job training, focusing on skills in great demand, has done extremely well. A nonprofit in New York City called Pursuit finds smart but struggling people in public housing or libraries—they average earnings of $18,000 a year, and half are on public assistance—and trains them in coding and business skills. Afterward, they work as software engineers and earn an average of $85,000 a year. Similar programs include Year Up, Per Scholas, TechHire and Skillful.

An organization called Social Finance is trying to scale up skills-training programs beyond computer coding to also include medical device programming, solar panel installation, truck driving and hospitality. As with Pursuit, the cost of a $10,000 training program will be funded by "career bonds," in which investors pay up front for the program and the students turn over a percentage of their earnings for a fixed period to repay the investors if their salary exceeds a certain minimum. Even in an age of automation, there will be jobs available for those who have the training. As Elon Musk, founder of Tesla, said in explaining the limits of automation: "Humans are underrated."

Yamhill-area schools are trying to provide a ladder up for children, including vocational and technical apprenticeship options, but they're finding it a challenge. The local economy is humming and the wine industry is helping to create jobs, but teachers are seeing more kids who have experienced trauma, post-traumatic stress disorder and anxiety.

"We're getting kindergartners right now who, locally, and this is across the state, people describe as 'feral,'" said Charan Cline, the superintendent of Yamhill Carlton School District.

Lauren Berg, the elementary-school principal, says that more kids are biting, screaming, kicking and throwing things. "I've sat many times at this table with a five-year-old saying, 'Why are you throwing chairs?

Lauren Berg, principal of the Yamhill Carlton Elementary School, meets with some of her charges. She says that a growing number of students come to the school "feral," profoundly neglected and difficult to control.
(Photo by Lynsey Addario)

What's going on? How do I help you?' but they can't tell me," Berg says. "We have kids that will run, kids that run out the door." Often the kids grow up neglected and absorb the lesson that the only way they can get attention is to have a tantrum. That has made improving the schools both harder and more necessary. As recently as 2014, only 73 percent of students graduated from Yamhill's high school, down from 80 percent when Nick was in school.

Superintendent Cline is trying to turn the schools around. He has a deep understanding of what some of the kids are going through because his own father spent three years in the state penitentiary for drug offenses, and Cline grew up enduring his share of trauma and emotional abuse. He became an escape artist through the army; he jokes that after his home life, basic training felt like a vacation.

"I know that no kid is responsible for their situation any more than I was responsible for mine, so we try to help everyone," Cline told us. "The enemy of our country is poverty and hopelessness." He has become a strong believer in equipping students with vocational skills, and he thinks that's the best model for overcoming poverty in places like Yamhill.

"Government programs should focus on empowering people with marketable skills that they can use to demand good wages or start businesses," he said. "By not helping students to get skills they can sell to an employer, we are adding to the problem."

Still, it's sometimes a Sisyphean struggle. The Yamhill County health department dispatched a full-time psychologist to each school to work with troubled students and reach out to families. But parents sometimes don't want help or don't sign permission slips for their children to get counseling. The school offered free parenting classes, but no one showed up. It organized a free program called Ready for Kindergarten, to help families get young children prepared for school, and at first about thirty families participated. By the end of the year, only a few families were left. In high school, some kids show up precisely once every ten school days. That's because if they receive government benefits, such as disability, the checks continue if the child shows up at least one day every two weeks, even if there's zero progress toward graduation.

The school system is trying new techniques. When Silas Halloran-Steiner, at the county's Health and Human Services Department, read a book called *The Nurture Effect* about how to help troubled kids, he invited the author, Anthony Biglan, to come to the area to see what he could do. As a result, the elementary school introduced the PAX Good Behavior Game, in which students decide on class rules. The aim is to promote self-regulation and reduce disruptive behavior, and randomized trials in Baltimore found that first and second graders who used the game were less likely to be arrested or smoke cigarettes in middle school, and later were more likely to graduate from high school and less likely to abuse drugs. Teachers loved the program and said it had made a significant difference.

The schools also now have a speech pathologist. One of Clayton Green's problems was a speech impediment for which he received no help, while children now would receive therapy to correct it. The school also used to expel problem kids like Clayton—that's why he left in ninth grade—while now there's a strong push to retain kids. High-school students are still expelled for dealing drugs, which happens once a year or so (one entrepreneurial high-school student hired others to go through their parents' medicine cabinets and bring in unused pills to sell). These days, however, students prone to fighting aren't reflexively pushed out but are diverted for half the day to a program where they learn anger management and how to resolve conflicts.

There is rebuilding at the high school as well, with two new giant domes, one for athletics and one for vocational and technical education, including pre-engineering, computer-aided drafting and fabrication, plus metal and wood shop. The building project reflects greater recognition in Yamhill—and in much of the country—that vocational education may be a way to keep students in school, and it is paired with a viticulture program to train students to work in local vineyards. So against all odds, the Yamhill-Carlton schools are making headway. The latest high-school graduation rate is back up to 80 percent.

Drew Goff takes his son Ashtyn everywhere, even when he gets another tattoo. (Photo by Lynsey Addario)

Yamhill Carlton High School invited Drew Goff to speak to a health class about his experience with drugs, as part of its effort to help students stay out of trouble. We sat in the back of the class to give him moral support. It was the first time Drew had ever spoken in public, and he was terrified. "My heart is beating like mad," he confided as we walked into the school. In fact, as soon as he began speaking he had the students in the palm of his hand. He talked movingly of feeling when he was a boy in school as if he didn't belong, of finding acceptance only when he got high. "Marijuana, meth, heroin, PCPs, I did it all," he told the students, and then he recounted how he had to steal to finance his habit, and his despair when he was sentenced to eleven years in prison. The students, most of whom knew someone struggling with addiction, peppered him with questions. One girl, who later came over to Drew and confided that she herself had tangled with addiction but had managed to stay away for four months, asked, "What would you tell yourself at age fourteen?"

"Say no," he said. "Talk to someone." He wrote down his phone number and email address and asked students to reach out if they wanted to talk further about drugs. "My message to you," he told the students, forgetting that he was in a classroom, "is it's just not fucking worth it."

20

America Regained

I know what I am asking is impossible. But in our time, as in every time, the impossible is the least that one can demand.

—JAMES BALDWIN

C layton Green's health deteriorated further in early 2019, with his heart and lungs failing. He spent most of his time sleeping and had trouble even walking around the house. When he fell inside, it took twelve people and the fire department to get him back on his feet. This was humiliating for Clayton, and it was difficult to reconcile the obese, sick man of 2019 with the vigorous boy on the Number 6 school bus a few decades earlier. Irene was soon caring for Clayton as if he were a child, and this was wrenching for both mother and son.

"Sometimes, I just want to run away from home," Irene told us once. Clayton was hospitalized periodically, but he hated hospitals and always came home within a few days. During one stay, he was caught with a meth pipe, unable to avoid using even in his hospital room. We spoke to him by phone from New York and tried to be reassuring, urging him to hang in there; he promised he would try. Soon afterward, Clayton became delirious, speaking to himself and imagining things. He was taken to the McMinnville hospital and died on January 29, 2019, at the age of fifty-seven. The official cause of death was congestive heart failure, but that medical term misses so much: his expulsion from school in ninth grade, his loss of good jobs as factories closed, his abuse of drugs and cooking meth, his criminal record from drugs, his genius for mechanics, his failed marriage, his loyalty to friends including us, his five grandchildren all taken into care by the state, his loneliness, his desolation. This was another death of despair, and Clayton was a casualty of America's social great depression.

Our journey of exploration for this book had begun in Yamhill, and in some sense it ended there when we flew back for Clayton's funeral. Rev. Rhonda Kroeker presided again, as she had for the services for Cindy and Kevin, and she recalled partying with Clayton and his contemporaries, "cruising" in his 1955 Chevy. "Having a lot of fun, causing trouble," she reminisced. "Things started out pretty innocent, pretty sweet. A lot of those people aren't with us anymore. They didn't know when enough was enough." She recalled that at Kevin's funeral she had

Clayton Green in the family kitchen near the end of his life
(Photo by Lynsey Addario)

asked, "Who will be next?" The empty seats in the pews answered her question: so many old friends of Clayton were gone. "This should have been packed with people," Rhonda told us afterward. "But we have some families that have lost a good percentage of their children." Some of those who came were struggling. One old friend, a former logger quite a bit younger than Clayton, needs oxygen because he has only 30 percent of his lung capacity left.

Many Americans see people like Clayton and perceive only "felons" and "junkies" whose struggles reflect their just deserts. Yet for those of us who knew Clayton, there was much more to him; he was a reminder that we all deserve to be remembered for more than our worst days. We counted Clayton as a dear friend, despite his mistakes, in part because of values that included unshakable loyalty. As writers, we have covered politicians and business leaders who are like weather vanes, shifting with the changing political winds. Clayton was the opposite. We always knew we could count on him to look after Nick's mom and the farm; even in his last week, he managed to come over to start our ailing Caterpillar tractor when no one else could. After his death, we found he had the keys to our farm gas tank, apparently to make sure that other workers didn't help themselves to free gas. For many years, Clayton had been a rock on whom we could depend, and we saw through his addiction, criminality and orneriness to his core values, which included utter devotion to those in his circle.

The Green farmhouse, once a symbol of upward mobility when Tom bought it with his mason's salary, was again shrouded in mourning as Irene prepared to bury her fourth child. We grieved for Clayton, for the Greens and for so many other kids on the old school bus. It would have been unimaginable back then that four Knapp kids and four Green kids, along with so many other children on the bus, would be dead so young. The "stairway to heaven" of the 1977 Yamhill prom had become a trapdoor to a Dantesque inferno. We thought the future would bring us flying cars; instead, it brought many of us lost jobs, broken families, illicit drugs and early death.

It was the luck of the draw—the lottery of birth—that placed some of us on the Number 6 school bus in Yamhill and others in private schools in Greenwich, Connecticut. It was wrenching to watch the Greens and the Knapps each lose four children, but it was also a bit frightening. We knew that what separated Nick from old friends was largely the good fortune of being raised by loving, educated parents who cherished Goethe more than carburetors, who subscribed to *The New York Times* by mail, who were tycoons in human capital. If instead he had been raised in the Knapp household, seething as a Gary drunkenly fired the .22 at Dee and whipped the children with a belt, then he, too, might have dropped out, cooked meth and died young. So often in America, we increasingly saw, our end point depends on our starting point. Robert Kennedy spoke shortly before his death about the damage to a society caused by "the breaking of a man's spirit by denying him the chance to stand as a father and as a man among other men," by "indifference and inaction and slow decay" and by "a slow destruction of children." Kennedy added that "only a cleansing of our whole society can remove this sickness from our souls." That leaves us at the conclusion of our journey committed not only to highlighting what has gone wrong but also to pointing to remedies.

The recent books *Hillbilly Elegy* and *Educated* unfold largely in Appalachia and Idaho, white working-class areas like Yamhill that embraced Trump and his efforts to undermine institutions from the courts to the media to the intelligence community. But as the writer Timothy Egan has noted, the protagonists of *Hillbilly Elegy* and *Educated*, J. D. Vance and Tara Westover, were able to escape oppressive circumstances because of lifelines from institutions—in Vance's case, the military, and in Westover's case, a university with an assist from the Mormon Church. Vance and Westover are both brilliant, hardworking individuals whose triumphs were possible in part because of institutional escalators that society had put in place, escalators that people like the Greens and Knapps simply couldn't manage to access.

The paramount lesson of our exploration was the need to fix the escalators and create more of them to spread opportunity, restore people's dignity and spark their ingenuity. Our conservative friends in Yamhill are understandably proud of their pioneer stock and of the exceptional courage their ancestors showed in taking wagon trains on the Oregon

Trail (or, in other cases, boarding ships to the New World). There is an exaltation of self-sufficiency that reflects the national popularity of the bootstraps narrative. Yet the pioneer spirit triumphed not only because of rugged individualism but also because of government policy. The pioneers didn't buy covered wagons and roll toward Oregon purely as actions of individual initiative; they headed for the Oregon Country because the Preemption Act of 1841, the Homestead Act and the territory's local laws allowed them to become farm owners. For landless workers in the East, it was a huge attraction that under local rules any white person who arrived in Oregon could mark off a square mile, improve it with buildings or fences, and then gain ownership just by living on it. The result was disastrous for Native Americans in the area but created the basis for a large landed middle class.* The Homestead Act was later supplemented with public education, land-grant universities, rural electrification and subsidies for home buyers and university students in the GI Bill of Rights. Time after time, government provided escalators, citizens jumped on board and America benefited. Yet in recent decades, that symbiosis has faded, and now it's time for America to get back in the escalator business.

THERE ARE NO MAGICAL SOLUTIONS to the issues we've described, and simplistic recommendations risk obscuring the depth and complexity of the challenges in policy, politics and implementation necessary to bring about change. One of the things we should have learned from the last half century is a certain humility, for helping people is harder than it looks.

Yet, imperfectly and unpredictably, a bit of help does transform

---

* Homestead opportunities were offered to just white Americans. Oregon specifically banned blacks from entering the territory beginning in 1844, stipulating that any black person attempting to settle in Oregon would be subject to a public whipping. The Oregon constitution, which took effect when statehood was granted in 1859, then barred blacks from becoming residents. Likewise, the federal Donation Land Act of 1850 declared that homesteading was for whites only, all across the country. Oregon not only banned whites from marrying blacks, Native Americans or Chinese but also provided for the imprisonment of anyone who performed such a wedding ceremony. That law remained on the books until the 1950s.

lives—especially when impressionable young people are at stake. When Nick was on the Number 6 bus each day in Yamhill, a brilliant working-class girl named Ann, who came from a military family, was attending a high school to the south in Ashland, Oregon. In the spring of her senior year, Ann was stopped in the hallway by her English teacher, Hattie Converse, an elderly woman with soft white curls. "Where are you going to college, Ann?" she asked. Ann explained that she wasn't going. She hadn't even applied. No one in her family had ever gone to college, and it would be unaffordable.

"Come with me," Converse said sternly, grabbing Ann by the arm. "I feared I'd done something wrong," Ann remembered, seeing that she was being led to the school office. Converse told her that she *must* go to college. She didn't give Ann a chance to argue. "She just kept insisting I had to go," Ann recalled. "It made me pretty emotional. On the one hand, it felt good that she thought I was smart enough. On the other hand, it was unnerving and scary." Soon it became a blur, and Ann found herself zoning out. The application deadline for most universities had already passed, but there were still a few options, and the front office gave her application forms. Ann tucked them into her book bag and rushed off, for she was late for her next class.

"At home I looked at the forms and almost didn't fill them out," Ann told us. "My family lived paycheck to paycheck. And I was the oldest of five children. But Mrs. Converse's insistence had gotten into my head and I decided to take a chance." To save on application fees, Ann applied only to the University of Oregon. It accepted her, the Carpenter Foundation in nearby Medford provided a scholarship and Ann was on campus in the fall. "The whole world opened up to me in college, and I fell deeply in its embrace, filling my mind with science and history, economics and anthropology, literature and the search for truth," Ann said.

It was a constant financial struggle, and Ann was never sure she would be able to make it through college. She worked during term time in the student cafeteria and each summer in whatever job she could find, including as a hotel maid in Las Vegas, taking out a loan as well. In the end, she finished college, and it was transformative. Ann studied journalism, met her husband of three decades and afterward vaulted into a job as a television reporter at KTVL in Medford—and then soared from there. Ann Curry became a star, one of the nation's best-known and most-admired television journalists, thanks to one small push. "I can remember the exact moment my life turned on a dime," she told us. "All because of Mrs. Converse. By the time I tried to track her down to thank her, she was gone. I wonder if she knew what I became because of her. I wonder how many other students she had to pull toward their potential. I wonder how she must have felt when her efforts failed. What I do know is that she's proof that just one person who takes action can change the future, even in a small town." America holds itself back when so much talent is left on the table, when so many opportunities are unrealized because talented young people like Ann Curry don't go to college or don't even finish high school—but a nudge can make all the difference. We can't guarantee a Mrs. Converse in every hallway, but we can try to institutionalize those nudges, as other countries do, to make it easier for young people to achieve their potential.

We have told stories in this book, more than explored policy alternatives, because we agree with Harvard's David Ellwood that the first step toward better policy is to amend our understanding of people's struggles so that it is less about individual irresponsibility and more about our collective irresponsibility in tolerating levels of child poverty that would be unacceptable in the rest of the developed world. Yes, the Knapps and the Greens and others made mistakes, but so did we as a society, and America is a lesser nation as a result.

We embrace the idea of Professor Victor Tan Chen of Virginia Commonwealth University that we should see the struggles of those left behind partly through the lens of a morality of grace. We need economic change but also cultural change, and ours would be a richer nation if it were more infused with empathy, above all for children.

While our journey of understanding has not focused on policy, we have also seen clearly how much difference policy makes. Laid-off autoworkers and their families fared better in Ontario than in Michigan because of Canadian efforts to get people back into jobs. People who abused drugs were far less likely to die in Portugal, where it was easy to receive treatment, than in any place in the United States. Moms were able to break the cycle of addiction, poverty and crime in Tulsa because of Women in Recovery, but not so easily elsewhere. America's future is not as bright as it should be because we rank number 61 in high-school enrollment. So while our own search into what went wrong has often felt harrowing, we have also been heartened to see that suffering is not inevitable. Solutions are difficult and imperfect, but the right programs make a big difference. There is a path forward out of the inferno.

Throughout this book, we've tried to argue that America has gone astray by perceiving poverty or drugs simply as a choice or as the consequence of personal irresponsibility. Yet in another sense, poverty *is* a choice. It is a choice by the country. The United States has chosen policies over the last half century that have resulted in higher levels of homelessness, overdose deaths, crime and inequality—and now it's time to make a different choice.

Many people we talked to seem willing to consider big steps, and the country may be ready for them just as it was during the Depression, the last time working-class families faced this kind of stagnation. There is a populist volatility on both right and left. The challenge will be to leverage the frustration so that we adopt helpful policies based on evidence—rather than on, say, feel-good scapegoating of immigrants.

A 2018 survey commissioned by the Democratic think tank Third Way found that 75 percent of voters agreed with the statement "We need an opportunity agenda for the Digital Age so that everyone, everywhere has the opportunity to earn a better life." For example, voters say they are more likely to support a candidate calling for universal broadband; it could bring the kind of opportunities that electricity brought in the 1930s, yet one-third of Americans still don't have access to broadband at home.

The National Academies of Sciences, Medicine and Engineering, tasked by Congress with investigating how to reduce child poverty in the United States, issued a landmark report in 2019 that concluded that each year child poverty costs Americans about $1 trillion in crime, education and welfare costs and related expenses. It estimated that child poverty could be cut by more than half in ten years with a series of steps costing about one-tenth as much, $100 billion a year, while also creating jobs—a bargain by any calculation. Outcomes can be far better. We need not boil like frogs in a beaker; we can leap out to safety. Borrowing from the National Academies and from other experts we've consulted, here are some big steps that we urge the country to take:

1. *High-quality early childhood programs.* This may be the single best thing we could do in the United States to help at-risk children. In the same way that America's mass education spawned a wave of industrialization and innovation, universal programs for toddlers are a promising investment in the country's future. Moreover, early childhood initiatives would also make it easier for moms and dads to get jobs. In 1971, Congress passed a bill to establish a national childcare program, and supporters expected President Nixon to sign it. Instead, he vetoed it, and it's time to remedy that mistake. For families living under the poverty level, childcare now consumes almost one-third of family income, and the United States hasn't done nearly as well as other countries in providing childcare options. New York City mayor Bill de Blasio told us that he initially advocated universal pre-kindergarten solely to help the children but later realized that this granted a huge boon as well to working parents by providing high-quality childcare. One factor holding back the U.S. economy as a whole is that we have gone from a leader in female labor force participation in 1990 to a laggard (we now rank number 20 out of 22 rich countries), partly because other nations have developed better childcare options. It's promising that support for early childhood education is bipartisan, with red states like Oklahoma among the leaders.

2. *Universal high-school graduation.* One child in seven doesn't graduate from high school on time (including almost one-fourth of black students), and these dropouts rarely have much of a future. By contrast, in Japan, Russia, Ireland and Finland, fewer than 3 percent of students don't graduate from high school. A starting point would be to require young people to stay in school until they turn eighteen or graduate from high school, whichever comes first. We can also do more with apprenticeship programs, vocational training, Career Academies and other efforts that increase the odds that students who stick with high school will be rewarded with a job at the end.

3. Universal health coverage. Seven decades after President Harry Truman tried to achieve universal coverage, let's not wait any longer to assure every American access to health care. This need not be a single-payer system that could force tens of millions of Americans to leave existing health insurance plans that they are happy with; rather, it could be a multipayer system like Germany's that mandates health insurance through a variety of plans. It could include a public option and expand Medicaid, while allowing people to buy into Medicare early if they are not otherwise covered. But the point is that we should no longer let Americans slip through the cracks in ways that impair national competitiveness, reduce life expectancy and lead to individual heartbreak.

4. Elimination of unwanted pregnancies. Teenage pregnancy is a major precursor of poverty, and ample evidence shows that free access to long-acting reversible contraceptives (such as implants and IUDs) and other contraceptives can reduce unwanted pregnancies. An investment of one dollar in such a program brings up to $7 in savings, not to mention improving the odds that teenage girls will graduate from high school and get good jobs. A bonus for social conservatives: fewer unwanted pregnancies would mean fewer abortions.

5. A monthly child allowance. Research shows that a government payment of about $250 a month to each household with a child would give poorer children a better start in life. A child allowance has been used successfully in Canada, Australia and nearly every European country—it is a major factor in the reduction of poverty in Canada—and research by H. Luke Shaefer, a welfare policy specialist at the University of Michigan, and others suggests that the allowance would virtually eliminate children living in extreme poverty in the United States.

6. An end to homelessness for children. We slashed veteran homelessness in half by making it a priority, so now let's fight homelessness for children. This means increasing affordable housing and using vouchers and evidence-based programs like Creating Moves to Opportunity that help families with kids move to better neighborhoods.

7. Baby bonds to help build savings. At birth, every American should be able to get an account with $2,000 that can be withdrawn only for education, to buy a home, to invest in a business or to retire. For low-income families, subsequent contributions to the account would be matched by the government to promote a savings habit. The idea is to help people build a productive nest egg. Various studies have calculated that baby bonds could reduce the black-white wealth divide by 80–90 percent. One variant of baby bonds is the individual development account, or IDA, and a condition for accessing the funds is completion of a financial literacy class. These seem to be very successful in increasing savings and should become part of school curriculums. In one randomized trial in the late 1990s and early 2000s, people with IDAs who lived on just $9,000 a year still managed to save 8 percent of their incomes by scrimping on coffee, alcohol, cigarettes and eating out; they also worked more hours. After ten years, the families with the accounts were much more likely to own their homes and have retirement accounts. But in 2017, Congress pulled the plug on funding for an IDA program.

8. A right to work. In 1944, Franklin Roosevelt proposed a right to work as part of a Second Bill of Rights for Americans, and he had a point. Government can do much more to move people into fair-paying work, even if we don't take this literally to mean that the government is the employer of last resort for all Americans. The message of a job is "Welcome to the world of taxpayers," and it is as empowering as welfare is stigmatizing. The best approach to help those who are struggling is to support better-paying jobs, either by raising the minimum wage or by giving earnings supplements along with job coaching. Partly that's for political reasons: "Where progressives made an error is in saying, 'We want to pay people who aren't working'—that's a killer politically," mused David Ellwood of Harvard. "If you say that a job should pay better, it's easier." For this reason, Senator Mark Warner of Virginia frames the message as, "We ought to give every American the opportunity to earn a good life"; he emphasizes the words "opportunity" and "earn." That's the idea behind raising the minimum wage, strengthening labor unions and worker protections, and expanding the Earned Income Tax Credit (EITC) or other earnings supplements. The EITC has bipartisan support, and scholars find that it largely pays for itself by turning people into taxpayers and reducing the benefits they receive. In contrast, we're skeptical of a universal basic income both because of the difficulty getting political support at a sufficient level and because of so much evidence that what matters for well-being is not just income but also the dignity and identity that come with a job.

Another smart step is wage insurance, to subsidize laid-off workers who accept lower-paying jobs rather than waiting for a job to come along that paid what the last one did. In experiments with wage insurance, both the United States and Canada have found that it results in workers becoming more likely to accept jobs that they otherwise would have scorned. That's better for those individuals and for the American economy as a whole. "Wage insurance may not be on your radar, but it should be," argues Robert Shiller, the eminent Yale economist, who advocates it as a way to reduce inequality. He notes that wage insurance has bipartisan support and was introduced in a very limited way by both George W. Bush and Barack Obama.

We should also experiment with programs to encourage people to move to areas where there are more jobs, or to subsidize employers for each new job they create in high-unemployment areas. There are also relatively new pay-for-success career- and technical-training programs to help disadvantaged youths get a foothold in the workforce. Another step would be a national service program to train at-risk young people with the discipline, work skills and self-confidence that come from the military track that has been so helpful to people like Dale Braden. The Defense Department estimates that 71 percent of young Americans would not be eligible to join the military even if they wanted to, because of felony convictions, drug use, obesity, failure to graduate from high school and other reasons—and those ineligible include many of those who would most benefit from military service. A year or two of national service would give these young people a better chance in the job market afterward.

A more dramatic step would be a federal job guarantee, but this faces difficult questions of implementation and enormous expense, with estimates in the hundreds of billions of dollars per year. It seems to make more sense to first try more modest measures, but if unemployment in some segments of the population is persistent, then a limited government jobs program of last resort would be preferable to the poverty, addiction and hopelessness that we see now.

These programs, which would require sensible partnerships with the private and nonprofit sectors, will cost money. Canadians and Europeans pay higher taxes and get universal health care, less poverty and homelessness, lower addiction rates and arguably more humane societies, and that's probably a worthwhile trade-off. Increasing taxes on the wealthy is an idea whose time may have come: polls find more Americans favor raising taxes on the wealthy than lowering them.

If we were simply to revert to the tax rates of the mid-to-late 1990s, when the economy was booming and people generally felt the country was on the right track, we would raise enough to finance much of this agenda. Those tax rates certainly didn't slow the economy; that was the last time we were paying down the debt and the economy seemed to be working well for everyone. So isn't that a conversation worth having?

Another way to raise significant sums would be a small financial transaction tax on trades of stocks, bonds, foreign exchange, commodities and derivatives, as proposed by John Maynard Keynes, James Tobin, Bill Gates and others. The Economic Policy Institute suggests that such a tax could raise more than $100 billion annually, which should be targeted to help pay for a child allowance, early childhood education or drug and alcohol treatment. There are many other ideas, including a wealth tax, curbs on the step-up basis for capital gains, a unified rate for capital gains and earned income, and a higher inheritance tax, that are worth exploring.

Outlays for people may seem like entitlements but actually are long-term capital investments in the country's human infrastructure. The education benefits in the GI Bill of Rights helped create a nationwide foundation of human capital in America, just as the interstate highways then under construction created a physical infrastructure. Both kinds of investments are crucial platforms that can help unleash market forces, just as in the nineteenth century new railroads spurred economic growth and mass education spawned cross-country entrepreneurial activity and vaulted America to the top of the world. Now, as other countries, such as China and India, build strong economic foundations and invest in their vast masses of people, the United States, with a much smaller population, risks falling behind. What holds the nation back in part is that tens of millions of people are underutilized because they lack the education or skill set to be more productive. Roads and bridges, along with stronger education, can build the kind of structural foundation that allows the nation to raise productivity, boost innovation and compete globally. To be a superpower, we must empower all Americans.

One challenge is that those suffering from these "workin' man blues," in the phrase of the conservative folk singer Merle Haggard, don't take up pitchforks to demand the end of loopholes for the rich. Instead, they may aim those pitchforks at the educated liberal urbanites in Washington or New York who seem condescending. It may seem odd that at a time of rising inequality, there aren't more vigorous efforts to help those who are struggling. But political scientists have found that even in a democracy, inequality awards the wealthy not only with more wealth but also with more political power. The rich then use this power to consolidate their own wealth. The upshot is that the more urgent economic justice becomes, the less likely it is to be pursued.

THE STORIES IN THIS BOOK have often been grim, but we remain optimistic about what is possible. We have seen great progress in the course of our lives: the gains in life expectancy, health care and living standards over the last century have been extraordinary, and we prefer to think of the troubles for the American working class in the last forty years as the exception rather than the new normal. Whether this *is* the new normal will depend in part on the steps we take as a nation. These difficulties have been driven partly by technology, trade and automation, it is true, but mostly they have been driven by policy mistakes and by a distorted obsession with personal responsibility. "As an economist, I am always asked: Can we afford to provide this middle-class life for most, let alone all, Americans?" notes Joseph Stiglitz. "Somehow, we did when we were a much poorer country in the years after World War II." Our answer is, yes, as a nation, we can recover our footing.

It is promising that there is a growing recognition that the country has gone astray and failed many Americans. Larry Fink, chairman of BlackRock, the global investment management company, in 2018 sent a letter to other CEOs warning that "to prosper over time, every company must not only deliver financial performance, but also show how it makes a positive contribution to society." The private sector has a role in unlocking human potential, just as government does. Starbucks is an example of a company that has found profit by doing good. It offers baristas health insurance, free college tuition and stock ownership, and there are enough Starbucks outlets that this has a significant impact. In the 1970s, executives like "Chainsaw Al" Dunlap and "Neutron Jack" Welch competed with one another to lay off workers, drop pension plans and outsource services; in the coming years, will some executives step forward to lead a competition to make companies more responsible members of society?

Companies are finding that if they want to recruit the best young people, if they want their brands to appeal to this young generation, then they must stand for values beyond share price. Tax policy could also easily nudge companies toward profit sharing, and this can be powerful. The 2009 auto industry bailout involved autoworkers giving up wages and benefits in exchange for future profit sharing, and in 2017, General Motors production workers received profit-sharing checks that reached $12,000. Companies could also provide more training. Even as jobs have become more technical since the 1990s, companies have significantly reduced both the amount of outside education they pay for and the amount of on-the-job training they provide. This may help short-term profits but undermines a company's future, its employees' morale and the human capital base of our country.

Inevitably, these big steps won't work as well as we might hope, for reality always intrudes. Funds will be scarce, particularly as we will have to dig ourselves out of debt and deficits. These proposals also do not address the political distortions that lead to a rigged economy. We do need to take steps to make our political system more responsive to ordinary citizens and less attentive to large donors and lobbyists. Making voting easier would also help. Still, experience in other countries suggests that these big steps can boost human capital, promote opportunity and mobility and create a more healthy society. Britain under Tony Blair made a concerted effort to cut child poverty, and in just five years it cut the rate almost in half—so it can be done. Some human tragedies may be inevitable, but over time there could be fewer kids headed toward crime, drugs, unemployment and early death.

In researching this book, we have discovered much money wasted subsidizing yachts, golf courses or private jets. But what has made our journey through America more painful has been to witness the waste of America's most important resource, its people. It has been wrenching to see old friends suffering and the dysfunction cascading down to their children and grandchildren. In our reporting over the decades abroad, we were pained to see talented Chinese, Bangladeshis, Syrians and Sudanese suffering unnecessarily in wars or refugee camps; it is even more harrowing to see unnecessary suffering among old friends who are capable of achieving much more, for themselves and for the country. Abroad, we've often cited the aphorism "Talent is universal, opportunity is not"—we've come to see that this is true not just of Congo, but also of America. As we were leaving Clayton's celebration-of-life service, Sheryl recalled the lines John Donne famously wrote almost four centuries ago:

> *No man is an island,*
> *Entire of itself.*
> *Each is a piece of the continent,*
> *A part of the main.*
> *If a clod be washed away by the sea,*
> *Europe is the less.*

Donne ended a few lines later, in a reference to the church bells tolling after someone's death, "Therefore, send not to know for whom the bell tolls; it tolls for thee." We no longer have church bells pealing in America at each death, but the point is the same. Whenever someone like Clayton dies an early death, whenever anyone falls from addiction, suicide, crime or despair, we all are diminished. We have the means to do better. We can shore up the American dream so that the children today climbing aboard the Number 6 school bus—and skipping into schools all across the country—achieve more of the dreams that animate them, so that this truly becomes, in Woody Guthrie's vision, "a land made for you and me."

Postscript

When *Tightrope* was about to be published, we were nervous about how it would be received by Yamhill and especially by the families featured in it. Would they feel we were undermining Yamhill's reputation as a vibrant wine tour destination? Would families wince at our descriptions of their loved ones—or of themselves? Truth be told, we felt a little awkward ourselves about our own book. We didn't want readers to perceive a community that we cherish as a caricature where people simply cook meth and die young. We wanted readers to also see its beauty and resilience and capacity to fix itself.

Perhaps some people in Yamhill were offended, but not many, and the families in the book embraced it. Irene Green came to New York for the book launch and spoke movingly about her family tragedies, almost exactly a year after Clayton had died; it was her first trip to New York, so we made sure that she also saw a Broadway show and met the mayor. As for the other Greens, Eathan's girlfriend, Ginnetta, left him, a major blow, but he is working hard to recover custody of his youngest child, Lilly. Every time we look at our farm's grapes and cider apples, we think of Clayton, who near the end of his life worked so hard to prepare for the plantings that he wanted to be a part of; we wish he could see them now.

Keylan Knapp, after the construction accident in which he fell off a roof in 2018, never fully recovered. He struggled to find work, couldn't make payments on his home and lost the house, and he grew depressed. Discouraged, he began to use heroin in addition to meth.

"I couldn't stand it," Dee Knapp told us. "I couldn't bear to see him do this to himself."

Keylan remained charming and endearing. We invited him to join us on stage at an event in Los Angeles, speaking to people in the television and movie industry about this book and those left behind, and he was thrilled to do so.

"I want to tell *my* family's story," he said. "It's *my* family, after all. It's *my* story."

The conference was postponed because of the coronavirus pandemic, but he reached out regularly to us for updates. Then in March 2020, his girlfriend left the house and, when she returned a bit more than an hour later, found him on the floor from a heroin overdose. He had collapsed against the door, apparently trying to get out to summon help. He died in the hospital a few days later, and there was no funeral because of the coronavirus outbreak.

"I think of him every day," Dee said. "He was doing so well when he first got out of prison. He was coming to church with me every week. He was off drugs. I thought he was going to be okay." And so Dee buried him on the hill above her home, and every day she walks up the hill to visit the graves of her five dead children. When we wrote *Tightrope*, we thought that Dee had already endured the unendurable after losing her four other children; it's difficult for us still to process that she has now lost Keylan as well.

Mary Mayor was also scheduled to join us at the entertainment industry event in Los Angeles, and she is doing very well. She attended a couple of our book events, and she brought her birdhouses to sell to people in the audience. If you're interested in buying one of Mary's lovely homemade birdhouses, you can find her at www.Facebook.com/cheeprentbirdhouses.

We held book talks in cities all over the United States, but the most meaningful was in McMinnville, just down the road from Yamhill. It was held in the community center and was full to the rafters, attended by many of the people in the book. Mary Mayor was in the front row with her birdhouses. Mike Stepp showed up briefly with his shopping cart. We wondered if the meeting would devolve into bickering about President Trump or about personal responsibility, but instead it was a lively evening in which a community searched for answers: What went wrong? How do we get lives back on track? What is our collective responsibility?

Provoking Hope, the organization in McMinnville that fights addiction, received many contributions from readers (thank you for that!), and that made some people in the book feel that their candor had achieved something important; they had bared their souls, and readers responded with empathy rather than condemnation. The Knapps thought that Farlan and his siblings would be glad that their stories had inspired support for drug treatment programs.

At a Provoking Hope benefit, we sat beside Drew Goff and his charming new wife. We had worried a bit about including Drew in this book, for he had been using drugs almost his entire life and had more felony convictions than he could count; what if he relapsed? But Drew has poured his intelligence and diligence into his new life. He now works as a manager at a moving company, in charge of a ten-person crew. As we watched that evening, people came up to him, asking for jobs. Drew's dad, our late friend Ricochet Goff, would be deeply proud of Drew—and he is a reminder why this book's subtitle includes the word "hope."

Yes, we mourn Keylan and Clayton and so many others, but because of people like Drew, we continue to feel hope.

Appendix

Ten Steps You Can Take in the
Next Ten Minutes to Make a Difference

1. Look into becoming a mentor. There's a particular need for men to mentor at-risk boys, with long waiting lists of boys who need a solid male role model. Check out organizations like Big Brothers Big Sisters or, if you want to help out online, iMentor.

2. Consider sponsoring a child in the United States through Save the Children, for about $30 a month. We associate child sponsorship programs with needy children in Africa, but Save the Children also has robust programs that help families in poor parts of the United States.

3. Visit the websites of some of the nonprofits we've described in the book: TOPPS helping underprivileged kids and youth in Arkansas (http://www.toppsinc.org/); Provoking Hope for people in Oregon with addictions (http://provokinghope.com/); Women in Recovery helping women with addiction in Oklahoma (https://www.fcsok.org/services/women-in-recovery/). You can contribute or spread the word about them by telling five friends, by following them on

268 | *Appendix*

social media or by posting on Facebook and Twitter about them.

4. Try supporting education for at-risk kids, especially in early childhood. It would be transformational if as many people gave to nursery schools for low-income children, like Educare (https://www.educareschools.org/), as to universities and business schools. A $20 donation to Reach Out and Read will cover the cost of bringing a new child into a national program that uses pediatricians to "prescribe" reading and hands out children's books during visits to the doctor's office. Reading Partners offers opportunities to volunteer to tutor a child in reading. You can also write to your members of Congress and urge them to fully fund early childhood programs for at-risk children. Tips on letter writing can be found at http://www.nea.org/home/19657.htm.

5. Become an ambassador for an organization you like or an advocate for these causes. Children are neglected in the United States because they can't vote, so they need others speaking up on their behalf. One excellent choice is RESULTS, which coaches citizens on how to lobby members of Congress effectively on issues like poverty and early childhood education. It's at www.results.org.

6. If you are reading this in a book club, consider harnessing the club for at least this session to tackle one issue. Maybe it's a call for your state to expand Medicaid, or for your local school district to do more for at-risk children, or for local prosecutors to support more diversion programs for drug offenders rather than just locking them up time and time again. It's always more fun to tackle problems together, and there are very successful models of "giving circles" like Full Circle Fund or Idaho Women's Charitable Foundation.

7. Consider volunteering at a homeless shelter. Information is available at the websites of the National Coalition for the Homeless and VolunteerMatch. Or volunteer at a health fair like those run by Remote Area Medical (they need all kinds of volunteers, not just doctors and nurses). This kind of volunteering may sound like a sacrifice, but it's also a rewarding adventure.

8. Break taboos! America tends to be at its worst in dealing with policy issues that are hard to talk about, like mental health, domestic violence or anything having to do with sex. So break the ice, for if we can't discuss these issues, we can never make progress on them.

9. Reward companies that have a moral compass, and punish those that don't. If more Americans supported companies that gave workers health care and reasonable wages and benefits, we could leverage American industry to provide traction for more workers. Likewise, consider investing in the class of socially responsible funds, with major fund companies like Vanguard, iShares and TIAA offering various options.

10. Start blazing your own path to make a difference. For example, as we were working on this book, our cherry orchard on the Kristof farm in Yamhill needed to be replaced, so after seeing the need for jobs in the area, we decided to plant the land with cider apples and wine grapes. Cider and pinot noir will employ more local people than other uses of the land, and we've already hired a couple of local people with troubled histories to clear the land and plant and nurture the apple trees. Our website for the project is www.Kristof Farms.com, so visit for updates. It'll be a risk and an adventure, but we're also excited to create a pathway that just might help a community that we cherish.

Acknowledgments

It has been a heartrending journey to report and write this book, and it has been possible only because so many people bared their souls to us. Clayton Green debated for a few months about whether to let us write about his meth dealing. "It's embarrassing," he said with a sigh. "What will the neighbors think?" Yet in the end he let us write about it because it was the messy truth and because he trusted us. That's a heavy responsibility, and we hope that the friends who appear in these pages find that we honored their trust. One of our concerns as we wrote this book was that our unsparing portrait of their lives might lead some readers to dismiss Clayton and others as screw-ups who deserve their fates rather than as the complicated friends we cared deeply about.

Some people, like Clayton, shared their stories partly because they had known us for decades. Mary Mayor, Nick's friend since seventh grade, had tried very hard not to let others know of her struggles with alcohol, drugs and homelessness, but after much reflection she told her story because she trusted us to help put a human face on homelessness in ways that would nurture more compassion and empathy. Others, like Daniel McDowell, the former soldier who became addicted after service in Afghanistan, didn't know us at all but told us every gritty detail of their humiliations simply because they wanted people to understand addiction better and appreciate the toll of failed policies. Daniel's willingness to speak up about his addiction is as courageous as anything he did in a firefight in Kandahar.

So we owe a huge thanks to those like Clayton, Mary and Daniel—and Irene Green and Dee, Keylan and Amber Knapp—who told us these stories out of some belief that the blunt truth would help formulate sounder policy and ease the suffering of others. It's particularly painful that Clayton, an old friend whose candor about his struggles helped inform our understanding of these issues, passed away before the book was completed.

Friends in New York sometimes ask us how old friends in Yamhill relate to us when they are struggling with unemployment, drugs or homelessness; is there resentment or an unbridgeable gulf? That's a question to pose to those friends themselves, but our answer is that our friendships are deeper than the divides. Yes, our experiences have diverged, and some old friends despair of our progressive politics or our lack of religiosity—just as they once despaired of Nick's poor welding or miserable auto repair skills. But they have forgiven our failings and welcomed Sheryl into their lives and hearts. "You're just the same as I am, a Yamhill kid," Clayton told Nick. "No matter how far in life you go, or where you go to, you're still part of Yamhill." It also helps that Nick's mom remains embedded in the community and is beloved by all. Ultimately, our bond with old friends arises because we all love Yamhill and because we're all aware that something has gone terribly wrong since that "Stairway to Heaven" prom.

Thanks to *The New York Times* for giving Nick a book leave for this project. Arthur Sulzberger, A. G. Sulzberger and James Bennet make magnificent bosses and partners at *The Times*, along with so many others during Nick's thirty-five years at the paper, ever since Abe Rosenthal and John Lee hired him as a young economics reporter in 1984. We also are very grateful to our publishing home of almost as many years, Knopf, and our longtime editor there, Jonathan Segal, who is an author's dream: smart, thoughtful, creative and reasonable. In contrast to many other publishing houses, Knopf truly edits and pampers manuscripts, and Jon sets the gold standard for book editors. We are lucky to have editors and publishers, in both journalism and books, so devoted to quality. At Knopf, thanks also to Markus Dohle, Madeline McIntosh and Sonny Mehta for nurturing books that start thoughtful national conversations. We are grateful for the daily help from Samuel Aber and Erin Sellers, and to so many others in the company who manage translations, illustrations, covers and so much more. Dan Novack provided wise counsel on legal and other issues. Chip Kidd designed this cover as he did our previous covers. Amy Ryan dazzled us with her copyedit of this book, repeatedly rescuing us from ourselves, and Ellen Feldman guided us through the production process and made it all seem easy. Paul Bogaards helps us reach you readers, along with Jessica Purcell and the publicity team at Knopf who will be sending us around the country to talk about this book, in conjunction with our lecture agents at American Program Bureau. It takes a village to produce a book, and Knopf is a remarkable community that we feel lucky to be part of.

Anne Sibbald has been our literary agent ever since we were young foreign correspondents in China in 1993 and faxed the legendary Mort Janklow at the suggestion of our colleague Bill Safire. We have been with Janklow & Nesbit agency ever since. Anne has been a wise, enthusiastic and patient cheerleader and read multiple drafts of this book. This trio of companies we have worked with—Knopf, *The New York Times* and Janklow & Nesbit—represent for-profit companies that also care deeply about quality, purpose and social mission. Anybody would be lucky to work with one of these, and we have been lucky enough to work with all three.

Huge thanks to Jennifer Garner for recording the audiobook version of *Tightrope*—and also for her tireless work on behalf of children. She serves on the board of Save the Children and is a passionate advocate for sounder policies to help kids left behind.

The Ford Foundation gave us a grant for the reporting of this book and the photography in it. Special thanks to Darren Walker, Noorain Khan, Dave Mazzoli, Kelsey Baker and Grace Añonuevo of the Ford Foundation for making that happen—and thanks to the Ford Foundation more broadly for its work addressing the issues we write about.

The photos in this book are mostly from Lynsey Addario, an old friend whose photography (and heart) we greatly admire. Lynsey has spent much of her career covering conflicts in places like Afghanistan, Iraq and Sudan, and we have worked with her abroad, so it was a treat to bring her with us to Oregon, Oklahoma and Alabama; it was particularly nice to work with Lynsey in a place without warlords and firefights. Alice Gabriner did a smart and meticulous job editing the photos.

Many experts discussed issues with us in the reporting of the book, or read parts of it. We are especially grateful to readers and commenters including Gordon Berlin of MDRC, Sheldon Danziger of the Russell Sage Foundation, Ken Levit of the George Kaiser Family Foundation, Isabel Sawhill of the Brookings Institution and H. Luke Shaefer of the University of Michigan. They are all experts on inequity whose comments were profoundly helpful. Other readers of all or part of the manuscript include Glenn Kramon, Liriel Higa and Natalie Kitroeff of *The New York Times*; Bob Bansen and Joni Marten from Yamhill; Jane Kristof, Darrell WuDunn and Katharine Miao; and our cousin George Apostolicas. Special thanks to our friend Josh Lewis, who offered excellent, detailed suggestions; he once helped rescue us from a rock in the Salmon River, and he proved himself as deft an editor as a kayaker.

The book was also informed by helpful conversations with Princeton University professor Alan Krueger, who died as this book was being completed, as well as George Kaiser of the George B. Kaiser Family Foundation and many others.

Several outstanding Princeton University students helped with fact-checking, research and early readings that led to excellent suggestions. They include Nathan Levit, who also worked with us in parts of Oklahoma, as well as Ethan Sterenfeld, Joseph Charney, Julia Hillenbrand and Seamus McDonough.

We were joined on this journey by a crew working on a television documentary in conjunction with this book, and the documentary team at Show of Force has been immensely helpful. The team helped us find Daniel McDowell and Police Lieutenant Steve Olson in Baltimore, in addition to Marquita Abbott in Washington, D.C., and a number of others we interviewed. The documentary team shared transcripts and was deeply committed to shining a light on these issues while preserving the dignity of those going through difficult times. The Show of Force team includes Maro Chermayeff, Josh Bennett and Jeff Dupre, with whom we worked on previous documentaries, and also Viva Van Loock, Paula Astorga, Christina Avalos, Lizzy Coplin, Erin Crumpacker, Wolfgang Held and Gina Nemirofsky.

With so much help, it's difficult to imagine that we could still mess up. But we refuse to engage in the customary piety that any remaining errors are solely the fault of the authors. If mistakes have crept in, we disclaim responsibility. Any errors are entirely the fault of our spouse.

Notes

1. THE KIDS ON THE NUMBER 6 SCHOOL BUS

5   only one migrant worker child in five hundred: The figure is from the powerful Edward R. Murrow documentary of 1960, *Harvest of Shame*, about migrant laborers. The documentary led to improved conditions for migrant workers.

8   the median American household is actually *poorer* in net worth today: David Leonhardt, "We're Measuring the Economy All Wrong," *The New York Times*, September 14, 2018. This is adjusted for inflation.

9   Median wages for the majority of the population: Weekly and hourly earnings data from the "Current Population Survey," Databases, Tables & Calculators by Subject, Bureau of Labor Statistics website, from 1979 to 2019. For workers with some college or an associate's degree, median wages in 2019 are about 15 percent less than they were in 1979, adjusted for inflation. It's even worse for high-school dropouts, whose median wages after inflation are about 21 percent less than in 1979.

9   "In fact, the levels of negative emotions": Julie Ray, "Americans' Stress, Worry and Anger Intensified in 2018," *Gallup News*, April 25, 2019.

10 Some 68,000 Americans now die annually from drug overdoses: "Provisional Drug Overdose Death Counts," National Center for Health Statistics, 2019. At the peak in 2017, more than 70,000 died of overdoses.

10 another 88,000 from alcohol abuse: "Alcohol Facts and Statistics," National Institute on Alcohol Abuse and Alcoholism.

10 and 47,000 from suicide: "Suicide," National Institute of Mental Health.

2. "WE'RE NUMBER 30!"

13 America ranks number 40: Joseph E. Stiglitz, Amartya Sen and Jean-Paul Fitoussi, "Report by the Commission on the Measurement of Economic Performance and Social Progress," 2009.

16 76 percent of the white working class expects: Patrick O'Connor, "Poll Finds Widespread Economic Anxiety" *The Wall Street Journal*, August 5, 2014; results from a *Wall Street Journal*/NBC News Poll.

16 Suicide rates are at their highest level: Jamie Ducharme, "U.S. Suicide Rates Are the Highest They've Been Since World War II," *Time*, June 20, 2019. The town of Herriman, Utah, endured the suicides of six high-school students, plus one recent graduate, in less than a year. Ian Lovett, "One Teenager Killed Himself, Then Six More Followed," *The Wall Street Journal*, April 13, 2019.

16 one American child in eight is living with a parent with a substance use disorder: Rachel N. Lipari and Struther L. Van Horn, "Children Living with Parents Who Have a Substance Use Disorder," *The CBHSQ Report*, Substance Abuse and Mental Health Services Administration, August 24, 2017.

17 Jeff Bezos, Bill Gates and Warren Buffett: Chuck Collins and Josh Hoxie, "Billionaire Bonanza," Institute for Policy Studies, November 2017. Collins and Hoxie say that the wealthiest 1 percent of all U.S. households own 39.7 percent of all private wealth. From 1860 to 1900, the wealthiest 2 percent of American households owned more than a third of the nation's wealth, while the top 10 percent owned roughly three-fourths of it.

17 "I don't believe modern American capitalism is working": Senator Warner believes in market economies, of course, but thinks that the current system skews incentives to invest in equipment rather than human resources. He also notes that venture capital overwhelmingly goes to white men in New York, California and Massachusetts and would like to see more efforts to broaden opportunities for struggling Americans to earn their way out of poverty. He would like to create more incentives to invest in human capital rather than machines. For example, he suggests that something like the R&D tax credit be applicable not just for buying a computer but also for training workers.

17 "even I think capitalism is broken": Ray Dalio said this in a tweet on April 7, 2019, https://twitter.com/RayDalio/status/1114987900201066496.

17 "The problem is that capitalists typically don't know": Dalio's comment is from an essay, "Why and How Capitalism Needs to Be Reformed," posted on his website, EconomicPrinciples.org, April 12, 2019.

17 more than two-thirds of Americans aged eighteen to twenty-nine: Frank Newport, "Democrats More Positive About Socialism Than Capitalism," *Gallup News*, August 13, 2018.

18 don't readily have the cash to cover a $400 emergency: J. Larrimore, A. Durante, K. Kreiss et al., "Report on the Economic Well-Being of U.S.

Households in 2017," Board of Governors of the Federal Reserve System, May 2018.

18 more unhappiness and psychological distress than low wages: Daniel Schneider and Kristen Harknett, "Consequences of Routine Work-Schedule Instability for Worker Health and Well-Being," *American Sociological Review*, February 1, 2019.

20 "a lot of little diamonds": Heather Long, "'Nobody Like You Has Ever Done It': How a High School Dropout Became President of the San Francisco Federal Reserve," *The Washington Post*, January 18, 2019.

22 ninety-three valedictorians: "The Valedictorians Project," *The Boston Globe*, January 2019.

22 about 8 million of these voters had supported Barack Obama: Geoffrey Skelley, "Just How Many Obama 2012-Trump 2016 Voters Were There?," University of Virginia Center for Politics, June 1, 2017, says there were 8.4 million such voters.

23 "an honest look at the welfare dependency": Kevin D. Williamson, "Chaos in the Family, Chaos in the State: The White Working Class's Dysfunction," *National Review*, March 17, 2016.

3. WHEN JOBS DISAPPEAR

32 a lifeline: The federal disability program is a lifeline for some but traps other people in perpetual poverty and makes it more difficult for them to return to the labor force when economic conditions or their own circumstances improve. After bottoming out in September 2015, labor force participation rates in the United States have risen, partly because some people who had been on disability returned to work, but they often lose benefits when they do. Federal Reserve chairman Jerome Powell has suggested that people on disability be allowed to work while losing fewer benefits. Another approach would be to give people a holiday so that they could return to the job market without losing disability payments for a certain number of years, or by allowing them to work more hours without facing a penalty. These steps would have given people like Kevin Green or Ricochet Goff more incentive to reenter the labor force.

32 The policy of confiscating driver's licenses: Justin Wm. Moyer, "More Than 7 Million May Have Lost Driver's Licenses Because of Traffic Debt," *The Washington Post*, May 19, 2018.

33 private wealth in the United States has increased: Board of Governors of the Federal Reserve System (US), "Households and Nonprofit Organizations; Net Worth, Level (TNWBSHNO)," retrieved from FRED, Federal Reserve Bank of St. Louis; https://fred.stlouisfed.org/series/TNWBSHNO, April 24, 2019.

33 The people in the top .01 percent: David Leonhardt makes this point in an excellent chart using income data (after taxes and transfers) from Thomas Piketty, Emmanuel Saez and Gabriel Zucman, as well as GDP data from the Bureau of Economic Analysis. David Leonhardt, "How the Upper Middle Class Is Really Doing," *The New York Times*, February 24, 2019.

33 The Wall Street bonus pool at the end of each year: "How Wall Street Drives Gender and Race Pay Gaps," Institute for Policy Studies, March 26, 2019. The latest report says that the total bonus pool for 181,300 New York City–based Wall Street employees was $27.5 billion—more than three times the combined annual earnings of all 640,000 U.S. workers employed full-time (at least thirty-five hours per week) at the federal minimum wage.

33 Average hourly wages: Drew Desilver, "For Most U.S. Workers, Real Wages Have Barely Budged in Decades," Fact Tank, Pew Research Center, August 7, 2018. This refers to average hourly wages for non-management non-farm private-sector workers. After 1973, these average wages declined modestly until the 1990s, then rose modestly afterward. Overall, they remain slightly below where they were in January 1973, after adjusting for inflation.

33 the median net worth adjusted for inflation: "The Demographics of Wealth: How Age, Education and Race Separate Thrivers from Strugglers in Today's Economy," Federal Reserve Bank of St. Louis, Essay No. 3: Age, Birth Year and Wealth, July 2015, Table 2: Median Wealth of Families by Age of Family Head, p. 7.

33 only half earned more than their parents had: Raj Chetty, David Grusky, Maximilian Hell et al., "The Fading American Dream: Trends in Absolute Income Mobility," *Science*, April 28, 2017. Another measure of economic mobility, intergenerational earnings elasticity, suggests that about 40 percent of an American's rank in the distribution of earnings is accounted for by his or her parents' incomes.

34 three more don't have jobs but aren't looking for work: Congressional Joint Economic Committee, Vice Chairman's staff, Mike Lee, Senator, Utah, "Inactive, Disconnected and Ailing: A Portrait of Prime-Age Men Out of the Labor Force," *Social Capital Project*, September 18, 2018.

34 the incidence of child neglect rose by 20 percent: Dan Brown and Elisabetta De Cao, "The Impact of Unemployment on Child Maltreatment in the United States," University of Essex, UK, working paper, March 2018.

34 in Flint, Michigan, where 35 percent of men of prime working age were not employed: Edward Glaeser, Lawrence Summers and Benjamin Austin, "A Rescue Plan for a Jobs Crisis in the Heartland," *The New York Times*, May 24, 2018. See also Benjamin Austen, Edward Glaeser and Lawrence Summers, "Saving the Heartland: Place-Based Policies in 21st Century America," Brookings Institution, March 8, 2018. There's growing interest in Congress in job-creation programs. But at a time of full employment, it

may not make sense to introduce such a program at a national level. Rather, because of the regional variations, we should target high-unemployment areas. We can also create incentives for employers who create jobs, expand the Earned Income Tax Credit and also target at-risk demographics like juvenile delinquents with special interventions like Career Academies that have an excellent record of job creation.

34 The OECD estimates that 38 percent of jobs in rich countries are at risk: Ljubica Nedelkoska and Glenda Quintini, "Automation, Skills Use and Training," OECD, working paper, 2018.

35 asked Americans recently to offer a word: Laura Wronski, "Top Words to Describe 2018: Great and Exhausting," Survey Monkey, Curiosity at Work, survey dates December 10–17, 2018.

36 between poor people who have a job and poor folks who don't: "We focus on not working, rather than income inequality, throughout this paper because we see it as a far greater problem. There is significant evidence suggesting that misery haunts the lives of the long-term not working," write three distinguished Harvard University economists, Benjamin Austin, Edward Glaeser and Lawrence H. Summers, in "Saving the Heartland."

37 Today 80 percent of American households living in poverty: Rachel Sheffield and Robert Rector, "Air Conditioning, Cable TV, and an Xbox: What Is Poverty in the United States Today?," The Heritage Foundation, July 19, 2011. Also see Derek Thompson, "30 Million in Poverty Aren't as Poor as You Think, Says Heritage Foundation," *The Atlantic*, July 19, 2011, which argues that productivity increases in electronics and other areas have made certain products very cheap, while health care, education and housing are still expensive.

39 same impact on lifespan as smoking fifteen cigarettes a day: Vivek Murthy, "Work and the Loneliness Epidemic," *Harvard Business Review*, September 2017. Murthy notes that we as a country have moved to confront the public health threat from cigarettes but have been largely oblivious to the threat from loneliness.

4. AMERICAN ARISTOCRACY

42 Children from the richest 1 percent of households: Raj Chetty, John N. Friedman, Emmanuel Saez et al., "Mobility Report Cards: The Role of Colleges in Intergenerational Mobility," NBER Working Paper No. 23618, July 2017.

44 it seems to work: We know about Ivy Coach's fee structure because it sued a family for paying only half of the $1.5 million owed for guiding a child into boarding schools and then an elite college. In that case, the child was accepted early at an Ivy League college. Scott Jaschik, "$1.5 Million to Get into an Ivy," *Inside Higher Ed*, February 12, 2018.

44   77 percent of kids in the top quartile of incomes: "College Affordability and Completion: Ensuring a Pathway to Opportunity," U.S. Department of Education, www.ed.gov/college.

44   a college degree on average is worth: Mary C. Daly and Leila Bengali, "Is It Still Worth Going to College?," Federal Reserve Bank of San Francisco, *FRBSF Economic Letter,* May 5, 2014.

44   low-income Canadian children are about twice as likely: Raj Chetty, "Improving Opportunities for Economic Mobility: New Evidence and Policy Lessons," Federal Reserve Bank of St. Louis, *Economic Mobility: Research & Ideas on Strengthening Families, Communities & the Economy,* March 2017, p. 37.

44   "an inequality machine": Karin Fischer, "Engine of Inequality," *The Chronicle of Higher Education,* January 17, 2016.

44   Today 15 percent of black students attend: "Segregation Then & Now," Center for Public Education, CenterforPublicEducation.org/research/segregation-then-now.

45   "Quietly and subtly, the opponents of integration have won": Rucker C. Johnson with Alexander Nazaryan, *Children of the Dream: Why School Integration Works* (New York: Basic Books, 2019), 2.

46   The public frets about cheating with food stamps: Emelyn Rude, "The Very Short History of Food Stamp Fraud in America," *Time,* March 30, 2017.

46   zillionaires hide assets abroad: Gabriel Zucman, "The Hidden Wealth of Nations: The Scourge of Tax Havens," University of California at Berkeley, presentation, September 2015. He calculates that $36 billion is lost to the Treasury each year because of hidden assets. This is only a small share of tax cheating. Overall, the IRS has estimated that people owe $458 billion annually in taxes that they don't pay, and follow-ups suggest that this underpayment is largely from very wealthy people.

46   "we confused the hard work of wealth creation": Joseph E. Stiglitz, Amartya Sen and Jean-Paul Fitoussi, "Report by the Commission on the Measurement of Economic Performance and Social Progress," 2009.

46   By some calculations, corporate subsidies, credits and loopholes: Mike P. Sinn, "Government Spends More on Corporate Welfare Subsidies Than Social Welfare Programs," Think by Numbers, 2013.

46   Amazon paid zero federal income tax: Institute on Taxation and Economic Policy, "Amazon in Its Prime: Doubles Profits, Pays 0 in Federal Income Taxes," blog post, February 13, 2019.

47   By late April 2016, Boeing had laid off: Jim Brunner, "For the First Time, Boeing Reveals State Tax Breaks: $305 Million in 2015," *The Seattle Times,* April 29, 2016.

47   "The United States invented antitrust": Luigi Zingales, "How E.U.'s Google Fine Explains High Cellphone Costs in the U.S.," op-ed, *The New York Times,* July 24, 2018.

47 More than one-third of all tax audits: Paul Kiel and Jesse Eisinger, "Who's More Likely to Be Audited: A Person Making $20,000—or $400,000?," *Pro-Publica*, December 12, 2018. For the fact that the top 5 percent of taxpayers account for a majority of underreported income, see Andrew Johns and Joel Slemrod, "The Distribution of Income Tax Noncompliance," *National Tax Journal*, September 2010, especially Table 3.

48 his attorney asked that the fine be canceled: "Manhattan DA Urges Jail for Dewey Exec, Alleges 'Fraud on This Court,' " *New York Law Journal*, November 13, 2018.

49 "Punishing and imprisoning the poor": "Report of the Special Rapporteur on Extreme Poverty and Human Rights on His Mission to the United States of America," United Nations General Assembly, Human Rights Council, May 4, 2018.

49 fewer than 7 percent of private-sector workers now in a union: "Union Members Summary," Bureau of Labor Statistics, January 18, 2019.

50 Noncompete agreements: "Non-compete Contracts: Economic Effects and Policy Implications," Office of Economic Policy, U.S. Department of the Treasury, March 2016.

50 40 percent have moved on to work on behalf of the finance companies: Jeff Stein, "Many Lawmakers and Aides Who Crafted Financial Regulations After the 2008 Crisis Now Work for Wall Street," *The Washington Post*, September 7, 2018.

5. HOW AMERICA WENT ASTRAY

55 "Secondary schools in America were free": Claudia Goldin and Lawrence F. Katz, *The Race Between Education and Technology* (Cambridge, MA: Belknap Press, 2008), 12.

56 top 1 percent now owns twice as great a share: These are real incomes after taxes and government transfers, based on data from Thomas Piketty, Emmanuel Saez and Gabriel Zucman. See David Leonhardt, "How the Upper Middle Class in America Is Really Doing," *The New York Times*, February 24, 2019.

56 who didn't graduate from high school do even worse: Isabel Sawhill, *The Forgotten Americans* (New Haven, CT: Yale University Press, 2018), 60–62.

56 in the United States it doubled to 20 percent: F. Alvarado, L. Chancel, T. Piketty et al., "World Inequality Report 2018," Harvard University Press, 2018.

58 not everyone, particularly those left behind: Some of the figures in the France-U.S. comparison come from Sawhill, *The Forgotten Americans*, 79–80.

59 a real Chicago woman, Linda Taylor: Josh Levin tells the story of Linda Taylor in *The Queen: The Forgotten Life Behind an American Myth* (New York: Little, Brown, 2019).

61 "solitary, poor, nasty, brutish and short": In political philosophy, there was a great debate about whether life in the natural state before governments was idyllic or horrific. Jean-Jacques Rousseau believed the former, Thomas Hobbes the latter. Hobbes famously argued in *Leviathan,* published in 1651, that individuals needed to surrender some rights to a powerful government to avoid a life that would be "solitary, poor, nasty, brutish and short."

61 "What began as a useful corrective": Steven Pearlstein, *Can American Capitalism Survive?* (New York: St. Martin's Press, 2018), 13–14, 22.

61 "Americans became a more acquisitive": Michael Tomasky, "The Real Legacy of the 1970s," *The New York Times,* February 3, 2019.

61 now the average CEO earns: Lawrence Mishel and Jessica Schieder, "CEO Compensation Surged in 2017," Economic Policy Institute, August 16, 2018.

61 A Walmart employee earning the median salary: Walmart Proxy Statement Schedule 14A, filed with the Securities Exchange Commission, May 30, 2018.

62 "What we have been left with": Oren Cass, *The Once and Future Worker* (New York: Encounter Books, 2018), 4.

64 to kick people out of the safety net: Catherine Rampell, "Arkansas's Medicaid Experiment Has Proved Disastrous," *The Washington Post,* November 19, 2018.

65 no correlation to increased employment: Jacob Bundrick and Thomas Snyder, "Do Business Subsidies Lead to Increased Economic Activity? Evidence from Arkansas's Quick Action Closing Fund," Mercatus Working Paper, Mercatus Center, George Mason University, 2017.

66 "morality of grace": Victor Tan Chen, *Cut Loose: Jobless and Hopeless in an Unfair Economy* (Oakland: University of California Press, 2015). The discussion of the Ford plant in Windsor and the nursing program is on page 61; the reference to sinking into "apathy, despair, and self-blame," on page 228. We strongly agree that what is needed is not just smarter policies but also a social narrative that is less judgmental and scornful of those who stumble.

67 Mississippi went from 30 percent of the per capita income: Paul Krugman, "What's the Matter with Trumpland?," *The New York Times,* April 2, 2018.

67 right-wing politicians in the South defend Confederate statues: These points are well made by Krugman, ibid.

68 "risks driving even more of the working class into the Republican camp": Sawhill, *The Forgotten Americans,* 13.

71 wrong for a man to beat his wife with a belt or stick: Steven Pinker, *The Better Angels of Our Nature* (New York: Penguin Books, 2012), 408.

71 A 1963 poll found: Karlyn Bowman, "Interracial Marriage: Changing Laws, Minds and Hearts," *Forbes,* January 13, 2017. See also Eleanor O'Neil, Heather Sims and Karlyn Bowman, "AEI Political Report: The Trump Presidency: Change, Change, Change," *AEI,* January 13, 2017.

71 fifteen states specifically banned: Hrishi Karthikeyan and Gabriel J. Chin, "Preserving Racial Identity," *Asian Law Journal* 9, no. 1 (2002).

6. DRUG DEALERS IN LAB COATS

73 "OxyContin is our ticket to the moon": Barry Meier, *Pain Killer* (New York: Random House, 2018), 41. Meier did pathbreaking reporting on Purdue Pharma, and his book remains a powerful chronicle of how drug companies peddle drugs at enormous human cost.

79 By official estimates, 2.1 million Americans suffer opioid addiction: "Health Insurance Plans May Be Fueling Opioid Epidemic," Johns Hopkins Bloomberg School of Public Health, June 22, 2018.

80 some scholarly estimates run many times higher: "Almost 18 million Americans are currently taking long-term prescription opioids," according to a joint statement by pain experts. "International Stakeholder Community of Pain Experts and Leaders Call for an Urgent Action on Forced Opioid Tapering," *Pain Medicine*, March 2019.

81 McKinsey & Company, the global consulting firm, advised Purdue: Michael Forsythe and Walt Bogdanich, "McKinsey Advised Purdue Pharma How to 'Turbocharge' Opioid Sales, Lawsuit Says," *The New York Times*, February 1, 2019.

81 Insys Therapeutics, a pharmaceutical company: "Justice Department Takes First-of-Its-Kind-Legal Action to Reduce Opioid Over-Prescription," U.S. Department of Justice press release, August 22, 2018.

81 Insys achieved 1,000 percent growth in earnings: Evan Hughes, "The Pain Hustlers," *The New York Times Magazine*, May 2, 2018.

81 "Every time a doc tells you they prescribed": "Fueling an Epidemic: Inside the Insys Strategy for Boosting Fentanyl Sales," U.S. Senate Homeland Security and Governmental Affairs Committee, Ranking Members Office, October 17, 2018, p. 8.

81 payments to doctors in a particular county correlated to overdose deaths: Scott E. Hadland et al., "Association of Pharmaceutical Industry Marketing of Opioid Products with Mortality from Opioid-Related Overdoses," *JAMA Network Open*, 2019.

82 prescribing it for chronic back pain is a recipe for addiction: The information on Insys comes largely from "Fueling an Epidemic."

82 McKesson Corporation, another giant pharmaceutical company: "Combating the Opioid Epidemic: Examining Concerns About Distribution and Diversion," House of Representatives, Subcommittee on Oversight and Investigations, Committee on Energy and Commerce, May 8, 2018. See also Stephanie Armour and Thomas M. Burton, "Opioid Shipments to Small Towns Come Under Spotlight at Hearing," *The Wall Street Journal*, May 8, 2018.

82 The government eventually fined McKesson: Erika Fry, "Big McKesson Shareholder, Governance Experts Say the Opioid Crisis Should Have Cost the CEO Some Bonus Pay," *Fortune*, July 10, 2017.

83 "The biggest drug dealers wear white lab coats": Jonathan Caulkins and Keith Humphreys, "Drug Dealers Among Us: Look for Those Wearing Lab Coats or Pinstripe Suits," *The Hill*, February 6, 2018.

7. LOSING THE WAR ON DRUGS

86 "The Nixon campaign in 1968": Ehrlichman made this comment about the drug war in 1996, many years after his White House years, to Dan Baum, who was writing a book about drug policy. Dan Baum, "Legalize It All," *Harper's Magazine*, April 2016. Partly because of this quote, liberals sometimes assume that the war on drugs and mass incarceration were simply a conservative plot; in fact, it's more complicated than that, and this was a bipartisan failing. James Forman Jr. notes in his Pulitzer Prize–winning book *Locking Up Our Own* (New York: Farrar, Straus and Giroux, 2017) that black leaders initially supported the war on crime and tough law-and-order measures because the cities they governed were so overrun by drugs and crime.

88 6,100 deaths from illegal drugs: Margaret Warner, Li Hui Chen, Diane M. Makuc et al., "Drug Poisoning Deaths in the United States, 1980–2008," *NCHS Data Brief*, No. 81, U.S. Department of Health and Human Services, December 2011, p. 1.

95 Back in 1971, President Nixon ordered: Nixon brought in Dr. Jerome Jaffe, who had run a drug treatment program in Chicago, to lead his drug effort, which in effect amounted to a decriminalization of addiction for those who wanted treatment. Likewise, American soldiers in Vietnam were treated before returning home, but were not court-martialed or otherwise punished. See an interview transcript with Dr. Jaffe by PBS *Frontline:* https://www.pbs .org/wgbh/pages/frontline/shows/drugs/interviews/jaffe.html.

95 Only one in five Americans: Substance Use and Mental Health Administration, *Key Substance Abuse and Mental Health Indicators in the United States*, 2018.

96 a dollar invested in addiction treatment programs: "Principles of Drug Addiction Treatment: A Research-Based Guide (Third Edition)," National Institute on Drug Abuse, January 2018.

96 Dozens of studies have found: Jennifer Ng, Christy Sutherland and Michael R. Kolber, "Does Evidence Support Supervised Injection Sites?," *Canadian Family Physician* 63, no. 11 (November 2017): 866.

96 One study estimated that a safe injection site: The Editors, "Addicts Should Be Able to Shoot Up Legally in Safe-Injection Facilities," *Scientific American*, July 1, 2018.

97 in 2016, doctors wrote more opioid prescriptions: Julie Mack, "Michigan Has More Annual Opioid Prescriptions Than People," MLive.com, June 2017. Michigan doctors wrote 11 million prescriptions for opioids in 2016. The population of Michigan was nearly 10 million.

8. UP BY THE BOOTSTRAPS

103 a growing empathy gap in America: Paul Bloom, a distinguished Yale professor of psychology, pushes back in a book called *Against Empathy*. Bloom declares himself on an "anti-empathy crusade" and warns that empathy can lead to depression or to irrational efforts to help a particular child with big eyes, rather than assisting larger groups who are more needy. Like many critics, we believe that Bloom defines empathy too narrowly and unfairly pits it against reason. Of course we're against irrationality, but we believe empathy is made of sterner stuff.

104 Varney's successful trajectory began: We learned of Varney's exchange in an excellent episode of the WNYC radio program *On the Media* about poverty. It's available at www.wnyc.org/poverty.

9. DEPTHS OF DESPAIR

111 Life expectancy rose in the United States: There are competing estimates of life expectancy in the nineteenth century, but see J. David Hacker, "Decennial Life Tables for the White Population of the United States," author manuscript, U.S. National Library of Medicine, 2011, Table 8. The figure for white males in the 1860s is 35.6; we know of no reliable figures for American life expectancy at that period that include the black or Native American populations, but they must have been considerably lower; hence we suggest an overall figure of "less than 35."

112 "We should take it very seriously": Lenny Bernstein and Christopher Ingraham, "Fueled by Drug Crisis, U.S. Life Expectancy Declines for a Second Straight Year," *The Washington Post*, December 21, 2017.

116 less significant than geography: James J. Lee et al., "Gene Discovery and Polygenic Prediction from a Genome-wide Association Study of Educational Attainment in 1.1 Million Individuals," *Nature Genetics*, July 23, 2018.

117 given hope that there is a way out: We discuss this in our book *A Path Appears* (New York: Knopf, 2014), in a chapter called "The Power of Hope."

119 cirrhosis-related deaths in the United States: Elliot B. Tapper and Neehar D. Parikh, "Mortality Due to Cirrhosis and Liver Cancer in the United States, 1999–2016: Observational Study," *British Medical Journal*, July 18, 2018.

10. INTERVENTIONS THAT WORK

129 93 percent of girls in the juvenile justice system: Malika Saadar Saar, Rebecca Epstein, Lindsay Rosenthal et al., "The Sexual Abuse to Prison Pipeline: The Girls' Story," Georgetown Law Center on Poverty and Inequality, c. 2016, p. 7.

129 79 percent of women in jails have children: Elizabeth Swavola, Kristine Riley and Ram Subramanian, "Overlooked: Women and Jails in an Era of Reform," Vera Institute of Justice, 2016, p. 12.

134 if offenders in state prisons received needed drug treatment: Gary A. Zarkin, Alexander J. Cowell, Katherine A. Hicks and Michael J. Mills, "Benefits and Costs of Substance Abuse Treatment Programs for State Prison Inmates: Results from a Lifetime Simulation Model," *Health Economics*, June 2012.

11. UNIVERSAL HEALTH CARE: ONE DAY, ONE TOWN

146 We're now behind Chile in life expectancy: "America's Health Rankings: 2017 Annual Report," United Health Foundation, p. 43.

147 Children in America today are 55 percent more likely to die: Ashish P. Thakrar, Alexandra D. Forrest, Mitchell G. Maltenfort and Christopher B. Forrest, "Child Mortality in the US and 19 OECD Comparator Nations: A 50-Year Time-Trend Analysis," *Health Affairs*, January 2018.

147 we lose fifty-eight children a day: Skeptics sometimes note that cross-country comparisons are complicated by differences in how data are collected. There is something to that, and we believe that China and Cuba sometimes do not count in infant mortality statistics newborns who die very soon after birth. But among advanced nations, reporting standards seem similar. One study examined this issue and found that fetal death rates are affected by the standard used, but that infant mortality rates are not materially affected. Ashna D. Mohangoo, Béatrice Blondel, Mika Gissler et al., "International Comparisons of Fetal and Neonatal Mortality Rates in High-Income Countries: Should Exclusion Thresholds Be Based on Birth Weight or Gestational Age?," *PLoS ONE*, May 13, 2013.

147 life expectancy rests so heavily on where a child is born: Robert M. Kaplan, *More Than Medicine* (Cambridge, MA: Harvard University Press, 2019), 96–98.

149 at least one life is saved: The study showing one life saved for every 830 people who gain insurance was conducted in Massachusetts. Baicker conducted a similar study with Benjamin Sommers and Arnold Epstein that found that in Arizona, Maine and New York the number of lives saved from insurance was even greater; there, insuring an additional 176 people saved one life per year.

150 in Spain, it's $2,003: International Federation of Health Plans, "2015 Comparative Price Report." The prices listed are averages in each country, with Spain and Switzerland consistently inexpensive for drugs and procedures and the United States consistently at the high end.

150 weight-related issues account for 9 percent of U.S. health-care spending: Kaplan, *More Than Medicine*, 128–29.

151 drained all their life assets over the next two years: Adrienne M. Gilligan, David S. Alberts, Denise J. Roe and Grant H. Skrepnek, "Death or Debt? National Estimates of Financial Toxicity in Persons with Newly-Diagnosed Cancer," *The American Journal of Medicine*, October 2018.

12. HOMELESS IN A RICH NATION

160 By even a conservative count: Meghan Henry, Anna Mahathey, Tyler Morrill et al., "Part I: Point-in-Time Estimates of Homelessness," *The 2018 Annual Homeless Assessment Report to Congress*, U.S. Department of Housing and Urban Development, December 2018. p. 1.

160 homelessness resulted in $8 billion in additional costs for children's health: Ana Poblacion, Allison Bovell-Ammon, Richard Sheward et al., "Stable Homes Make Stable Families," Children's HealthWatch What If? series, July 2017.

161 These are areas lacking adequate affordable housing: Andrew Auramd, Dan Emmanuel and Diane Yentel, "Out of Reach: The High Cost of Housing," National Low Income Housing Coalition, 2018.

161 one shouldn't spend more than 30 percent of one's income on housing: Edward L. Glaeser and Joseph Gyourko, "The Impact of Zoning on Housing Affordability," NBER working paper, March 2002.

164 "our evidence suggests": Ibid.

164 "zoning and other land-use controls contribute significantly": "Housing Development Toolkit," The White House, September 2016, p. 7.

165 financial literacy programs have had a mixed record: See Daniel Fernandes, John G. Lynch Jr. and Richard G. Netemeyer, "The Effect of Financial Literacy and Financial Education on Downstream Financial Behaviors," *Management Science*, August 2014. Careful studies have found that financial literacy is helpful with individual development accounts, and some school programs have also found good outcomes.

166 twice as much on subsidizing housing for mostly affluent homeowners: Kathy Orton, "Federal Government Spends More Subsidizing Homeowners Than It Does Helping People Avoid Homelessness," *The Washington Post*, October 11, 2017. Also see: Michael Novogradac, "Once Again, Homeownership Gets Far More Tax Subsidies Than Rental Housing," *Novogradac Journal of Tax Credits*, July 2, 2018. The cost of the mortgage interest deduction is expected to drop to $41 billion in 2018 from $66 billion in 2017 after that year's tax reform law; the exclusion of $500,000 from capital gains on home sales amounts to another $36 billion annually.

166 provided $1.3 billion to Stockbridge Capital: Peter Whoriskey, "A Billion-Dollar Empire Made of Mobile Homes," *The Washington Post*, February 14, 2019.

13. THE ESCAPE ARTISTS

170 children raised in religious households were less likely to suffer: Ying Chen and Tyler J. VanderWeele, "Associations of Religious Upbringing with Subsequent Health and Well-Being from Adolescence to Young Adulthood: An Outcome-Wide Analysis," *American Journal of Epidemiology*, June 29, 2018.

173 military particularly helped black men: W. Bradford Wilcox, Wendy R. Wang and Ronald B. Mincy, "Black Men Making It in America," American Enterprise Institute, 2018. The same study also found that black men were more likely to reach the middle class if they were married, were church members or had a sense of agency as teenagers or young men. And not surprisingly, higher education and full-time work also correlated to success.

14. A SHOT IN THE FACE

178 Beginning in the early 1970s, our incarceration rate: Jeremy Travis, Bruce Western and Steve Redburn, eds., *The Growth of Incarceration in the United States: Exploring Causes and Consequences* (Washington, DC: National Academies Press, 2014), 33.

178 now it has 1.4 million: "Fact Sheet: Trends in U.S. Corrections," The Sentencing Project, Washington, DC, June 2018.

178 Barr issued a report: U.S. Department of Justice, "The Case for More Incarceration," with opening statement by Attorney General William P. Barr, dated October 28, 1992.

178 one in seven Americans in prison today: Ashley Nellis, "Still Life: America's Increasing Use of Life and Long-Term Sentences," The Sentencing Project, 2017, p. 5. The one in seven figure includes an additional 44,311 individuals who are serving "virtual life" sentences of fifty years or more. For life imprisonment costs, see ibid., p. 26.

178 in Germany, it's 6 percent: Danielle Allen, "How Should We Deal with Wrongdoing? And You Can't Say Prison," *The Washington Post*, May 16, 2018.

180 home visitation reaches less than 2 percent: Edward Rodrigue and Richard V. Reeves, "Home Visiting Programs: An Early Test for the 114h Congress," The Brookings Institution, February 5, 2015. See also National Home Visiting Resource Center, *2018 Home Visiting Yearbook*, which says that evidence-based home visitation programs served 300,000 families in 2017, out of 18 million that would have benefited.

182 Judges are more likely to rule against defendants: Shai Danziger, Jonathan Levav and Liora Avnaim-Pesso, "Extraneous Factors in Judicial Decisions," *PNAS*, April 26, 2011.

182 disproportionately applied to black defendants: Ozkan Eren and Naci Mocan, "Emotional Judges and Unlucky Juveniles," *American Economic Journal: Applied Economics* 10, no. 3 (September 2016): 171–205.

183 our justice system acts in racist ways: This point has been made powerfully by Michelle Alexander, *The New Jim Crow: Mass Incarceration in the Age of Colorblindness* (New York: New Press, 2010).

183 One way researchers measure bias: Marianne Bertrand and Sendhil Mullainathan, "Are Emily and Greg More Employable Than Lakisha and Jamal? A Field Experiment on Labor Market Discrimination," *American Economic Review* 94, no. 4 (September 2004): 991–1013.

183 A survey found that 92 percent of black youths: Orlando Patterson with Ethan Fosse, eds., *The Cultural Matrix: Understanding Black Youth* (Cambridge, MA: Harvard University Press, 2015).

183 In a 2015 CNN poll: Kaiser Family Foundation/CNN Survey of Americans on Race, November 2015.

184 That's one reason the median black family: Lisa J. Dettling, Joanne W. Hsu, Lindsay Jacobs et al., with assistance from Elizabeth Llanes, "Recent Trends in Wealth-Holding by Race and Ethnicity: Evidence from the Survey of Consumer Finances," Board of Governors of the Federal Reserve System, *FEDS Notes*, September 27, 2017.

184 educational discrimination continues: Jonathan Rothwell, "Housing Costs, Zoning, and Access to High-Scoring Schools," Brookings Institution, Metropolitan Policy Program, April 2012, p. 8.

185 As a young adult: Stephanie Saul and Matt Flegenheimer, "The El Paso Homecoming That Set Beto O'Rourke's Star on the Rise," *The New York Times*, April 27, 2019.

186 The graduation rate at high schools: "Synopsis of Reprogramming," Bureau of Indian Education website, www.bie.edu.

186 The Indian Health Service: "IHS Profile," Indian Health Service, 2015–2018 data.

186 less than half what the Bureau of Prisons spends: "Bureau of Prisons: Better Planning and Evaluation Needed to Understand and Control Rising Inmate Health Care Costs," GAO-17-379, published June 29, 2017, publicly released July 31, 2017.

15. GOD SAVE THE FAMILY

190 Newt Gingrich rose to become Speaker of the House: Bonnie Goldstein, "What Newt Gingrich's Three Wives Tell Us About the President He'd Be," *The Washington Post*, January 2, 2012.

191 the judge scolded Moore: See Jon Swaine and David Smith, "Trump Fed Pick Was Held in Contempt for Failing to Pay Ex-Wife Over $300,000," *The Guardian*, March 30, 2019.

193 Forty percent of American kids: Joyce A. Martin, Brady E. Hamilton, Michelle J. K. Osterman, et al., "Births: Final Data for 2016," *National Vital Statistics Reports*, January 31, 2018, Table 9, p. 31.

193 four out of five of them will experience the stress: Maria Cancian, Daniel R. Meyer and Steven T. Cook, "Stepparents and Half-Siblings: Family Complexity from a Child's Perspective," *Fast Focus*, Institute for Research on Poverty University of Wisconsin–Madison, September 2011, p. 3.

194 Same-sex couples seem to have slightly better outcomes: Some studies have found that children of same-sex couples have modestly worse outcomes, but that seems to be because these children often were in households that divorced; typically, the child was born in a heterosexual marriage, then one parent came out as gay and the couple divorced. Divorce is an ACE, and so has an impact on child outcomes in the aggregate. However, other researchers have found that children raised *from birth* by a same-sex couple do slightly better than average. In all likelihood this, too, has no relationship to the sexual preference of the parents. Rather, same-sex parents who have children are somewhat more affluent and have higher socioeconomic status than the average. In addition, because same-sex parents have to actively seek a child and invest considerably to have one, such children are less likely to be neglected. See Deni Mazrekaj, Kristof de Witte and Sofie Cabus, "School Outcomes of Children Raised by Same-Sex Couples from Birth: Evidence from Administrative Panel Data," Conference of the American Economic Association, January 5, 2019.

196 only 5 percent rise to the top quintile: Richard Reeves and Joanna Venator, "Saving Horatio Alger," Brookings Institution, Social Mobility Memo, August 21, 2014.

198 Foster care costs: Nicholas Zill, "Better Prospects, Lower Cost: The Case for Increasing Foster Care Adoption," National Council for Adoption, *Adoption Advocate*, May 2011.

198 only 58 percent graduate from high school: "Supporting Older Youth in Foster Care," National Conference of State Legislatures website (www.ncsl.org), February 25, 2019.

198 six times more likely to end up homeless: "Aging Out of Foster Care," National Foster Youth Institute website (www.nfyi.org), May 26, 2017.

198 "it makes it harder for me to get a job": Resentment of Latino immigrants was rooted not only in lost jobs but also in frustration that the social status of white working-class men had plummeted, with demographic and cultural changes making them feel a little like, in Arlie Russell Hochschild's phrase, "strangers in their own land."

16. THE MARRIAGE OF TRUE MINDS

204 success for black men was marriage: W. Bradford Wilcox, Wendy R. Wang and Ronald B. Mincy, "Black Men Making It in America," American Enter-

prise Institute, 2018. Of course, that is correlation rather than causation, and some of the unmarried men had risk factors that also made them less marriageable.

204 two-parent households have more social capital: Consider low-income black men growing up in two different neighborhoods in Los Angeles. Of young black men who grew up in the lowest-income families in Watts, 44 percent ended up incarcerated on a single day (the day of the 2010 census). But of young black men who grew up similarly poor in Compton, two miles to the south, only 6 percent were incarcerated that day. One difference between the two neighborhoods is family structure: when these men were children in the 1980s, single parents made up 87 percent of households with kids in Watts and only 50 percent in Compton. All this underscores Pat Moynihan's point about the importance of family structure, not only for children but also for adults and the larger society.

207 policies have made low-income men less attractive as marriage partners: See David Autor, David Dorn and Gordon Hanson, "When Work Disappears: Manufacturing Decline and the Falling Marriage Market Value of Young Men," NBER working paper, revised December 2018, and Daniel Schneider, Kristen Harknett and Matthew Stimpson, "What Explains the Decline in First Marriage in the United States?," *Journal of Marriage and Family*, May 8, 2018.

207 Lifting the minimum wage: Research on cities that have raised the minimum wage to $15 an hour has so far not shown a significant corresponding loss in jobs, perhaps partly because of slightly higher loyalty and reduced turnover. Sylvia A. Allegretto, Anna Godoey, Carl Nadler and Michael Reich, "The New Wave of Local Minimum Wage Policies: Evidence from Six Cities," Institute for Research on Labor and Employment, University of California, Berkeley, September 6, 2018. Other research shows that higher minimum wage has some negative effects, including more automation by companies. David Neumark, J. M. Ian Salas and William Wascher, "Revisiting the Minimum Wage–Employment Debate: Throwing Out the Baby with the Bathwater?," The National Bureau of Economic Research, June 2013.

208 Some 70 percent of pregnancies among single women under thirty: Mia Zolna and Laura Lindberg, "Unintended Pregnancy: Incidence and Outcomes Among Young Adult Unmarried Women in the United States, 2001 and 2008," Guttmacher Institute report, April 2012.

17. WE EAT OUR YOUNG

210 More children die each year in the United States from abuse: By official figures, 1,600 die each year, although experts suggest that the real total is twice that.

211 five-year-olds who have experienced serious adversity: Poor boys are twice as likely to be arrested and poor girls are six times as likely to have a child out of wedlock before age twenty-one. Greg J. Duncan and Ariel Kalil, "Early-Childhood Poverty and Adult Attainment, Behavior, and Health," *Child Development*, February 4, 2010.

211 they will be much more susceptible to substance abuse: Ju Lee Oei, "Adult Consequences of Prenatal Drug Exposure," *Internal Medicine Journal*, January 3, 2018.

211 a 1,220 percent increased chance of adult suicide: Vincent J. Felitti, Robert F. Anda, Dale Nordenberg et al., "Relationship of Childhood Abuse and Household Dysfunction to Many of the Leading Causes of Death in Adults," *American Journal of Preventive Medicine*, May 1998, 245–58.

212 We've reduced teen pregnancies by 67 percent: "Teen Pregnancy Prevention," National Conference of State Legislatures website (www.ncsl.org), October 11, 2018.

212 We've raised high-school graduation rates by 5 percentage points: "Common Core of Data: America's Public Schools," National Center for Education Statistics; graduation rates for the 2016–17 school year reached 84.6 percent, up from 79 percent in 2011. And see Moriah Balingit, "U.S. High School Graduation Rates Rise to New High," *The Washington Post*, December 4, 2017.

216 through genetics or epigenetics: In high school, you probably learned that Lamarck's theory of evolution—that animals change during their lifetime and pass those changes to their offspring—was wrong. For example, ancient giraffes did not stretch their necks to reach tall branches and then have longer-necked babies. But epigenetics is a new field of science that suggests that environmental factors can affect the expression of genes so that acquired traits may sometimes be transmitted to the next generations. This is not Lamarckian genetics, but it is not quite clear what it is; this is a revolutionary discipline in its infancy.

216 each dollar invested in reducing child disadvantage: Michael McLaughlin and Mark R. Rank, "Estimating the Economic Cost of Child Poverty in the United States," *Social Work Research*, March 30, 2018.

217 cost of a single murder is $3 million: Some estimates of the costs of murders are higher, including one that reached $17 million, but most estimates are in the range of $3 million to $5 million where the murderer is convicted and imprisoned. Matt DeLisi, Anna Kosloski, Molly Sween et al., "Murder by Numbers: Monetary Costs Imposed by a Sample of Homicide Offenders," *The Journal of Forensic Psychiatry & Psychology*, August 2010.

217 crime is caused by 5 percent of the population: Örjan Falk, Märta Wallinius and Sebastian Lundström, "The 1% of the Population Accountable for 63% of All Violent Crime Convictions," *Social Psychiatry Psychiatric Epidemiology* 49, no. 4 (2014): 559–71.

217   diminish the well-being of an entire society: Richard Wilkinson and Katie
       Pickett, *The Inner Level* (London: Allen Lane, 2018), xxi. Wilkinson and Pick-
       ett also explored these issues in their previous book, *The Spirit Level*.

218   64 percent less likely to attempt suicide: Chloe Reichel, "Suicide Prevention:
       Research on Successful Interventions," *Journalist's Resource*, Harvard Kennedy
       School of Government, 2019.

219   4 percent of pediatricians screen for ACEs: Vanessa Sacks and David Mur-
       phey, "The Prevalence of Adverse Childhood Experiences, Nationally, by
       State, and by Race or Ethnicity," *Child Trends*, February 20, 2018.

220   devastating for their children as well: See H. Luke Shaefer and Kathryn J.
       Edin, *$2 a Day: Living on Almost Nothing in America* (Boston: Houghton Mif-
       flin Harcourt, 2015). There is a vigorous debate about how to make these
       international comparisons. Some note that extremely poor families abroad
       often are villagers who raise their own food and pay nothing for housing in
       a way that is not possible in the United States; others observe that broke
       Americans, especially children, can get food stamps, emergency medical care
       and help from private charities.

220   sometimes having unintended consequences: One of the dangers, for exam-
       ple, is that by offering benefits for households with children, the government
       will create an incentive that results in a surge in births to low-income single
       moms. The economist Paul Collier argues that this is what happened in Brit-
       ain in 1999. Paul Collier, *The Future of Capitalism* (New York: HarperCollins,
       2018), 160. Other British studies found no impact on births to single women
       but an increase in births to low-income couples. Reviews of the United
       States are mixed, with Robert Moffitt finding fertility effects ("The Effect
       of Welfare on Marriage and Fertility," Institute for Research on Poverty
       discussion paper, 1997), while Hilary Hoynes reaches the opposite conclu-
       sion in "Work, Welfare and Family Structure," in Alan Auerbach, ed., *Fiscal
       Policy: Lessons from Economic Research* (Cambridge, MA: MIT Press, 1997).
       Studies in Canada and Europe have found that welfare offerings have little
       or no effect on fertility among low-income women; Australia had a tempo-
       rary bump in fertility that then disappeared. To us, the balance of evidence
       internationally suggests that we should be vigilant about fertility effects aris-
       ing from benefits for children but that they are unlikely to be a significant
       problem.

220   "millions of Americans whose suffering": Angus Deaton, "The U.S. Can No
       Longer Hide from Its Deep Poverty Problem," *The New York Times*, Janu-
       ary 24, 2018.

221   70 percent said they had been affected by prescription drug use: Deborah
       A. P. Hersman, "How the Prescription Drug Crisis Is Impacting American
       Employers," National Safety Council, 2017, p. 8.

18. RAISING TROUBLED KIDS

226 an incarceration rate that is the highest in the world: H. Luke Shaefer, Ping-hui Wu and Kathryn Edin, "Can Poverty in America Be Compared to Conditions in the World's Poorest Countries?" National Poverty Center Working Paper Series, #16-07, August 2016.

233 The case went through endless appeals: *Kenneth Reams v. State of Arkansas*, Arkansas State Supreme Court case, 2018 Ark. 324, majority opinion by Judge Karen R. Baker.

234 each dollar invested in the programs saved up to $30: Sara B. Heller, Anuj K. Shah, Jonathan Guryan et al., "Thinking, Fast and Slow? Some Field Experiments to Reduce Crime and Dropout in Chicago," NBER Working Paper No. 21178, May 2015.

19. CREATING MORE ESCAPE ARTISTS

236 the collective impact model: John Kania and Mark Kramer, "Collective Impact," *Stanford Social Innovation Review*, Winter 2011.

20. AMERICA REGAINED

249 "the breaking of a man's spirit": Robert F. Kennedy, speech to Cleveland City Club, April 5, 1968. The transcription on the John F. Kennedy Presidential Library website is not entirely accurate, so we relied on our own transcription from the recording.

254 a bargain by any calculation: National Academies of Sciences, Engineering, and Medicine, *A Roadmap to Reducing Child Poverty* (Washington, DC: National Academies Press, 2019).

254 other nations have developed better childcare options: Francine D. Blau and Lawrence M. Kahn, "Female Labor Supply: Why Is the United States Falling Behind?," *American Economic Review: Papers & Proceedings*, 2013. See also Catherine Rampell, "Paid Family Leave Isn't Just a Women's Issue," *The Washington Post*, February 14, 2019.

255 the allowance would virtually eliminate children living in extreme poverty: See H. Luke Shaefer, Sophie Collyer, Greg Duncan et al., "A Universal Child Allowance: A Plan to Reduce Poverty and Income Instability Among Children in the United States," *The Russell Sage Foundation Journal of the Social Sciences* 4, no. 2 (February 2018): 22.

256 Various studies have calculated: Chuck Collins, Darrick Hamilton, Dedrick Asante-Muhammad et al., *Ten Solutions to Bridge the Racial Wealth Divide* (Washington, DC: Institute for Policy Studies, 2019).

256 Congress pulled the plug on funding for an IDA program: These individual development accounts are extensively discussed in Robert E. Friedman, *A Few Thousand Dollars* (New York: The New Press, 2018).

257 wage insurance has bipartisan support: Robert J. Shiller, "How Wage Insurance Could Ease Economic Inequality," *The New York Times*, March 11, 2016.

257 federal job guarantee: L. Randall Wray, Flavia Dantas, Scott Fullwiler et al., "Public Service Employment: A Path to Full Employment," Levy Economic Institute of Bard College, April 2018.

259 "As an economist, I am always asked": Joseph E. Stiglitz, Amartya Sen and Jean-Paul Fitoussi, "Report by the Commission on the Measurement of Economic Performance and Social Progress," 2009.

Index

Page numbers in *italic* refer to illustrations.

Made in the USA
Las Vegas, NV
22 January 2023

66062650R00177